Praise for *Dynamic Reteaming*

Heidi's wisdom will change how you think about, form, re-form, and participate in teams. Her stories, whether from the three successful startups she's
guided through hypergrowth or the dozens of teams she's interviewed
across the globe, delineate the power, intelligence, and joy of reteaming.
If you seek a healthier, happier, more harmonious approach
to teaming, study this book.

—*Joshua Kerievsky, Industrial Logic,*
author of Refactoring to Patterns

I used to think, in fact I was certain, that long-lived teams with very stable
membership were the best way for software development organizations to
deliver fantastic software. Heidi and her book encouraged me to challenge
and reevaluate this notion. She explains the many perspectives, virtues, and
advantages of deliberately and thoughtfully changing up teams. This book is
a must for software development leaders looking to create a development
culture of engagement, connectedness, resilience, and opportunity.

—*Chris Smith, head of product delivery at Redgate Software*

For most of us, our image of teamwork needs to be updated—the stable,
familiar groups of people who learn how to work together well are being
replaced by fluid, porous teams that have to work together in new ways. Helfand provides inspiration and practical insights for how to do this well.

—*Amy C. Edmondson, Harvard Business School,*
author of Teaming *and* The Fearless Organization

Building effective teams is hard. A good team is a dynamic thing that changes all of the time. Understanding this and using it to help to guide your team is a cornerstone of any approach to continuous improvement. Heidi's book describes powerful, real-world patterns based on her extensive experience that will help you to reflect on what is happening in your team and give you a guide for what to do next.

—*Dave Farley, coauthor of* Continuous Delivery

If you want to weather the comings and goings, the hits and misses, the ups and downs of team life, this book is the guide. If you want to understand a more accurate and complex model of team life cycles, read deep from this book. Drawn from experience with her real engineering and product development teams, Heidi is the voice of engineers. She stands up for what they need in team life and offers sage advice for organizations who want to give it to them so they can create products that matter.

—*Lyssa Adkins, coach of difficult problems,*
and author of Coaching Agile Teams

High-performing teams are simultaneously powerful and fragile. Changes to the team can quickly disrupt their flow, but can also bring new insights and better ways of working in the long run. *Dynamic Reteaming* is a fundamental book for anyone involved in the fine art of balancing team evolution with team health in the real world. The author's immense experience is in full display here, backed by meaningful examples and concrete patterns.

—*Manuel Pais, coauthor of* Team Topologies: Organizing Business and Technology Teams for Fast Flow

Like it or not, knowledge work is a team sport. The essence of being a professional knowledge worker, then, is the ability to be a good team player. But how does one engage on a team when teams today are undergoing constant change? Isn't "change" the opposite of "team"? The established Agile paradigm is to try and stabilize teams as much as possible, but this advice flies in the face of the reality that most of us experience. That's where Heidi comes in. Rather than to resist team change, she teaches us to embrace it.

Recognize your context, apply appropriate patterns, and watch outcomes follow. Especially here, in early 2020, the idea of what a team is and what it means to be on a team is evolving. Thankfully, Heidi is here to help us.

—*Daniel S. Vacanti, CEO of* Actionable Agile, *and author of* When Will It Be Done? *and* Actionable Agile Metrics for Predictability

"Whether you like it or not, teams are going to change. You might as well get good at it." This is the premise of Heidi's book, which is a treasure trove of stories and anecdotes from practitioners from all over the world. The author brings to life her extensive research coupled with deep personal experience. I highly recommend this book as a source of inspiration and guidance for anyone working with teams in a world of change.

—*Sandy Mamoli, Nomad8, coauthor of* Creating Great Teams

For organizations building software-enabled services today, the team is the fundamental means of delivery. But a team is not a loose collection of individuals with the same manager; instead, a team has a shared goal, shared working practices, and shared sense of purpose. Above all, a team needs to nurture and develop its ways of working, its very being. This is where *Dynamic Reteaming* by Heidi Helfand is so valuable: this book provides tried and tested techniques for helping to nurture and evolve a team over time. Changes to team composition can be disruptive, but the *Dynamic Reteaming* patterns provide ways to turn these changes into positive experiences for individuals, teams, and organizations. This team-first book is vital for every organization today.

—*Matthew Skelton, coauthor of* Team Topologies: Organizing Business and Technology Teams for Fast Flow

There is no question that the future belongs to the curious learner. I can easily say that the future belongs to Heidi Helfand and those lucky ones that are her students. In *Dynamic Reteaming*, Heidi takes on some important big ideas with great wisdom, humility, and curiosity. We are all better for her efforts. Read, learn, experiment, grow!

—*Richard Sheridan, Menlo Innovations, author of* Joy, Inc. *and* Chief Joy Officer

Dynamic Reteaming

SECOND EDITION

The Art and Wisdom of Changing Teams

Heidi Helfand

Beijing · Boston · Farnham · Sebastopol · Tokyo

Dynamic Reteaming

by Heidi Helfand

Published by O'Reilly Media, Inc., 1005 Gravenstein Highway North, Sebastopol, CA 95472.

O'Reilly books may be purchased for educational, business, or sales promotional use. Online editions are also available for most titles (http://oreilly.com). For more information, contact our corporate/institutional sales department: 800-998-9938 or *corporate@oreilly.com*.

Acquisitions Editor: Melissa Duffield	**Proofreader:** Kim Cofer
Development Editor: Melissa Potter	**Indexer:** nSight, Inc.
Production Editor: Kate Galloway	**Interior Designer:** Monica Kamsvaag
Copyeditor: Piper Editorial	**Cover Designer:** Randy Comer
	Illustrators: Kristin Romano and Rebecca Demarest

July 2020:   Second Edition

Revision History for the Second Edition

2020-06-11:   First Release

See http://oreilly.com/catalog/errata.csp?isbn=9781492061298 for release details.

978-1-492-06129-8

[LSI]

Contents

Foreword by John Cutler

I first met Heidi while working at AppFolio, a company Heidi mentions in this book. Soon after I joined the team, I began to hang out with Heidi, Paul, and the other coaches. There was something about their work that I found very interesting and inspiring—and challenging, especially during a period of rapid growth.

Behind the office, near the train tracks, was an out-and-back walking path. Team members often did one-on-ones on this path, and while Heidi wasn't on my immediate team, she was always willing to lend an ear. Heidi's many superpowers—her curiosity, patience, storytelling, and deep care for the humans she worked with—were in full effect. You'd need to be a *Star Trek: The Next Generation* fan to get this, but picture ship counselor and empath Deanna Troi as a coach at a SoCal tech company. That's Heidi.

I didn't realize it at the time, but interacting with that group of coaches, and Heidi in particular, would have a profound impact on my career. They encouraged me to start speaking and writing. They showed me that it was OK to nerd out about certain things like team health and what Heidi would later describe as dynamic reteaming. They inspired me.

It was a year or two later that Heidi started telling me about this book project. In 2016, the seeds of *Dynamic Reteaming* appeared as an AppFolio experience report for Agile2016. Heidi didn't stop there. You could tell she had found her groove. She was mining her amazing network, deep in research mode, picking up stories and patterns like a sponge.

Santa Barbara has a small but thriving tech scene, and Heidi has worked at many of the real standouts. They appear in this book, but like any tech hub, Santa Barbara has a unique cultural fingerprint. So she cast a wide net—New Zealand, Iceland, London, New York, San Francisco, and beyond—to do more research. Every time I checked in, she had more stories, and more conviction about the topic of dynamic reteaming.

And here we are. The second edition.

This is an important book. It is important because it discusses real-world change and real humans trying to do their best work. So many books in this domain treat teams as either stable and static, or disposable and interchangeable. Or they discuss scaling (and downsizing) in mechanistic terms, more suitable to talking about software architecture. No stories. No gradient.

Meanwhile, the real world of product development is beautiful and messy. Heidi takes a pattern-based approach rooted in relatable stories and makes sure to leave us with actionable tips on the first read. But she doesn't gloss over the nuance and humanity inherent in the work. Reteaming is always happening—for better or worse—and Heidi tackles that head on.

I'll close with a theme that punctuates the book. We often talk about reorgs in violent terms. Big and bold. Broad strokes. I'd like to think that much of what Heidi presents here is a safer alternative. She doesn't shy away from the fact that big changes are sometimes necessary or happen outside of our control. But I'm confident that by exploring the ideas in this book—by strategically reteaming and gracefully responding to reteaming—we can replace this violence with joy and productive adaptability.

I trust you'll end up reading this a couple times. I did. Thank you, Heidi, for sharing your curiosity and care and concern for us geeks.

—*John Cutler*
Product Team Coach, Amplitude

Foreword by Diana Larsen

Heidi Helfand notices. That's one of the first things I learned about her as we became better acquainted. I've enjoyed getting to know Heidi. I've also received side benefits of her ability to notice what's going on and to discern the response needed.

Heidi notices what's going on in a situation and then dives deeply into making sense of it. She discerns patterns in personal, group, and organizational dynamics. But she doesn't stop there. She recognizes how she can contribute to our learning about those patterns. Heidi helps us see what she sees.

This book, *Dynamic Reteaming*, demonstrates this attribute of noticing. Heidi noticed that the conventional wisdom about teams didn't match reality. She became curious. Heidi is also bravely willing to challenge conventional wisdom. In this way, she adds "role model for leaders" to her role as author.

She understood a generalization that many of us take for granted—team members work better together as they interact over time. She also recognized the flaw in its corollary—strive to keep team membership stable. Heidi saw it differently. While this is an interesting ideal, it's not the lived reality in most organizations. People and organizations are not tidy, and unexpected stuff happens.

Team members (a.k.a. people who have lives) leave teams for a variety of reasons. New people join growing teams. Products undergo changes based on customer needs and shifting business directions. New products emerge. New versions need team members with institutional and system memory to work on them. Where do those folks come from? Prior team assignments.

Once she noticed these realities, Heidi didn't just shrug her shoulders and say, "Oh well, too bad, that's just the messy way things are." Nope. She researched the many reasons that team membership can shift. Then she codified them and offered them to her readers. She wants to help us see the situation and work through it well. Heidi categorized more than a dozen drivers for reteaming and five patterns in ways team membership shifts. Her work enables us to think more clearly and deeply as we anticipate change in the makeup of our teams.

So Heidi shares good reasons for reteaming. Including the word *dynamic* in the title tells us that we must understand and apply good practices for implementing it. In some instances, many new teams are needed all at once. At other times a single team loses or gains a new member. Heidi gives us guidance on why and suggests how to reteam as a conscious process. She adds examples of effective ways to help newly formed teams accelerate into shared performance.

I particularly appreciated the reports about teams forming, adjourning, and reforming. Heidi has collected experiences from our colleagues all around the world. Heidi's many current and former coworkers offered their accounts. Generous practitioners from around the world shared theirs as well. I enjoyed reading stories from Rachel Davies, Christopher Lucian, Sandy Mamoli, Elaine Bulloch, Cristian Fuentes, Kristian Lindwall, Evan Willey, Jason Kerney, and many more. These stories add rich narrative. They give us insight into the many reasons for reteaming and the many forms it takes. The examples recognize the many ways that reteaming can be effective and fit for different purposes and functions.

Heidi has grown her own practice and skill at leading production and business outcomes through teams. Along her path, she has accumulated a formidable list of resources. Throughout the book I found familiar references to most books or articles relating to teams that I have in my own library. I also found many more that are now on my "order this one next" list.

Finally, I appreciate the way Heidi's *Dynamic Reteaming* work extends my professional interests. We share this devotion to fostering healthy, productive teams. This book includes applications for retrospectives, team liftoffs and chartering, and teams' shared learning and skills building. I also recognized examples that describe teams seeking fluency in all the zones of the Agile Fluency™ Model, as well.

If you have software development teams in your organization, you owe it to yourself to read this book. Whether you know it or not, your next "reteaming" is just around the corner. Be prepared.

—Diana Larsen
Cofounder, Agile Fluency Project LLC
Coauthor of Agile Retrospectives: Making Good Teams Great;
Liftoff: Start and Sustain Successful Agile Teams;
Five Rules of Accelerated Learning;
and "Agile Fluency Model: A Brief Guide to Success with Agile."

Preface

Expertcity was about to die! Conceived as the eBay for tech support, this startup that my colleagues and I poured our hearts and souls into had failed in the marketplace. By 2001 our leadership team said it was time to stop all development. I cried.

Fortunately, our cofounder Klaus Schauser had a plan. His plan involved a pivot that would ultimately lead us to breathtaking success with two best-selling products. To get there, we needed to begin with what I now call *dynamic reteaming*.

Klaus asked me to join a small, isolated team to work on a brand-new product. Because we reteamed, we were a new team and were able to work differently. We could innovate. We were given explicit permission and encouragement to abandon the Waterfall way of working that we had grown accustomed to. We had process freedom. It was liberating.

The team was comprised of software engineers. I was along as a writer. We didn't have any other roles, unlike other teams at our company, who were told to leave us alone. Not having the standard roles meant that we had to do it all. Developers designed the interface and didn't have to wait for pixel-perfect mockups illustrating the frontend design. We named the product Easy Remote Control—or ERC for short. Those initials would live on in the codebase for years. The product was later named GoToMyPC after a company contest was held.

If we had not reteamed at that time and had gone down a different path, I think we would have never created these successful products—GoToMeeting and GoToWebinar—that enable anywhere from two to more than a thousand people to connect online for meetings and webinars. Our success later turned into the acquisition of our startup by Citrix in 2004, and we were renamed Citrix Online.

Nearly 10 years later, when I was working at a startup called AppFolio, Inc., this isolation reteaming pattern happened again. In this case, the company wasn't about to go under, but rather invent a new product line to diversify its offerings.

The product this team invented was also successful. It wound up becoming an entirely different company called SecureDocs, which offers a secure, online virtual data room for storing your company's files for sharing with others later, such as during mergers and acquisitions. It exists today and is headquartered in Santa Barbara, California. Reteaming is so powerful that it even starts companies.

I was exposed to this isolation reteaming pattern yet again back at Citrix Online with a product called Convoi. A close friend was part of this team, where she and other innovators got together and were encouraged to disrupt their flagship product, GoToMeeting. The result of *that* reteaming was another isolated team that validated the acquisition of a company called Grasshopper.

The three isolation examples mentioned here form what I'm calling a pattern. They are examples of the same type of team changes that I came across three or more times in my experience and research for this book.

This is a book about dynamic reteaming, also known as team change. Team change is real, and this book proves it. It feels like I'm stating the obvious; however, there is a bias in the software industry toward having stable teams. That message has been so strong it's as if you might feel like you're doing it wrong if you change up your teams deliberately. You might read quotes like, "Teams with stable membership perform better,"[1] or you might try to heed advice like, "Keep your teams the same for predictability."[2] For many of us, however, team stability is more like a pipe dream. Our teams are more like moving targets than unchanging entities. It's time that we acknowledge that team change is real and that we share stories and ideas for how to not only get good at it, but also dominate it—the essence of this book.

After working in three successful, fast-growing companies since 1999, and after interviewing countless people at other software companies, I present to you a variety of team-change stories and patterns that you can leverage when thinking

---

1 Hackman, *Leading Teams*, 55.

2 Scrum PLoP, "Stable Teams"

about how to grow your company, or attempt to change it in your pursuit of excellence.

The topics in this book vary depending on geography, company type, and size, and aren't always pretty. Included are stories of quite emotional mergers, layoffs, and anti-patterns for unskillfully done reteamings. When the team members choose or catalyze the reteaming, it might be positive. When reteaming happens to us, we might not like it—at least not initially, especially when it's done in a top-down, command-and-control manner.

In Part I you will discover some background information on dynamic reteaming. This includes the evolution of teams, basic definitions to get an understanding of teams, and the power and politics involved in dynamic reteaming. I also detail why you might consider deliberate forms of reteaming in your company to reduce risk and to promote sustainability.

Part II gets into specific reteaming patterns and stories. These "transformations" show up as five base dynamic reteaming patterns: one by one, grow and split, isolation, merging, and switching. I also include a discussion of what I consider to be anti-patterns for reteaming.

Part III includes more practical ideas for how you can make things easier before, during, and after your reteaming. I'll share how to design and prime your company for reteaming so when it happens later, it's easier. I'll also share my favorite tools for planning large-scale reteaming initiatives and explain how to run calibration sessions to get your teams up and running after they change.

No matter what your opinion is on dynamic reteaming, you *will* face it in the future whether you like it or not. People will come and go from your teams and your company. Your company might reorganize or get taken over by a competitor. Key players will join, and at some point they will leave. You might even decide to completely switch up your teams to accomplish a new company goal. No matter what your opinion is on this topic, reteaming is inevitable, so you might as well get good at it.

Approach

My research approach is qualitative and is inspired by the emergent nature of grounded theory as written about and used by Brené Brown in her book *Daring Greatly*.[3] Much of what I have written about in this book has been discovered in

---

3 Brown, *Daring Greatly*, 251.

my interviews. To collect qualitative perspectives from others, I spent an hour with each person and asked them to tell me stories about how their teams had formed and changed over the years. I then had the conversations transcribed, and I coded the data for themes that emerged and composed this book. Some of these respondents have permitted me to use their company names in the book examples. Others told me stories with the agreement that I would keep their company names confidential.

From these stories, I've derived unique patterns and themes that illustrate the concept of dynamic reteaming. All of these organizations are quite adaptive. That means that what I present here is really a snapshot in time for these companies. *Today* they might do things differently than described in this book. And that's a good thing. We need to reflect on our teams and organizational structures in our companies. What worked *yesterday* might not be appropriate *tomorrow*. In addition, these companies range in size from 30 people to thousands of people. What is shared here is not necessarily representative of the organizational patterns within all parts of their companies.

Audience

This book is for people who make decisions about how teams are formed and changed in their companies, or for companies with whom they consult. When writing this book, I imagined that I was speaking to people with titles like vice president of engineering, chief executive officer, founder, chief technology officer, director, manager, or consultant. This book is also for the many people who influence reteaming decisions in their companies, such as software engineers, quality assurance engineers, user experience engineers, ScrumMasters, and coaches.

Participants

My sincere thanks goes to all of the participants who have graciously shared their stories with me:

- Richard Sheridan: Founder and Chief Storyteller at Menlo Innovations (Michigan, USA)
- Jon Walker: CTO and Cofounder of AppFolio, Inc. (California, USA)
- Comron Sattari: Founder and Architect at SecureDocs (California, USA)
- Andrew Mutz: Chief Scientist at AppFolio, Inc. (California, USA)

- Kristian Lindwall: Engineering Site Lead at Spotify (California, USA)
- Chris Lucian: Engineering Lead at Hunter Industries (California, USA)
- William Them: Delivery Manager at Trade Me (Wellington, New Zealand)
- Sandy Mamoli: Agile Coach and Consultant at Nomad8 (Aukland, New Zealand)
- Damon Valenzona: Engineering Director at AppFolio, Inc. (California, USA)
- Mark Kilby: Agile Coach at a DevOps tooling company (Florida, USA)
- Rachel Davies: Agile Coach and Engineering Lead at Unruly (London, UK)
- Evan Willey: Director of Program Management at Pivotal Software Inc., Pivotal Cloud Foundry (California, USA)
- Carey Caulfield: Principal Product Manager at LogMeIn (California, USA)
- Thordur Arnarson: Agile Coach Lead at Tempo Software (Reykjavik, Iceland)
- Cristian Fuentes: Engineering Manager at Jama Software (Oregon, USA)
- Thomas O'Boyle: Software Engineer at Procore Technologies (California, USA)
- Jason Kerney: Full Stack Software Engineer at Hunter Industries (California, USA)
- Elaine Bulloch: Manager, Interactive Program Management at FitBit (California, USA)
- Paige Garnick: Engineering Manager at Procore Technologies (California, USA)
- Andrew Lister: Senior Director of Engineering at Greenhouse Software (New York, USA)
- Mike Boufford: CTO at Greenhouse Software (New York, USA)
- Chris Smith: Head of Product Delivery at Redgate Software (Cambridge, UK)

O'Reilly Online Learning

O'REILLY® For more than 40 years, *O'Reilly Media* has provided technology and business training, knowledge, and insight to help companies succeed.

Our unique network of experts and innovators share their knowledge and expertise through books, articles, and our online learning platform. O'Reilly's online learning platform gives you on-demand access to live training courses, in-depth learning paths, interactive coding environments, and a vast collection of text and video from O'Reilly and 200+ other publishers. For more information, visit *http://oreilly.com*.

How to Contact Us

Please address comments and questions concerning this book to the publisher:

O'Reilly Media, Inc.

1005 Gravenstein Highway North

Sebastopol, CA 95472

800-998-9938 (in the United States or Canada)

707-829-0515 (international or local)

707-829-0104 (fax)

We have a web page for this book, where we list errata, examples, and any additional information. You can access this page at *https://oreil.ly/reteam*.

Email *bookquestions@oreilly.com* to comment or ask technical questions about this book.

For more news and information about our books and courses, visit *http://oreilly.com*.

Find us on Facebook: *http://facebook.com/oreilly*

Follow us on Twitter: *http://twitter.com/oreillymedia*

Watch us on YouTube: *http://www.youtube.com/oreillymedia*

How to Use This Book

If you want an introduction to what dynamic reteaming is, read Part I.

If you want to read about the patterns and anti-patterns, read Part II.

If you want to dig into practical ideas for how to make reteaming easier now or in the future, read Part III, as well as the rest of the book where practices are described in context.

Acknowledgments

I want to thank everyone who has supported this learning quest. In particular, I'd like to thank Leanpub, the publishing platform that empowered me to release the first version of this book, which I later shared with O'Reilly, who published this edition. Without both companies, this material would not be in your hands. Special thanks to editor Melissa Duffield, who believed in me and gave me many opportunities to showcase my ideas, and Melissa Potter, my development editor, who helped me refine and craft this edition. Kate Galloway helped me become much more articulate in expressing so many important details in this book, and I thank her immensely for that. I also thank Chris Smith of Redgate Software and Mark Kilby for their detailed feedback on this edition.

I also want to thank all of the contributors listed in the previous section, who shared their reteaming stories with me. Their stories as well as my personal experience are what revealed the five patterns of dynamic reteaming and brought them to life.

Diana Larsen contacted me about writing the original book's foreword, which has been republished for this version. It still means the world to me that she did that! John Cutler is a friend and former colleague of mine from AppFolio. He is one of the most thoughtful and creative people I know, and I am delighted to have his foreword for this edition.

Back in 2015, Joshua Kerievsky encouraged me to write this book in its entirety so that I would write the book that I wanted to write before approaching publishers. That let me work at my own pace and shape my thoughts and research into something complete. I now give that incredible advice to other aspiring writers.

Klaus Schauser and Jon Walker were two key managers and mentors in my career, and they are also the cofounders of AppFolio. I am so grateful to have learned software development with them. We built two amazing companies together—Expertcity, where we invented GoToMeeting and GoToWebinar, and

AppFolio. They gave me a solid foundation to apply at other companies. I share many of our stories and philosophies in this book.

Sam Crigman, now head of R&D at Procore Technologies, told me, "Don't slow down," and encouraged me to speak about dynamic reteaming at industry events. His ongoing support has helped me to pursue the concept of dynamic reteaming to a greater level of understanding.

My parents have always been very supportive and encouraging. In particular, I want to thank my father, Alan Shetzer, who always advised me to pursue the work that I would love to do and look forward to doing every day. You can find his influence in this book.

Michael Feathers was the original inspiration for my writing about the topic of dynamic reteaming. He might have even named the topic in our early conversations. I am so grateful for our life together.

Most of all I'd like to thank my children, Samuel and Julia. I hope that through my example I have instilled some sort of work ethic that will inspire them now and in the future.

PART I

What Is Dynamic Reteaming?

Whether you like it or not, your teams are going to change. People will join your team, and people will leave your team. It takes the addition or removal of only one person to have a new team system.[1] And sometimes it is more than that. Multiple people join the company. It feels different. When a company goes through hard times, it could be that many people are dismissed. This is all dynamic reteaming. It is all part of the general concept of team change. We might catalyze our own team change and, therefore, desire it. At other times, the changes happen to us. Recognizing team change as a natural occurrence is a key point of this book. In essence, team change is inevitable, so we might as well get good at it.

Our teams evolve. Time passes and transformations occur. Let's dive into the nature of teams.

---

1 See Rød and Fridjhon, *Creating Intelligent Teams*, for an expanded perspective on this concept.

What Is Dynamic Reteaming?

The Evolution of Teams

Think of a team that you were a part of in the past. Can you remember when you joined or when you left that team? Many of us aren't on the same teams forever—our team experiences have beginnings as well as endings. And other people might come and go from our teams in the middle of all that. An ecocycle, like the example shown in Figure 1-1, is a useful metaphor for thinking about the evolution of a team and how it changes over time.

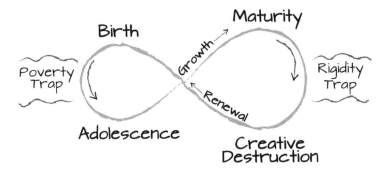

Figure 1-1. An ecocycle based on the adaptive cycle by Lance H. Gunderson and C.S. Holling, Panarchy; *and Keith McCandless, Henri Lipmanowicz, and Fisher Qua,* Liberating Structures

Here's a short example from forestry to illustrate the general concept of an ecocycle that I will then relate to dynamic reteaming. In the Los Padres National Forest near where I live in California, we can witness the ecocycle of oak trees firsthand. At a very high level it works like this: Acorns drop from the trees. They find their way underground and take root–like a birth phase. Next is the adolescence phase, in which the young oak trees grow and grow and grow. Then there is an accumulation taking place as the forest becomes denser. The trees that thrive get really thick and develop canopies—they are in the maturity phase. The trees that do not do well might never get to adolescence and will instead struggle and probably die off. This is akin to being in a *poverty trap*, or a situation where there is a failure to thrive.

After a while, in a mature forest, the trees might get brittle and their growth might be slowed. It's like a rigidity trap, where the life appears stifled or not as expansive. It could even appear stagnating. All of this is the opposite of thriving. In times of drought it can be even more pronounced, incredibly fragile, and even dangerous. Just a small spark can cause a catastrophic wildfire and burn the trees to the ground. This is the place in the ecocycle that evokes some kind of disruption or destruction.

Researchers who apply this ecocycle concept beyond forestry sometimes call the phase after maturity *creative destruction*, a term coined by economist Joseph Schumpeter in 1950.[1] It's the death and disturbance phase. But nature is clever. Through this grand disruption, it finds new beginnings. Wildfires enable the release of new seeds and other matter that catalyzes incredible renewal. What takes root and survives will start this ecocycle again, regenerating the forest and the life around it in all kinds of interesting ways until the next time a large disturbance or even a catastrophe happens.

So how does a forestry ecocycle relate to dynamic reteaming? I think it helps to provide an awesome context for it. Let me explain. But first a caveat—keep in mind that this dynamic reteaming ecocycle is only a metaphor. Like forestry ecocycles, it's not meant to be a prescriptive path for all teams or organizations.[2] I view the dynamic reteaming ecocycle as a sensemaking tool. Inherent in this metaphor is an evolutionary approach to teams instead of a predictive or linear one.

I joined AppFolio, the second startup I was a part of, in 2007 as the tenth employee. I was on the first engineering team. When I joined, that team was more or less in its birth phase, depicted in Figure 1-2.

---

1 Gunderson and Holling, *Panarchy*, 34.

2 Gunderson and Holling, *Panarchy*, 51.

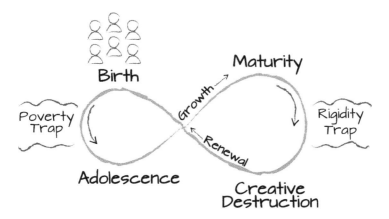

Figure 1-2. A new team

After a while, that first team gained more experience and got bigger. It grew into adolescence and continued to grow. The hiring ramped up. Team members were added on gradually using the dynamic reteaming pattern that I call *one by one*, described in Chapter 5. You could say that particular team was in its maturity phase, like in Figure 1-3.

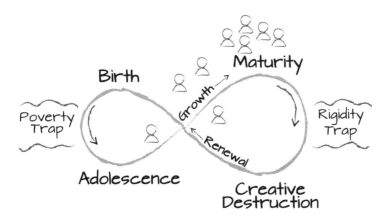

Figure 1-3. One-by-one addition of new team members

Time passed, and that team felt too big for many of us. It became very difficult for us to make decisions together. Meetings started taking forever. It was as if we were stagnating. Something had to change. This is the rigidity trap idea shown in Figure 1-4.

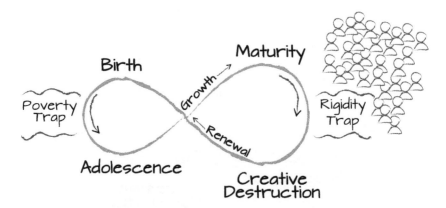

Figure 1-4. A team is that growing so big is probably going to fall into a rigidity trap or stagnate

After a while it got even more challenging, and we realized that we needed to change our team composition. We needed to disrupt ourselves. At that point, we essentially dynamically reteamed into two new teams. Following that structural split, our people started again as two brand-new teams, and then the cycle continued, as shown in Figure 1-5. We focused on different areas of work. We reinvented our meetings. Things felt different and fresh.

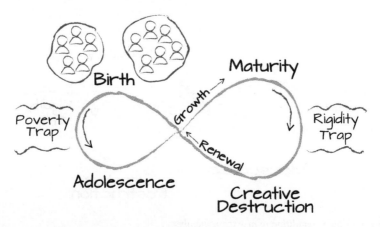

Figure 1-5. A team that grew big and then split in half and is now two teams

Not all teams are fortunate enough even to grow big and split, or get anywhere near a maturation phase. A team that doesn't succeed might be thought of as getting stuck in a poverty trap. Maybe the chemistry is off, and the people together on the team don't gel. So, the team dissolves, or you disband it. It could also be that the product the team is working on doesn't take off. From my perspective, the Expertcity marketplace product I described in the beginning of this book was in a poverty trap. No one would buy it! So we quickly started a new team off to the side, using what I call the *isolation pattern*, described in Chapter 7, and the team ecocycle started anew for those people. You might view the poverty trap as an early exit point out of the dynamic reteaming ecocycle.

The nature of ecocycles is that they are multilevel, which brings us to the concept of *panarchy*.

Panarchy

Extending the ecocycle metaphor even further, let's entertain it as being present simultaneously on multiple levels of context. In the English language, the word *team* itself is lexically ambiguous. When I say *team*, I might be referring to the immediate, cross-functional software development team that I'm on, or I could be referring to my company as a whole. I could even be referencing some level in between—such as referring to my R&D organization as my team. The concept of *team* is multilevel and multidimensional.

This reminds me of a concept related to the ecocycle, an idea called panarchy, which is depicted visually by multiple ecocycles at different scales. Authors Gunderson and Holling describe panarchy as "linkages between systems dynamics and scale," and they elaborate on that in a cross-disciplinary fashion in their 2002 book called *Panarchy: Understanding Transformations in Human and Natural Systems*. The intent of their work is to develop a cross-scale, integrative theory to help people understand global transformational, adaptive systems in nature, economics, and organizations. The name *panarchy* pays homage to the Greek god Pan, who they say "captures an image of unpredictable change and [...] notions of hierarchies across scales to represent structures that sustain experiments, test results, and allow adaptive evolution."[3]

Applying panarchy to dynamic reteaming brings the idea that we are essentially going through multiple, relatively unpredictable dynamic reteaming ecocycles concurrently, at different levels and at different speeds or dynamics. When thinking of dynamic reteaming, I apply this concept by imagining three levels of panarchy: the individual level, the team level, and the company level. I'm sure you can imagine other levels in between and beyond—think about how

---

3 Gunderson and Holling, *Panarchy*, 5.

COVID-19 impacted us at the world level and influenced all the way down and around the levels. For the sake of simplicity and focus, I illustrate this concept using only three levels, as depicted in Figure 1-6.

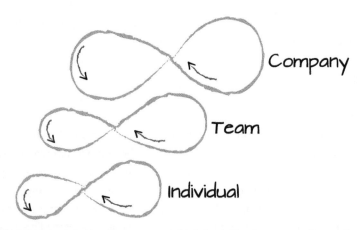

Company

Team

Individual

Figure 1-6. Dynamic reteaming happens on multiple levels like the concept of panarchy (Gunderson and Holling, Panarchy, *2002)*

At any time, we as individuals are going through our own dynamic reteaming ecocycles. It's like when you join a company. You're in the birth phase of your individual experience there, and will continue on through your ecocycle of experience until some type of event occurs and you are disrupted. Maybe others join your team and that renews your experience. Maybe you change teams. Maybe the work changes. Maybe you change roles in your company. You might even leave the company. It could be that the changes happen to you without your input. You might even catalyze creative destruction, or sometimes it seems to just emerge. There are lots of possibilities.

We also go through the ecocycle at a team level. When a team is created it's in the birth phase. As time passes on it might grow and change in adolescence. Whether or not the team gets the addition of new people, with time it might feel as if it is becoming mature. Then at some point the team might go through its own transformation and dynamically reteam in a myriad of patterns. In essence, teams have their beginnings, and as time passes, these teams might thrive, grow, change, die, and so on.

As we get more macro with our application of panarchy to dynamic reteaming, we look at company entities themselves. They too can be viewed as going through an ecocycle. I was at my first startup, Expertcity, for eight years. I was there as the company grew from 15 to about 700 employees. I was there around birth and left at some point of maturity. The company was disrupted when acquired by Citrix in 2004, and the whole organization changed and reassembled with a newly stated identity and leadership. We were called Citrix Online, a separate and, for a while, independent division of that company. So, theoretically, it started over in the ecocycle. In 2017, this team was acquired by another company, LogMeIn, and morphed into that identity. This is the *merging pattern*, described in Chapter 8.

According to Gunderson and Holling, the speed at which changes occur in ecocycles differs based on scale. The authors write that when large, the ecocycle goes slower, and it goes more rapidly at a smaller scale, like at the team level. The slow pace of a large-scale ecocycle suggests that if you can keep things stable at the company level, then you can endure more dynamic reteaming at the team level due to that contextual anchor. The authors note, "In essence, larger and slower components of the hierarchy provide the memory of the past and of the distant to allow recovery of smaller and adaptive cycles."[4] The role of story and the connectedness to shared experience and purpose at the company level might just be the glue that keeps organizations with dynamic teams together. I can see that as true from my experiences at AppFolio. We had strong traditions, such as representing company milestones on whitewater rafting oars that we'd all sign, which related back to two whitewater rafting trips taken by team members early in the company. We would have repeated events at the company level that provided a rhythm, such as an annual guacamole-making competition on Cinco de Mayo. The traditions, culture, and symbols of the larger entity gave continuity to the smaller team entities.

The stories in this book illustrate the complex nature of individual-, team-, and company-level changes that many of us experience in the software industry. The five patterns show the structural and transformational nature of the changes. If I were to describe the essence of dynamic reteaming, it is defined as a myriad of changes catalyzed or occurring on multiple levels, for multiple reasons, and expressed in multiple patterns. The biggest challenges to dynamic reteaming, however, are related to human factors, which we will cover throughout this book. You can't just install reteaming into your company without respect and consideration for the people. Before we get into that, let's take a look at some basic definitions of teams and apply them to dynamic reteaming.

---

4 Gunderson and Holling, *Panarchy*, 20.

2

Understanding Teams

We just looked into the nature of teams and how they change and evolve through time. As previously described, sometimes the changes emerge and happen naturally. Other times people try to catalyze the changes. This is a key concept to understand about dynamic reteaming.

This chapter details other basic concepts like the definition of *team* and how it relates to the concept of change in general. In addition, we discuss the base transformation of dynamic reteaming, which is the addition or removal of one person from the team. That's the "smallest" type of reteaming, and it might sound easy; however, depending on the person who is either moving in or out, it can be quite disruptive.

Let's take a look at the basics, then, and dig into some preliminary concepts.

What Is a Team?

If you read a definition of the term *team*, you might read that it is "a bounded and stable set of individuals interdependent for a common purpose."[1] But what if the team composition is not stable? What if it is highly changeable, as in the case of a startup engaged in hypergrowth? Is this still a team? To this I say yes. Changeable teams are teams.

The smallest unit of a team is a pair, as depicted in Figure 2-1. The pair is defined as two people working together to build something valuable for their customers. They are thought partners.

---

1 Wageman et al., "Changing Ecology of Teams," 305.

Figure 2-1. The base unit of a team is a pair

How the pair works together is important. Is the pair a "team" when they pair program? Are they still a team if they coordinate on shared goals and do the work in parallel? I would say yes for both cases, and I would add that what makes them a team is the *shared goal and the joint ownership of the outcome*. If they are both responsible for the outcome, then they are a team. If they take responsibility for their joint work, then they are a team.

But it feels quite different when people are pairing with one computer versus working in parallel, separately, toward the same goal. There is a different notion of proximity and collaboration when you are pair programming versus when you are working in parallel. I dig into this idea in "Collaboration Dynamics that Restrict and Enable Reteaming" on page 156.

Now that we have a working definition of what I mean by the concept of a *team*, let's talk about team change, or dynamic reteaming.

Dynamic Reteaming

Dynamic reteaming is when your teams change. It could be as simple as the addition or removal of one team member. It could be as radical as pulling team members off of multiple teams to form a new team. It could even be the dissolution of the team. Dynamic reteaming happens at different rates and on different levels within our organizations. Here is our overarching definition of *dynamic reteaming*:

Dynamic
> (Of a process or system) characterized by constant change, activity, or progress

Reteaming
> To bring (people) together or apart in work or activity

Dynamic reteaming is the structural transformation of your teams. These structural transformations occur as five base patterns, which I'll describe in detail in Part II of this book. Besides structural changes, when reteaming happens other social changes happen.

In particular, dynamic reteaming creates a new "team system" or "team entity." The new people added to the team bring their interests and talents to the mix, impacting the collective intelligence present on the team.[2] They bring new learning potential and ideas to the team as a whole, as depicted in Figure 2-2.

Figure 2-2. When a new person joins, they bring new ideas to the team

Reteaming helps teams learn together and do things they couldn't do before. Reteaming brings possibility. Comron Sattari, architect and cofounder of Secure-Docs, reflected on his time at AppFolio when it was a startup. When talking about reteaming, he said, "We could play to the team's strengths. There was a team with experience doing X, and the product team could say, *Okay, let's give this project to that team because they have a lot of experience with it.* So we were able to

---

2 Rød and Fridjhon, *Creating Intelligent Teams*, 13.

work on things that we were good at, and new people would come in and change the makeup of the team, and then all of a sudden the team was good at something else, and we would work on that." People bring new ideas and perspectives when they change teams. There can be great intellectual power to team change.

Furthermore, Comron notes, "If the team stays stagnant, the abilities you have stay stagnant. We have people on the global engineering team for a reason: they're good at certain things, they're good team members, and mixing that up all the time is important."[3]

I would echo that importance. When you view your company as a learning community, you can collaborate with many of the people in the setting, by creatively reteaming. When you deliberately plan out the reteaming in your organization, you can provide new learning opportunities for people. People can get bored if they're not learning. Avoiding stagnation in this way can help you retain good employees.

The loss of team members—whether to another team internally or to an organization outside the company—causes a reteaming of a different kind. When a team member goes away for whatever reason, the team system is smaller, and the character and personality of the person who left is not physically there anymore. This could be a good thing if the individual was annoying or disruptive. In that case, the team could be in a better place and quite possibly ready to move on. It could also feel like a huge loss if this person was a key player with special influence in the team, such as a founder. It might take a long time to get over the loss of this person.

In either case, sometimes it "feels" like that person is still there as the thought of them lingers on almost like a ghost, as shown in Figure 2-3. Maybe others expect that any new person in their place should act just like the person who left. Or maybe you can't stop thinking about the person who left the team.

---

3 Comron Sattari, in an interview with the author, March 2016.

Figure 2-3. When a person leaves an existing team, the team system is different. However, the thought of that person might linger like a ghost (Rød and Fridjhon, Creating Intelligent Teams, *104–106)*

Deliberate activities to acknowledge feelings when people leave teams can help. See "When People Leave, You Have a New Team" on page 61 for ideas.

Regardless of how the dynamic reteaming happens, the feel of the team—the social dynamic—is impacted because the team system is different. It has changed its structural composition. There is often a disconnect between the structural changing of teams and the acceptance of it by the people involved. This is related to the idea of transition from William Bridges, which we will address in Chapter 13. You can't expect to change your teams and have the humans all "snap into line" and get over it quickly. In many cases, there is a delay between a structural change and the acceptance or transition into the new team structure, and so you can pay attention and try activities to help the people acclimate to their new structures.

That being said, dynamic reteaming is not easy. When people hear about the concept they might be excited because in theory it sounds great. "Let's mix up all of our teams right away! Let's implement *dynamic reteaming!*" That would be entirely shortsighted. The truth is, dynamic reteaming can be very challenging, which makes it worth your time to study. Know what you're getting into. Be prepared to deal with it when it happens naturally.

DOES DYNAMIC RETEAMING ALWAYS WORK OUT?

If you go forth and just mix up all your team members in an effort to reteam, you could cause panic, fear, and confusion. It doesn't always work out for the best. What you need to remember is that you're dealing with humans. Humans have preferences and individual personalities. We don't like to be moved around abstractly like pieces on a chessboard. Our thoughts and opinions matter. In other words, what if the people do not want to change teams? What if they feel that they are learning a lot on their existing team? It might be better to keep some teams unchanged. See the anti-patterns described in Chapter 10 for ideas about when to leave teams alone.

Reteaming done well takes great care and respect for people. There is no one-size-fits-all "installation" of reteaming. Catalyzing dynamic reteaming is challenging and nuanced. In this book, I will teach you my best tactics for success, and show you some pitfalls to avoid. I think success or failure in dynamic reteaming is impacted by several variables, such as those described in "Variables That Impact Dynamic Reteaming" on page 160. Success also has something to do with the chemistry of the team—that is, the social dynamic created by the mix of human personalities that are brought together as a team. Let's explore this.

The Social Dynamic of a Team

People talk about *chemistry* and whether it's present or not in love relationships. The term *soul mates* might come to mind. There's something mystical and magical about certain humans together, and I think there's an element of this in teams.

A team's social dynamic can answer the questions "What is that team like?" or "What is that team's personality?" Jon Walker, CTO and cofounder of AppFolio, described what a high-functioning team and low-functioning team feels like, in his experience. He said of high-functioning teams, "You feel their enthusiasm and excitement when a team is working really well. They get really excited about what they're doing. To be honest, I had one sitting outside my office. All the time they are noisy and celebrating stuff, talking with each other. But you can feel it and it feels really different."

In terms of a low-functioning team, he said, "I think the energy feels low. If you're in meetings with them it feels like, *Ah, we've got to get through this,* versus

Hey, there's new stuff that we're excited about and can learn here...What if we did this, what if we did that?"[4]

This phenomenon was noticed at MIT's Human Dynamics Laboratory by Alex "Sandy" Pentland and his staff, who study the communication patterns of teams. In a *Harvard Business Review* article, he wrote, "We noticed we could sense a buzz in a team even if we didn't understand what the members were talking about. That suggested that the key to high performance lay not in the content of a team's discussions but in the manner in which it was communicating."[5] There is something almost inexplicable about this kind of chemistry.

Damon Valenzona, an engineering director at AppFolio in San Diego, compared teams to a musical band: "You feel that magic when you're brainstorming and you kind of think like a jam session when people are riffing, right, and the drummer starts and everyone's kind of, oh, Yeah! Yeah! Yeah! And they're adding their own like playing the guitar and then the bass comes in. They're all starting to feel it, and they're all very different things, but they're kind of like adding their special sauce to this thing and it's kind of like creating something together."

The opposite to jamming, in Damon's words, is when you have more of the "command and control–like team where you have this team or project lead and then everyone else is kind of just following along and shaking their heads and then they're the ones who actually go and execute on it."[6]

Being able to identify the feel of a team just by visual cues or reading the energy is certainly not as simple as described here, and I don't mean to trivialize it. There could be a quiet and serious team that is highly engaged, but you look at the members and think they're all bored. Or you find a loud, boisterous team and assume it is delivering value continuously, but the members are goofing off most of the time and aren't producing much. But not everything lasts.

AS TIME PASSES, OUR TEAMS CHANGE

At one point our team is thriving. Later on it might degrade. Circumstances around us change. What we are working on changes. Whatever it is, the feel or dynamic of the team does not stay the same forever. Team change is a natural occurrence, as detailed in Chapter 1. As time passes in your team you might

---

4 Jon Walker, in an interview with the author, February 2016.

5 Pentland, "New Science," 1.

6 Damon Valenzona, in an interview with the author, October 2016.

think, "Why aren't we as effective as we used to be?" Or, as things change around your team, maybe due to extreme growth or acquisition by another company, people might notice the shifts and wonder what happened to the company they knew before because now it "feels so different." See "What It Means When You're Asked, "How Do We Maintain Our Culture?"" on page 87 for an exploration of this topic.

At other times, when we feel that things are less productive or stagnating, we might try to change the teams deliberately in order to feel refreshed or renewed. We might try to intentionally reorganize our teams in the quest for greater effectiveness. But that's no easy endeavor. Reteaming can be very tricky and downright risky.

I like to encourage teams to reflect on their own compositions and determine how they might shift into greater effectiveness. How can they change their structure to be more effective? By asking questions like this, a team can become more self-aware as an entity, and when given the go-ahead by the powers that be, team members can even be empowered to change their *own* team composition in order to solve problems. I think that's the spirit of a self-organizing team as a concept. This concept is not readily taught with the stable-teams dogma that has permeated the Agile and organizational development spheres. I have found that it takes a bit of brain rewiring on the part of executives to trust teams to do this. It is worth the plight. It can be done. It can be coached.

Different combinations of people yield different team chemistry. You could get lucky and get the right team members together. If you do, and if they are delivering awesome value at a great cadence to customers, by all means, keep them together. However, if you have teams in a funk for months on end, and things don't seem quite right collaboratively, switching things up might be just what you need.

The bottom line to dynamic reteaming is this: Start where you are. Visualize your team structures. Observe and get to know them. Agree to pursue incremental reflection and adjustment to your teams. Experiment and learn. Adjust your team compositions accordingly. See Chapter 14 for an exploration of retrospectives as a tool to shift your teams.

We've taken a look at basic team definitions, and we've seen how dynamic reteaming is, in essence, about the structural change of teams. So how do people get on teams in the first place, and how do they get off of teams? Let's dig into the power dynamics surrounding team assignment and change.

3

The Power of Team Assignment

There are different ways in which people arrive to their teams and later change teams. Some companies are open to having the team members decide where they go. For others it's more of a controlled management decision. Things vary and depend on the context. A humanistic approach to team assignment takes the interests and learning needs of the individual into account when they arrive to teams, as opposed to yanking people out of teams without their input and placing them into situations that they do not want to be in. Sometimes we have a say in when we change teams, but other times we do not. There is an inherent notion of power in team assignment—ranging from very command-and-control, "from the top" decision making, to bottom-up, self-organized decision making that is made by team members. I think about this as a continuum, as shown in Figure 3-1.

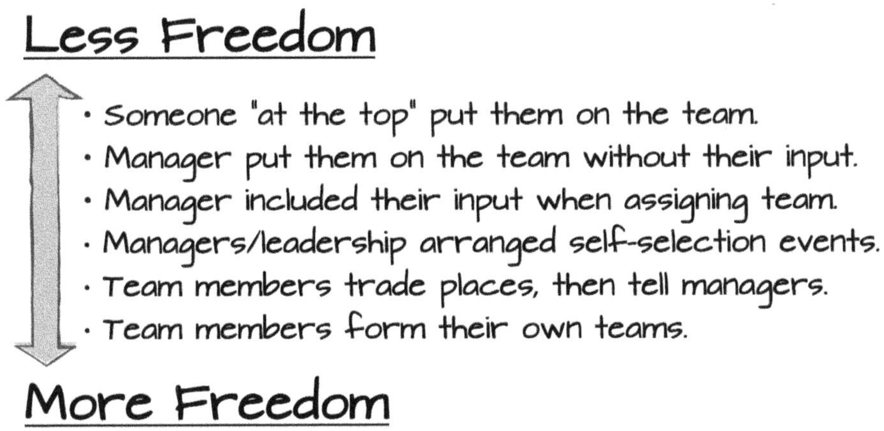

Less Freedom

- Someone "at the top" put them on the team.
- Manager put them on the team without their input.
- Manager included their input when assigning team.
- Managers/leadership arranged self-selection events.
- Team members trade places, then tell managers.
- Team members form their own teams.

More Freedom

Figure 3-1. Continuum of team assignment and change

Let's start at the top of Figure 3-1. I think that when we are put into teams, or removed from teams by decisions made by people we don't know, there is a sense of abstraction. I've seen this happen in my career during acquisitions. I've been on both sides—I've been at companies that got acquired, and I've been at companies that have acquired other companies. I've witnessed teams get combined, and code ownership moved from one location to another. I've watched managers get reassigned, and people lose their jobs after others explored around to "find synergies" across both companies. You might feel like a cog in a wheel during these times if you are far from the decisions being made. This is the abstraction part. "Someone" has decided which changes are happening. It's out of your control. That's what I mean by *less freedom*.

Moving down the continuum of team assignment and change, more power is in the hands of the people to determine their team destinies. Managers can form close relationships with their people and thoughtfully put them on teams. They can help them learn and grow, and give individuals more freedom to choose their team and work assignment. At the furthest end of the freedom spectrum, the people act as responsible agents of their own team change and formation. They just go and form teams. No one is holding them back, and I would imagine that there is a lot of freedom and safety in this context. Let's explore the politics of team assignment in closer detail, from less freedom to more freedom.

Someone "At the Top" Put Them on the Team

As a consultant, I was at a client site that was taken over by one of its competitors. We were told that 5% of the company would be laid off globally. We had to wait a couple of weeks to have our meetings in engineering to find out who would be losing their jobs. How the decisions were made, and how they trickled down to the people, was very opaque. The average individual contributor was not privy to this information. People just waited to see if they were getting the email inviting them to a meeting that would seal their fate.

At one point, someone decided to shut down the San Francisco office. Part of my team was up there. Two of my team members were laid off, but were given a month to transfer knowledge and find another job. Why was it them and not the other team members? It was unclear and unspoken. No one talked about it openly—this was reteaming by abstraction.

The San Francisco office had been bustling at one time. People were happy, and there was a sense of community in that small office of about 45 people. With this turn of events, when I visited during the layoff time, there were just about five people left, surrounded by empty desks. The mood was somber, and the dynamic felt so heavy. The remaining people wound up moving to a separate office in another part of the city that had better access to public transportation and better restaurants. At least they had that to look forward to. A change of location sounded like the best thing for the remaining people, in my opinion.

Layoffs like this kill communities. They just do. I know there are business reasons why these things happen, but the human aspect of it can just be really, really difficult to deal with. It takes a while to heal from this, especially if it is your first time experiencing a layoff. It relates to the concept of transition. There's a structural change in the team composition, but there is a human lag to process and integrate the change, and that takes time. Not all humans respond the same. See Chapter 13 for ideas on how to deal with unexpected dynamic reteaming like this, and how to move on from it in your company.

The Managers Decide the Team Membership

One way that teams were formed and reteamed at AppFolio was by managers getting to know people's needs and interests on a one-on-one basis and putting them into a team where they could have a great mentor who was willing to help them learn the basics.

I spoke with Andrew Mutz, chief scientist at AppFolio, about reteaming, and he shared several stories with me. AppFolio has a very solid, learning-focused approach. Managers learn what engineers are excited to work on and pair them with people who are willing to be their mentors across their feature teams. Andrew called this a "fit operation."[1] Every new hire gets a mentor who helps them get up to speed with the current work and the environment as a whole. They pair program together as a strategy for sharing information and growing the new person into their role.

All along the way, the manager and the engineer have a continuous conversation about how the engineer is doing and what they are passionate about. As time goes on, that conversation helps to determine if the engineer should stay on the same team or switch to another one. This process is very fulfillment focused. It acknowledges that, as people, we grow and change with time. It's about having engineers who are excited to come to work each day, are energized by what they

---

1 Andrew Mutz, in an interview with the author, April 2016.

are doing, and have the opportunity to learn and grow without being stuck on the same team forever.

The People Take a Survey to See if They Want to Change Teams

Sending out a survey to team members is one way to find out if people need a change to feel more engaged at work. Rachel Davies told me about how for the past four years at Unruly in London, for example, team members had the opportunity to submit an electronic survey indicating how much they would like to switch into another team, and on what timescale. Unruly sent out a survey roughly every three months, and it was up to the managers or team leads to make the final team-switching decisions.

The survey idea came about at Unruly after its first team split into two, and in less than a year, one of those teams split in two again. The split of the first team enabled the development of a brand-new analytics product that could be built while maintaining the core product set used across its business. The next split was the core product team, which enabled an expansion of the existing product set. Each time they split, the teams found that a smaller team led to a better work experience for both teams because they had shorter standups and the feeling that they were all more productive.[2]

Following this experience of team splitting, Unruly's team leads decided to encourage regular reteaming in order to share knowledge and create more resilient teams. This approach also provided an opportunity for developers to learn about new system areas, and to gain experience developing different products. At that point there were three teams, and people were able to, in Rachel's words, "work their way around all of the teams."[3] A couple of team members did just that.

When an engineer wanted to expand their experience in another coding language or develop a new part of the product, they could request to change teams via conversations with the coach or team lead, or via the team rotation survey. People were drawn to a team by both the technology and the culture. Some people avoided teams when they didn't like the dynamic—such as a team with a loud, opinionated person who dominated the conversation.

---

2 A *standup* is a 15-minute daily huddle meeting for teams.

3 Rachel Davies, in an interview with the author, December 2016.

The survey helped managers to avoid typecasting people into one team forever. As Rachel said, "People that joined the company as Java developers ended up in the JavaScript team, and other people gravitated away from it. There were people who didn't want to learn about frontend work and preferred the familiarity of Java code." It's nice to provide people with the ability to grow and learn at their workplace. Giving the opportunity to change teams can help retain people.

Besides surveying people to find out if they want to switch teams, you can just announce an opportunity and see who reaches out in response; that's what Kristian Lindwall and team did at Spotify when reteaming around a cross-team challenge, which is described in the following section.

Managers Encourage People to Volunteer for a Team

Kristian Lindwall, engineering site lead at Spotify San Francisco, told me how some of its teams came to be. Spotify had different platform teams dedicated to developing on different clients, such as iOS, Android, and so on. At Spotify, groups of squads are referred to as tribes (*https://labs.spotify.com/2014/03/27/ spotify-engineering-culture-part-1*). In one of its tribes related to app development productivity, there were some performance issues that came about across all of these platforms. It was not surfacing as a priority to solve these issues from within the individual client teams, so a new team came together with a mission to improve cross-platform performance challenges. The members of this group, which included a product owner, fleshed out what the initial mission would be, and then—using existing channels in the company like email and chat—advertised that there was a new team forming with the mission they had prepared, and that they were looking for team members who would be interested in working on those challenges. Those who were interested could volunteer to join, and leave the teams that they were currently on.[4]

Beyond surveying and inviting volunteers, another structure that companies use to get people onto new teams is by having an event—sometimes called a *self-selection event*. Let's dig in.

---

4 Kristian Lindwall, in an interview with the author, September 2016.

Managers Arrange Team Self-Selection Events

Sandy Mamoli, coauthor of the book *Creating Great Teams: How Self-Selection Lets People Excel*, told me about a few different ways that she has seen teams form and reform. These include managers just putting people onto teams at random, and managers forming teams of people based on the skills they have without consideration for the people's interests, needs, or relationships with others. She has also seen managers work with their people to understand their interests and needs, similar to the stories Andrew shared earlier in this chapter. She does think that manager-formed reteaming breaks down when you reach a larger scale.

In her book she writes that "managers might still know their direct reports' skills and personalities, but it becomes increasingly difficult to understand the intricacies of relationships among people as the number of relationships increases almost exponentially. In our experience the breaking point is around ten people."[5] Imagine having to do that with 150 people! It was this situation in particular that led her and her colleagues to try something different—the people would be asked to place themselves on teams, which she calls *self-selection*, as the next story illustrates.

HOW A COMPANY REORGED WITH SELF-SELECTION

In the case of the example with the 150 people, Sandy was at Trade Me, New Zealand's biggest e-commerce provider and online auction marketplace. This was in 2013, at a time when the company did not have a team-based structure. In her words: "People were *resourced* on a project-by-project basis, but we had this one group of people, a tribe of four teams that were stable and they were doing incredibly well and they loved it. And we had the rest of the company be really, really envious." So she and others talked about making that transition happen—a reorg. To get started, they gathered the managers into a room and attempted to start the switch to teams like they had done with other "resource assignments" in the past—manager selection. Sandy said, "We wasted an incredible amount of time. And we said, why are we actually talking about this? We are not the people affected. We are not the people who know who wants to do what, and we are not

---

5 Mamoli and Mole, *Creating Great Teams*, 5.

the people who know who gets along with whom, so we decided why not ask the people who actually know this...so we did."[6]

There was excitement, but also fear and concern about asking people to put themselves into teams. Questions came up: "What if it's like the school yard where some people are not going be picked? What do we do if people can't figure it out? What if no one chooses to work in a particular work area?" Sandy and her coauthor and business partner at Nomad8, David Mole, worked together on this challenge. They decided to have a self-selection event—one that would really plant the seed for many events like this—that they still use in their consulting work at Nomad8 to this day.

After a lot of thinking and planning, they created a comprehensive facilitation plan and decided that they really had nothing to lose. If the self-selection event failed, at least they would have gathered a lot more information than they had before, which they could then feed into a management selection of teams. But then they thought, what if? What if they take this risk? Wouldn't it be amazing? It would be incredible if all of these 150 people were able to self-select into their own teams. After all, as they described in their book, the idea of self-selected teams matched the research they had read and believed in from Daniel H. Pink's book *Drive* and from research done by management consultant Margaret J. Wheatley.[7] Furthermore, they had experiences at Trade Me as part of their 24-hour hack days in which they self-selected teams across 80 people. That served as a test case for this larger self-selection event. So because of all this, they went for it!

When you organize any event with 150 people, you need to be really, really organized—you need a solid plan. At a very high level, Sandy and David facilitated an event where there were posters all over the walls displaying externally focused work purposes or missions like "Make the experience better for the top sellers in the marketplace" or "Make the internal legal team's work as easy as possible." Focusing on purposes or missions is thought to be "longer living than just a project because you get domain knowledge, you start to love what you are building," according to Sandy.[8] The people arrived at the event and were given a photo of themselves to use for the self-selection. They got an overview of the

---

6 Sandy Mamoli, in an interview with the author, October 2016.

7 Mamoli and Mole, *Creating Great Teams*, 7.

8 Sandy Mamoli, in an interview with the author, October 2016.

event process, and then product owners described the purpose of their work. The attendees then worked in iterations to figure out which team they wanted to select, and which type of roles each team needed to fulfill its purpose—like engineer, user experience designer, and quality assurance engineer. Sandy and the event organizers put a constraint on team size, insisting that there should be seven or fewer people on each squad.

Every six months or so, this team at Trade Me ran a reteaming event via self-selection. At that point, all the names were removed from existing teams, and people had the opportunity to decide again where they wanted to focus their time for the subsequent six months. They could choose the same mission they were on, or a different one. In Sandy's words: "It's a good way of keeping teams from getting stale."[9] Some of the missions might have been completed, and some were still in progress. The people were given the freedom to move around as they saw fit.

Other companies give this ability to reteam even more directly to the people involved. It might not be at the scale of an entire department, but at the team level, as we will see next.

Teams Strategize and Form Their Own Team Structures

At the closer end of the freedom spectrum, some companies let their teams figure out how they might morph on their own, in order to be more effective. There is a high level of trust, as the following two stories demonstrate, and there is also a lot of respect for the professionals involved. First, we hear Elaine's story about her team at Fitbit and how they reteamed after open conversations about it. Following that, we hear a story from Hunter Industries, where the company enabled team switching at the discretion of the engineers doing the work.

RETEAMING AS THE TEAM'S PROBLEM TO SOLVE

Getting people to participate and decide how to scale out a team from roughly 10 to 50 people who are able to work on multiple concurrent projects is what Elaine Bulloch and her Device Cornerstone team at Fitbit accomplished in 2016. According to Elaine, Fitbit designs products and experiences that fit seamlessly into your life so you can achieve your health and fitness goals. When I talked with Elaine, she said that in 2015 the original team had about 9 to 12 people and it was comprised of cross-functional, full stack engineers working on embedded

---

9 Sandy Mamoli, in an interview with the author, October 2016.

devices that deploy to multiple platforms, including iOS, Android, and web clients. As demand for its wearable devices grew, this leadership committee needed to find a way to reorganize so it could meet the consumer demand and ship devices more frequently to its customers.

So first, in Elaine's words: "We put a lot of thought into how we would reteam, and we heard from our engineers and got ideas from them. We created a leadership committee that included myself as a ScrumMaster, our product owner, our technical leads, engineering managers, and our QA leads and managers and really just talked, and talked, and talked about really what would make sense moving forward."[10] It was clear from the start that the committee wanted to have a separate team, what Elaine called a "vanguard" team, to create and envision the future architecture for Fitbit's devices. After several months, this isolated team had a viable plan, and the existing team had gotten a lot bigger, and accordingly, the committee needed to figure out its new structure.

Figuring out this new structure was like a puzzle to solve, and Elaine's leadership committee took the challenge directly to the team. Elaine told me, "We really wanted to hear from the actual team members themselves, all of the developers, the design folks, all of the QA folks—every person involved in the engineering stack." In order to attain the outcome of having a new team structure that people would be happy with, Elaine facilitated a workshop that she called the Reteaming Exercise.

It worked like this: she invited all of the team members into a large room for a couple of hours. During this reteaming exercise, Elaine had all of the team members write on whiteboards everything that each person and team owned. She said to the group, "Let's write down what we do from areas of code that we own and are responsible for." The mobile and client teams worked on one whiteboard, and the backend team worked on another.

After all of the work and ownership was revealed by the teams, Elaine asked questions like, "How are these groupings going to inform us around how we should group ourselves? What would an optimal team size be, and what would that look like? What would a team of today look like knowing what it is that we are working on today versus the team of tomorrow, three months, six months, nine months, a year from now down the line? What would that look like, knowing what's coming up on our product roadmap?"

---

10 Elaine Bulloch, in an interview with the author, July 2017.

Using this approach, Elaine posed the reteaming puzzle to all the members of the current team. It was a problem for them to solve together. In the end, they concluded that a series of smaller "pods" with ownership over naturally occurring areas of work that they had identified and laid out made the most sense, and whenever possible, the "pods" would have their own leads that could keep aligned on architectural design and implementation decisions on initiatives moving forward. They also crafted mission statements for each of the "pod" teams. At the time of our interview, these same teams had been in place for more than six months, and they continue to be built upon today.

What I really like about the approach described here is that Elaine and others brought the challenge of restructuring for the future to the people who best understood the work of those teams. There is a great deal of respect in reteaming this way. That kind of respect is also present in the next story from Hunter Industries, where the people are able to initiate their own reteaming in concert with the input of their team members.

TEAM MEMBERS TRADE PLACES, THEN TELL MANAGERS

Hunter Industries, a sprinkler manufacturer located near Carlsbad, California, practices mob programming, which is programming that is done by a group of people using one computer. Mob programming is a movement in the software industry that actually originated at Hunter Industries, catalyzed by Woody Zuill and his team. Hunter was going through a growth spurt and had been hiring about two people per month for a period of eight months when I interviewed Chris Lucian, the director of software development, back in summer of 2016. He told me about the flexibility that existed in the different mobs, or groups of people, coding at the same place in the office—complete with large screen, chairs on wheels, shared computer, and keyboard.

They had the idea that "anybody can go and work on whatever they want, and then eventually we realized that some things are way more interesting than others at times so we needed, at least, to have kind of a minimum headcount in place for certain projects." He went on to say that for each identified project they would determine the number of people to work on that project. For example, "we essentially say eight people in this project, eight people in this project, and five people in this project and then you can form the mobs..."

From that start, people were able to move from mob to mob in an open and fluid way. After retrospecting on how things were going in the teams, Hunter discovered that "it's kind of going too fast, and people aren't retaining some information between them." They needed a change. And from there, what Chris called a "negotiation-based reforming" started. It worked like this, according to Chris:

> If you feel like you want to go on to another team, you just have to find somebody else on another team that wants to switch with you, and then you can switch [...] so the idea is that you could switch once every three months, or less frequently, or more frequently. And then as long as the people that are switching on and off those teams are okay with the exchange, then we won't really be going too fast for others because the nature of mob programming is that you kind of have that support and you have that group knowledge, the group memory that's there when you switch.[11]

Notice that this shift in how the team is organized is driven by a retrospective. That is a key idea in team-based change, as discussed in Chapter 14.

Furthermore, negotiating with other team members to switch teams has been a pretty regular occurrence at Hunter Industries. It really depends on the person. As Chris told me, "There are a few people that like to switch every three months, and there are a few people that like to just stay on the same project for a long time. And that's another thing; we get feedback from some people that they do not want to switch teams, but inevitably, because new people will be coming on and off their team, that's essentially a new team. So regardless, they maybe don't want to switch the technical and business logic material that they're working on, but their team will be different."[12] The nature of dynamic reteaming, as we saw in Chapter 1, is that it really is inevitable. It will happen to you. It's not just about catalyzing your team change.

When you do want to catalyze your own team change at Hunter Industries, however, there is help to do that. Full stack software engineer Jason Kerney told me that help is available for people who want to trade places, but need assistance to get the trade to happen.

> They look at whichever team they'd like to move on, and then if they feel comfortable with it, they go over and negotiate it. If they don't, they talk to one of the senior developers who will negotiate for them. Then we will

---

11 Chris Lucian, in an interview with the author, August 2016.

12 Ibid.

take it upon ourselves to go to the other team and say, "Hey look, there is someone who would like to try this out, is there anybody willing to trade with them to go to this other place?" And almost always it's a yes. I don't think we've had anyone say "Absolutely not." I think we've had a couple say, "Well, not right now, but can you come back in a couple of weeks? We're in the middle of something..."[13]

Hunter Industries is committed to fostering an environment of continual retrospectives and learning. In fact, on a daily basis teams have an hour of mob-style learning, and two hours of it on Fridays. During these learning sessions, people get together from across their teams to solve programming exercises together and to learn new skills. When I visited them eight months prior to our interview, they were doing more rapid reteaming. Through retrospectives, they learned that they should reteam at a different rate and in a completely different way. Hunter is a great example of how you can build an adaptive organization powered by retrospectives. You can tune and adjust your reteaming based on this reflection. It's how you become a generative, learning organization.

This chapter detailed different ways that people get on teams. There are different degrees of freedom, from a more controlled, top-down reteaming, to more of an open, bottom-up reteaming. There is not really a one-size-fits-all reteaming process. I think that in general it feels a lot better to people when they have a say in their reteaming. It doesn't feel good to be moved around without any input. It's a competitive advantage to be able to reteam well, with the people in mind. In fact, you can reduce a wide variety of risks to your business as a whole if you get good at reteaming. So let's explore how reteaming, when done well, can reduce risk and encourage the sustainability of companies.

---

13 Jason Kerney, in an interview with the author, January 2017.

4

Reduce Risk and Encourage Sustainability

There are several ways that changing up your team compositions can reduce risk in your company and strengthen the ties between the teams so that information is not lost if teams disband or if people leave. You can proactively manage the spread of information, the development of people, and the cohesion between teams through dynamic reteaming. Let's explore.

Reteaming Decreases the Development of Knowledge Silos

The notion of "bus count" or "bus factor" is not new in the software industry. If you increase your bus count, which is the number of people who know about something—like a specialized technology in your company—you are safer.[1] If one of those people leaves, someone else knows enough about the technology to carry it on into the future, hopefully without too much pain. It's building in redundancy of knowledge, which is better for your company—kind of like a group memory.

But it's not good enough to just add people to teams to be safe. After all, you don't want your individual teams to be too big because that can bring other problems unless managed and facilitated well. These problems might include longer meetings where not everyone speaks or is engaged, lack of visibility on work, difficulty making decisions, and poor coordination.

---

1 Wikipedia, "Bus factor." (*https://en.wikipedia.org/wiki/Bus_factor*).

Within a team, pair programming and test-driven development (TDD) are ways to facilitate a more effective bus count within a team. The quality of interactions on the bus matters! If all the people are sitting on the bus in separate seats with their headphones on working alone, it's quite different than when they are in rows of two people sitting side-by-side working with each other, like pairing. Switching pairing seats on the bus is even better because each mind learns from other perspectives. It's even more diverse and probably safer when all the people on the bus are collaborating with each other, like in mob programming.

On a team-to-team level, you can reduce the risk of developing knowledge silos by reteaming. Spreading knowledge out from one team to another is a great way to keep your company safer and your developers less siloed. We had collective code ownership at AppFolio. As the years went on, pockets of specialization emerged on teams. Trends would develop. Team A would get assigned work on the same feature set over and over again. The members became the experts in that feature set. It was a critical feature set. After a while, we started reteaming to spread the knowledge out deliberately so that Team B could work on the feature set, too. It gave the organization more flexibility and safety.

There is a tension here, however. You want enough code ownership so that people can progress quickly on their work and care about the bigger picture, but you don't want to typecast people or teams so that they are stuck working on "that feature" only. Silos are emergent. Be mindful of them and notice when they occur so that you can proactively reteam.

Beneficial silos are another story. You want to create them for a different purpose. See Chapter 7 for more on this.

Reteaming Reduces Team Member Attrition by Providing Career Growth Opportunities

Your organization can become "stickier," and people might be less likely to leave it, if you provide people with opportunities to learn from others by reteaming and re-roleing.

At AppFolio, engineers had the opportunity to switch into other teams from time to time to provide anti–career stagnation. For example, engineers could leave a feature team and then go over to the data center development team to learn something completely different. Or they could move over to an infrastructure team to work on some systemic code challenges. Tech support engineers could spend time over on feature development teams as well. Some of the engineers who explored something different decided to go back to their original teams, while others stayed in their new team.

Sandy Mamoli talks about how tribes reteamed every six months at Trade Me in New Zealand. Even if there was still work continuing on at that six-month marker, people had the opportunity to work on a completely different team and mission if they so desired. It anchored with their company's important value of autonomy. William Them, who worked within a particular tribe at Trade Me, shared how they do that in his teams every few weeks, which I discuss in more detail in Chapter 8.

As humans, we change with time. If we have the mindset of lifelong learning, we are never really "finished" developing ourselves. Companies can be compatible with visions like this and enable team and role movement for their people. It helps retain them. Why wouldn't we want to retain good people in our companies?

Reteaming Decreases Inter-Team Competition, Fostering a Whole-Team Mentality

The last thing you want in your company is to have multiple teams at war with each other, competing and comparing themselves. We need to work together across our teams. Especially if we share a huge codebase that has cross-team dependencies that need to be worked out with close collaboration.

Having the ability to switch teams and work across them is important, according to Comron Sattari, who reflected on his time at AppFolio. As he recalled to me, "Mixing up team members all the time is important. You don't want to break up the overall engineering teams into the smaller teams, and then have this tribal warfare where this team gets good projects because there are senior members in it. For example, like allowing one team to work on database stuff while the other team doesn't. So if you mix them around there is not necessarily team loyalty so much, and it just makes communication easier."[2] You decrease the notion of *us* versus *them* with reteaming. You can foster a greater sense of a whole collective team.

At Pivotal Software, Evan Willey also talked about how reteaming helps to reduce inter-team competition via its ability to help teams build empathy for each other. When switching teams and working on different areas of the codebase,

---

2 Comron Sattari, in an interview with the author, March 2016.

you help to build generalism—that is, the opposite of being a specialist in only one area of the code. He said, "Generalism also leads to empathy. So we are not creating my team versus that team because I might be on that team in a month."[3] So beyond sharing code, we share the sense of being on the same team.

Reteaming Yields Teams That Aren't Ossified, Making It Potentially Easier to Integrate Newcomers

New teams made up of people who don't know each other are a challenge because you want the teams to gel and collaborate well to accomplish their goals. The opposite challenge is when teams are together too long. In that case, you have a greater chance of people having stronger bonds and being less open to change. The team culture is more solidified. People know what to expect, have "inside jokes," and share a history. This is an obstacle to integrating new people into the team system. It's hard to break into the culture that has formed.[4]

During periods of hypergrowth in a company, when reteaming might feel rampant, this problem seems to take care of itself. The reteaming feels commonplace, as detailed in examples in this book from AppFolio in particular.

We'll see later on that companies such as Pivotal Software and Menlo Innovations, which both deliberately reteam either at regular cadences or due to the emergence of new work, might have an easier time assimilating new employees because of these practices. The change cadence is baked in.

Regardless, as time passes, teams age and change, so preparing for it is key.

Reteaming Is Going to Happen

In this section we've gone over how reteaming helps decrease knowledge silos, reduces attrition, provides career growth opportunities, decreases inter-team competition, and makes it potentially easier to integrate new hires. These are all good reasons for why we might catalyze or start team change to reduce the risk that we will lose people or have challenging situations later. However, this is only part of the story of dynamic reteaming. Reteaming becomes riskier when you're impacting more than one person. Proceed with extreme caution when

---

3 Evan Willey, in an interview with the author, February 2017.

4 Moreland and Levine, "Socialization in Small Groups," as quoted in Kozlowski and Bell, "Work Groups and Teams in Organizations," 19.

attempting a batch reteaming, such as a reorganization of hundreds of people or more. See Chapter 12 for ideas on how to approach this challenge.

In the words of scholars Ruth Wageman, Heidi Gardner, and Mark Mortensen, "Bounded and stable membership is less and less the norm as teams become more dynamic and are frequently overlapping."[5] I've seen this for 20 years, and it shows up in predictable patterns described in this book. People are going to come and go from teams due to their own life circumstances. Your company could get acquired by another company, and through a reorg, you might suddenly find yourself on a different team. Your company might change directions next quarter, and you might get reassigned to work on something different. You might even catalyze team change for yourself. Whatever the case, team change is inevitable. You need to prepare for it. This book is your guide. Study the patterns and stories we'll cover next in Part II, and get ready for dynamic reteaming.

---

5 Wageman et al., "Changing Ecology," 308.

PART II

Dynamic Reteaming Patterns

Dynamic reteaming involves structural changes to your teams, as well as tactics for humans to transition over to the changes. These structural changes, if you pay close attention to them in particular, show up as regular base patterns. These patterns will be illuminated and explored in this section through industry stories and a weaving of tactics.

From my research, I derived five main dynamic reteaming patterns, which are as follows:

1. One by one

2. Grow and split

3. Isolation

4. Merging

5. Switching

While reteaming follows these base patterns, teams also change for a variety of reasons: for company growth; for the work; for learning, fullfilment, and sustainablity; for the code; and to liberate people from undesirable situations. This part of the book is organized by the patterns, but I'll also show that specific patterns work well when reteaming for some of the reasons I just listed. Let's get started, then, with the one-by-one pattern.

5

One-by-One Pattern

When our companies grow, our teams change. We hire in people one by one. When we are fortunate in hiring, we have the challenge of bringing multiple people onboard in close proximity. On the other hand, sometimes we face the opposite situation. We lose people. People quit, are fired, and at times are laid off en masse.

I think there's an inherent joy when our companies grow. Things are good. We have the money to hire in new people. Conversely, when someone leaves the company it's not typically a happy situation, unless for some reason we're glad they're leaving because maybe we perceived them as hard to work with or difficult. Maybe the feeling then is more like a feeling of relief or is an expansive feeling—without the "difficult person" around we feel like we can now do more in our jobs and are not as held back.

Joining and leaving are both part of the one-by-one dynamic reteaming pattern. This chapter addresses both facets of the pattern, starting out with when someone joins a team, as shown in Figure 5-1.

Figure 5-1. One-by-one pattern

Depending on the personalities of the people coming in and out, this "adjustment at the edges" of teams can be a less risky team-change pattern. Keeping the crux of the team the same brings continuity. When you add new people to the existing teams, they can get a sense of what the existing culture is like. This is helpful when you want your existing team culture to persist. If you don't want your existing team culture to persist, you might try starting up a new team with the isolation pattern and grow it from there. Then at some point you can deprecate the previous team structure. See Chapter 7.

The one-by-one pattern of reteaming covers the addition of people to teams as well as the departures. This chapter details a variety of strategies for getting better at this pattern, starting with figuring out where to allocate the new hires.

Add People to Existing or New Teams?

As Figure 5-2 shows, sometimes when you have a batch of new people, you can have more of this "edge reteaming" strategy on a larger scale by weaving the new people in across multiple teams. This might seem like a big disturbance, and it is; however, I've seen organizations like AppFolio manage this quite well and be very successful with mentoring and pairing. When your team doubles in size, you might consider this approach.

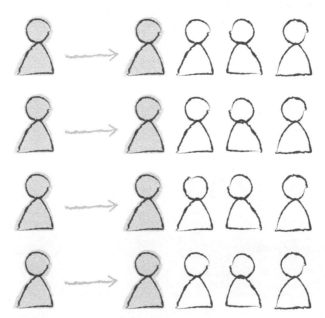

Figure 5-2. Spread out new hires to different teams

Besides sharing the load of weaving in the new hires, there is more maintenance of the existing culture by spreading new people across various teams. Rachel Davies, a team lead and coach at Unruly, expressed it like this when reflecting back on an influx of money at her company (which led to a lot of new hires): If you make a team of just new hires, "you don't get the continuity of culture."[1]

In the same way, if your existing teams practice things like extreme programming (XP), test-driven development (TDD), and other beneficial code practices, you might worry that if you start new teams with people not yet skilled in those practices, then you would degrade your overall organization. This could be the case for other practices that you want to maintain at your company. Seeding new teams with existing people and then adding in new people is a strategy you might apply. But it's not without some challenges. There is a cost to seeding teams, especially when the result is partial teams "waiting" for people to be hired. Let's dig deeper into seeding teams.

SEEDING TEAMS

Sometimes you're moving so fast that you start up new teams without the perfect team composition that you might have throughout the rest of your organization. I've been at more than one company that would seed a team with the first couple of members and then hire in the rest. So who are the people that can seed new teams?

Mike Boufford, CTO at Greenhouse Software, learned that it's important to seed new teams with experienced engineers because, as you grow, it could be very challenging to start a bunch of teams that only consist of new hires. He said, "We would take a couple of people who knew what they were doing and use them as seeds on the new teams that were being formed. We couldn't take a whole batch of new people and say, *You are now a team,* because then no one knows what they are doing and they don't have any resources inside of the team in order to ramp people up."[2]

So why seed teams? Why not just grow your company and integrate new hires into existing teams all the time? Well, it might be that the business opportunity is just so great that you can't wait for a fully staffed team. So you think strategically, and seeding becomes part of your growth strategy. But it could take

---

1 Rachel Davies, in an interview with the author, December 2016.

2 Mike Boufford, in an interview with the author, January 2020.

time to fully staff up the teams until you have whatever team composition you are used to having, or that you want to have. For example, maybe you typically have teams comprised of a product manager, user experience designer, quality assurance engineer, and four developers. When you seed a new team, the intent is to build out this new team by hiring or by reteaming.

So how does this play out? In my experience, it can either go really well or be really challenging. It depends on who the developers are that are running with this new team. Regardless of their rank, if they are entrepreneurial, they will run with the idea of the new product or feature and will most likely relish the freedom of the position—the freedom to launch the new team. They will go out of their comfort zones to help push forward the work to attain the initial business objective. This could be a thrilling ride for them, with enough support. You need to pay extra attention to seeded teams.

Conversely, if the members you seed onto this new team are less entrepreneurial and really have become accustomed to working with the roles not present on the team (typically product management, UX, or quality assurance), then they might feel challenged in this "partial" team structure. If that complete structure is all they have known, they might fall into the trap of "waiting" for others to do the services that these roles typically provide to the team. Coaching can help in this scenario. Individuals can be encouraged to develop new skills beyond their original role expertise and see the situation as a learning opportunity. In addition, coaches or managers can help the team move forward, if the seeded team appears to be stuck.

Think carefully when you seed new teams. Validate that the seeded people are up for the challenge and have the gumption to be catalysts. I've seen seeded teams work well when the leadership pays enough attention to them so that they feel supported. Paying attention to seeded teams and spending time with them can go a long way. Providing weekly updates on recruiting progress can help seeded teams feel that staffing their team is a priority.

We want not only to pay attention to, but also be inclusive of, the people in our teams so that they feel ownership over the direction the organization is going. The people on the teams are closest to the work, and their perspectives are valuable to consider when determining your future organization.

INCLUDE YOUR PEOPLE IN THE ORGANIZATIONAL DESIGN

It sounds really obvious to include people in organizational design; however, it needs to be said that if you plan to expand the team, you should have a deliberate conversation with the existing team about that topic. People need to know that you're looking for more people so they can play a part in helping to recruit the new people. This is one way to expand the ownership of the change.

Early in my career, when I was a web editor at a startup, I encountered a job ad in the local newspaper for a web editor at the startup where I was working. It was essentially an ad for the job I was already doing. Being inexperienced, I jumped to the conclusion that the company was trying to replace me. I had a lot of fear and anguish about this situation. I was the only one in the web editor role at the time. I didn't know that the plan was to have multiple web editors. I was not part of discussions about how our group was going to grow. I wound up asking my manager directly about this, and it became clear that the idea was to have more than one editor. This kind of situation should be avoided. It felt terrible because, as someone just starting my career, I stewed over this situation for an inordinate amount of time before having the courage to bring it up. I was so fearful.

Instead, get together with the team and discuss how to grow. You can vision out on a whiteboard what you see the organizational structure becoming. Then you can put the team members to work thinking of who they might invite in to the company. See Appendix A for a tactical approach to consider.

At AppFolio, in the early stages of the startup, we really leveraged our employees' connections to expand our growing team. We would talk to our friends to see if they had friends who wanted to join our startup. Each person we brought in for an interview had strong recommendations from existing employees, or from friends of existing employees. The same pattern took place at Greenhouse Software, according to CTO Mike Boufford. He said, "I think most people at an early-stage startup with no brand recognition and limited budget to spend on people, I mostly recruited from my network and then started learning how to recruit from a broader pool of people to create a more diverse team as we grew."[3]

At another startup I was at during the hypergrowth phase, it was made clear by our upper management that we were growing and would continue to grow fast for the foreseeable future. Having an official proclamation mandating this growth helped us understand our future a little better. Sharing more specific hiring plans in an open fashion is recommended to increase inclusion and to share opportunities to change teams. At one point when we were still very colocated, we shared hiring opportunities openly on a whiteboard. This let existing employees know about the other opportunities that were there for them at our company.

---

3 Mike Boufford, in an interview with the author, January 2020.

Even if you're distributed, you can still do this in your online communication channels.

Sometimes you hire from within, especially if you share new opportunities as discussed already. Other times you recruit from outside your company. There are some wonderful examples of companies that try to have parity with their hiring practices and the way that they work, which helps to sustain the way they work, as discussed in the next section.

HIRING TO SUSTAIN CULTURE AND DEVELOPMENT PRACTICES

Having parity or consistency with interview practices, onboarding practices, and actual development practices, is valued at many of the companies I interviewed while writing this book. Here are some examples from Menlo Innovations, App-Folio, Pivotal Software, and Hunter Industries.

At Menlo Innovations, one of the keys to sustaining its experimentation-focused, *pairing culture* might contribute to the parity in its recruiting and onboarding of new people. The day I interviewed Richard Sheridan, Menlo's cofounder and chief storyteller, there was a potential new hire going through the process. It worked like this.

When someone is going to join the company, they first go through a one-day trial during which, as Richard joked, "We test you for good kindergarten skills." If they pass that, the candidate then comes in for another day during which they are paired with someone doing real work, just like they would do as a full-time employee at Menlo. Once they pass out of that, the candidate embarks on a three-week trial. During that time frame, they continue to pair up on work with their potential future coworkers. These recruits are doing a wide variety of activities, which may include leading tours of the company, presenting work to clients, or going on client visits. The safety net in all of this is the pairing situation. The pair, and the wider team, are the people who ultimately decide whether the recruit becomes a full-time employee or not. It's not the management deciding this. As Richard put it, "The team builds the team." And the recruits know this. Transparency about the process is built in.

This idea of trying out the workplace by using the methods that regular employees use is paramount to sustaining the strong pair programming culture at Menlo. I view this as *culture priming*. In a similar vein, Damon Valenzona, a director of engineering at AppFolio in San Diego, told me that he practices *culture seeding*.

When culture seeding, Damon meets with each new person and goes over engineering principles and values that are important at AppFolio. He emphasizes to people that "they have ownership over this and that they're now a part of our culture and that individuality is an important thing, but they're also joining a big family." He goes on to explain the reason he has these discussions with new hires: "I tend to share it with people before we even hire them because I think that it's important for them to know what they're getting themselves into."[4]

To me, this type of culture seeding—as Damon calls it—sounds like good risk management. We want people to be successful when they join our companies. We might as well be explicit with them about what we want to sustain in our culture. That's not to say that new people would not influence and change the culture because, as we will see later, when teams double in size, people have a kind of identity crisis with their "former" culture, as described in the section "What It Means When You're Asked, "How Do We Maintain Our Culture?"" on page 87. Nevertheless, we might as well try to sustain what we have if it's working for us, at least when hiring is sporadic.

Menlo Innovations and AppFolio aren't alone with this culture-priming concept. It also takes place in the interview process at Pivotal Software. At Pivotal, where there is 100% pair programming, the interviews of new team members involve pairing. This helps to preserve Pivotal's pairing culture. According to Evan Willey:

> When we hire, we actually have a thing called an RPI, or **Rob Pairing Interview**. Rob is our CEO, and he kind of invented this. It's a fairly objectively scored pairing session with the candidate, and we're basically looking for the ability to listen, to learn, to ask questions, to be empathetic, and to show an aptitude to learn. If you pass that, you come in for an all-day pairing session. On the first half of the day you are with one team, and the second half on another team. So we're really focused on your ability as a candidate and as a hire to exist within the system and to learn quickly. We're more focused on aptitude and empathy as critical skills for a new hire than we are for existing deep subject matter expertise.[5]

---

4 Damon Valenzona, in an interview with the author, October 2016.

5 Evan Willey, in an interview with the author, February 2017.

Collaboration is important in software development. I like how this company emphasizes not only technical expertise but also the ability to communicate with empathy.

In a similar vein, conducting interviews via mob programming is a clever way to teach potential new hires what it's like to mob program, and it also helps to preserve the mob programming culture at Hunter Industries. Full stack software engineer Jason Kerney gave me a brief description of how it worked in early 2017:

> So the idea is, you come in and there are four to five people, two who are your team, and one of which who is a proctor or guide. Their job is to keep the interview moving fluidly. If the person gets hung up on something, help them. Make them feel comfortable. Talk to them through the whole process. The last person is a recorder. They're there to kind of record events, and their notes are used in the retrospective on how we can improve the interview process.[6]

The candidates get a taste of what it's like to work in Hunter Industries' highly collaborative and communication-rich environment. The people in the mob get an idea of the communication style and potential contributions of the candidate. "We want to see how they talk to different people at different skill levels," said Jason, "They're given one to five small problems to solve, and they do it in rotation. I think right now we are favoring rotating per question...and the candidate does most of the navigation."

These hiring and interview practices help to make a one-by-one reteaming, as well as the follow-up onboarding of the new hire, run more smoothly with less risk of failure.

Because development team members are involved in these activities, they will know if the potential new hire gets the job or not. Other times in our companies, people are hired by our teammates, and unless we are told that they are joining, we might have no idea. Hence the next section, which discusses the importance of telling the teams when someone gets hired.

---

6 Jason Kerney, in an interview with the author, January 2017.

PLAN AND COMMUNICATE ABOUT THE ARRIVAL OF THE NEW TEAM MEMBER

The team should know that a new person will be arriving. If it is a surprise to the team, that is an awkward and rough start for the new person, the existing team, and the budding new team system.

Patrick Lencioni, a management consultant who has written numerous best-selling books on team development, insists in his book *The Advantage* that over-communicating is a must. Leaders should be "chief reminding officers" and communicate new ideas *seven* times—and I'm applying it here to the addition of new people in your company.[7] So how might you do that?

If you're in the same location, you can do it on a whiteboard. Put the name of the new person on that big visual board. Then when people walk by and look at the board, they can notice that a new person will be coming. We did this for years at AppFolio, and it encouraged communication around this topic, which I really think helped people feel more comfortable with the changing teams along the way.

Use other virtual communication channels to let others know a new team member is coming. Send an email. Announce it in standup. Announce it in all-hands meetings. Announce it in your online chat tool.

If the new person will be joining the company after a few months, you can do what I call "keep warm" activities. Send company swag, care packages, and special things to the person if they have a delayed start. That raises the positivity they feel about your company, and it might help keep them from dropping off and joining another company. I used to send frozen Chicago-style pizzas to people finishing up their final college exams before they started at AppFolio. One of our team members who received the pizzas from me would talk about it for years after.

It feels awful if you start at a new job or a new team and you don't have a place to sit, and it feels even worse if you start but people don't know you're supposed to be there. We need to be ready for the new hire when they show up at the office. The idea is to reduce anxiety for the new person. Here's what I like to do before the new hire's first day.

---

7 Lencioni, *The Advantage*, 141–143.

GET THINGS TOGETHER FOR THE NEW HIRE BEFORE THEY ARRIVE

Email or text the new person and be clear about what time they should arrive and what to expect on the first day and week. Someone should take the new person to lunch on their first day, or at least offer to do so. If the team is virtual, you can prearrange some quick get to know you (GTKY) calls for the new hire to increase the welcoming vibe.

Order the equipment you need for the new person before they arrive, have it on their desk, and if you label desks with people's names at your company, try to do that in advance of the person joining. Get the new person's input as appropriate before ordering. You can also put company swag on their desk, too. Ship it all to the person in advance if they're distributed. Order key books that illustrate the philosophies you want to promote in your environment. Have them ready for the new person in the same way.

It makes a great first impression when you arrive on your first day and people are overprepared for your arrival! And speaking of people waiting for your arrival, imagine how it feels when you arrive at your new job and your manager is nowhere to be found. Having the manager welcome the new hire and spend time with them on day one is recommended, as discussed in the next section.

ENCOURAGE MANAGERS TO PAY ATTENTION AND INFLUENCE THE NEW HIRE

It seems so obvious to point out that the manager should spend time with the new hire once they have started at the company. Is that always the case? Or is the new hire offloaded to someone else who is tasked with bringing them up to speed? I recommend selecting mentors for new hires, as you will read in this chapter, and I think that they can be responsible for providing the most attention to the new hire. That doesn't mean, however, that the manager shouldn't make time for the new hire, especially in their early days at the company. In fact, when managers pay attention to the new hires, the new hires experience less psychological stress during their job transition.[8]

And don't forget to pay attention to even the highly skilled senior developers who join your team. They have worked elsewhere, but never in your context. We want to increase the sense of belonging.

It's also good risk management for the manager to pay attention, answer questions, and address those needs that only they as the manager can address.

---

8 Anderson and Thomas, "Work Group Socialization," 9, citing Nelson, "Organizational Socialization."

Reality shock, a concept discussed by organizational psychologists Kozlowski and Bell, is when new hires, sometime after joining, feel that the job isn't matching what they thought it would be, or they have unmet needs for getting acclimated to their new job.[9] Having an active manager who is nearby and available to the new hire can help to mitigate this. Just schedule the time on the calendar with the new hire—or better yet, be present for them from day one.

Further, the manager can really help the newcomer to understand the social system of the team they are joining by modeling the socially appropriate level of self-disclosure. This can help aid in the process of belonging and social acceptance that new hires yearn for when they join the company. It can help reduce the amount of social ambiguity present when first joining a team.[10] Tech leads within a team can do this as well, and so can mentors.

Speaking of the social system the new hire is joining, sometimes it can be hard for the current team members when a new hire starts. And when there are a lot of new hires, questions around culture and identity come up, as described in "What It Means When You're Asked, "How Do We Maintain Our Culture?"" on page 87. Nevertheless, there are things we can do to support the people who are already there when the new hire joins.

SUPPORT THE NEW HIRE AS WELL AS THE PEOPLE AROUND THEM

It can be daunting, intimidating, and maybe even scary to change jobs and to join a new team. There is also a sense of excitement. It is a position of vulnerability as well, as the new person may wonder if their new team will accept them.

What many people might forget is that people around the new person are also processing the new hire's arrival. They may be wondering how their job might change due to the addition of the new person. And, it might feel different based on the role or the rank of the new hire.

It can feel threatening when someone comes into the company in the same role but at a higher rank. Having conversations with the existing people about job safety and role safety is important. In the case of a more senior person joining your company when there is a junior person already in that role, you can emphasize that there is great learning potential available to the junior person. It's hard when you're the first person there, and you think you will get promoted to manage a group, let's say, and then the department hires someone who has been

---

9 Kozlowski and Bell, "Work Groups," 19.

10 Kozlowski et al., "Dynamic Theory," 270.

doing a similar job for years at another company to be the new manager. The situation is one that requires deliberate attention. You need to coach the junior person so that they can make sense of the situation.

It could also feel threatening when someone is proactively hired with the best of intentions to "lighten the load" of another team member. If that other team member is not ready to give up an area of work or responsibility, there could be animosity toward the new person. On the other hand, if you are open with your existing team about the hiring plans, you are essentially creating more safety and inclusion, and are on the way to fostering healthy conversations about team expansion.

Getting the existing team involved in the hiring and onboarding of the new hire, even one who is entering a type of leadership role, helps. And so does setting up mentoring programs.

ASSIGN THE NEW PERSON A MENTOR

You want to try to prevent awkwardness for the new person after they join the team. Their transition into work should not be sitting at their desk wondering how to get into the code or how to interact with the team. They should be supported. Feeling included is very important at this stage in a new hire's journey, because team members have an intense need to be accepted by others on the team, and they are afraid of rejection, according to Sir John Whitmore in his book *Coaching for Performance*.[11] Cultivating a sense of belonging and comfort on the team is critical.

At AppFolio, putting new people on teams with experienced engineers and assigning each of them a specific mentor within their team was a deliberate way to grow the skill sets of all the engineers working at the company. You learn by teaching and mentoring, and you learn from being taught and mentored. Furthermore, writing self-testing code, whether via test-driven development (TDD) or otherwise, was an incredible accelerator of learning in this context. For more on TDD and reteaming, see "Test automation, or lack thereof" on page 164.

In the first nine years of AppFolio, it was rare to have teams of all senior engineers or all junior engineers. The team compositions would be designed for maximum mentorship among the individuals. And this was just a snapshot in time. It could very well be different at this company now.

As chief scientist Andrew Mutz told me in the summer of 2016:

---

11 Whitmore, *Coaching for Performance*, 136.

So as the company is growing we have new people—which is a really common occurrence—and so we want to be adjusting our team compositions a little here and there to make sure that a new engineer gets the right mentorship because it's super important for that person's growth to have a great mentor. If a new engineer joins a team and they have the perfect mentor, and the situation with that mentor can give them a lot of interaction and a lot of learning and feedback, then a year later, two years later, they are going to be a much better engineer than they would have been if they just joined any random team, a team that didn't have time for them, or a team where there wasn't enough mentorship.[12]

As an engineering group we aligned on what it meant to be an engineering mentor. We came up with a one-page checklist of what the mentor should go over with the new hire—the mentee. The checklist consisted of things like setting up the mentee's development environment, teaching them the basics of test-driven development, giving them a walkthrough of the code, giving them an overview of the software we were building, and even encouraging the pair to go out to lunch together or to spend social time together online. In turn, the mentee had a one-page description of what it meant to be a mentee, which encouraged them to ask questions and had general pointers on the work environment.

Gathering mentors together to dream up this list is a start. Then you can iterate on it after each new person starts. Here are some basic things to consider adding to your checklist. Talk with your team members about what else to add to this starter list, and what to remove. You can use it as a default:

- Overview of their first week and any special, upcoming events for the department
- Pointers on how to set up the development environment
- Overview of the software and team mission
- Conventions for using tools
- Tour of the office/facility
- Reminder to take the new person around and introduce them to other team members

---

12 Andrew Mutz, in an interview with the author, April 2016.

- Reminder to share team events with the new person so they know where to be and when

- Instructions to get them into the appropriate chat channels for the team and other groups of interest, as well as email lists

- Pointers on where to go for frequently asked questions, such as on an intranet

- Invitations to shadow key team members in similar roles at the company

Once you start and get a mentor checklist going, make it the new hire's job to get these materials ready for the next person. They should have some empathy for the next new hire considering they were just in that position themselves.

If it's a software engineer that is coming on board, having a supportive entry into the codebase is essential. Pair programming helps with this.

USE PAIR PROGRAMMING TO ONBOARD NEW DEVELOPERS

For new hires joining your teams as software engineers, pair programming is a great way to bring them up to speed. It helps them ease into your codebase with a helpful in-the-moment guide, and it helps to share tribal knowledge and the technical practices that you want to be consistent across your codebase.

Cristian Fuentes, an engineering manager from Jama Software in Portland, Oregon, told me how pairing helped ease the transition for new joiners. He said, "You couldn't just bring in someone new and expect them to be [productive]. Things like code review are too late in the process for any kind of correction, and it's hard too, through osmosis, to get what the team's technical processes are or technical consistency things or just general culture." Then the company decided to start pair programming to onboard new people. He said, "It introduced them to our codebase. There's a lot of legacy parts of the system that you have to weed through. It's better not to just guide them by yourself. If you're working with somebody else that can kind of help guide some of that, but also if you're pairing, you're also contributing to it so you're learning yourself."[13] Pair programming in this way is how you can transfer the tribal knowledge that has emerged in your context over time.

---

13 Cristian Fuentes, in an interview with the author, April 2017.

Thomas O'Boyle, a software engineer at Procore Technologies, explained how pairing and switching pairs was helpful to bring up a new team member who joined his team.

> When my squad onboarded a brand new dev who had never dev'd [sic] anywhere else before, we started doing promiscuous pairing to get him up to speed. Promiscuous pairing is a concept that you pair for a certain set time and then you rotate to a new pair so all of the partners switch.[14] You have those anchors that will stay on the same feature, and then new ones rotate in and then those anchors rotate off so that everybody gets some exposure to each feature. We played with the interval all the time, changing it from an hour, to 20 minutes, to 2 hours each sprint…through pairing, everybody on my team got to be really good friends, and we saw learning happen really quickly—and that new dev got onboard in no time at all.[15]

In addition to pair programming, it's also helpful for new hires to observe other team members in similar roles as they attend meetings and interact with key partners in the organization. This is shadowing.

ENCOURAGE SHADOWING

Shadowing is when you are new to a team and you follow and observe someone else who is doing the same role. It could be that you are new to the company, or that you are new to the particular role.

Shadowing unearths the cultural norms and behaviors of a role. For example, by shadowing, you can observe someone in the same role participating in team meetings. If you are the person being shadowed, you can first brief the new person on the meeting purpose and goals beforehand, and then you can debrief with them afterward. You can have discussions about what your role was like in that particular meeting, why you spoke when you did, and why you didn't speak if that was the case.

I've seen this done quite successfully with quality assurance team member onboarding and training. Agile QA is an art. Learning the ropes of building the

---

14 For more information on promiscuous pairing, see Arlo Belshee's paper "Promiscuous Pairing and the Beginner's Mind." (*https://www.researchgate.net/publication/4231053_Promiscuous_pairing_and_begin ner's_mind_Embrace_inexperience*)

15 Thomas O'Boyle, in an interview with the author, February 2018.

relationships necessary to thrive as a proactive QA team member who is involved in the early parts of work, such as coauthoring stories and acceptance tests, is key to succeeding in this role—especially if you come from a traditional quality control background where you are involved later in the development process.

You can shadow with in-person teams, and you can also do it with virtual teams by connecting through video conferencing software. In either case, the mentor should ask the team that is being shadowed if it's okay to do so, and let team members know when it will take place. That sets the context so people aren't wondering who the new person at the meeting is.

Shadowing does have downsides, however. If you have too many shadowers in a team, people on the team might feel uncomfortable, like they are under a microscope. Team members might clam up and not want to talk. This could happen, in particular, if the shadow people are in nontechnical roles, and the events that they are shadowing have to do with team estimation. It can feel like way too much pressure to estimate with "watchers and lookers."

Too many extra people causes bloat. If the extra people start to speak up in these events, then the communication could get too cumbersome and the events can become inefficient. So there is the need to strike a balance with how many shadows you allow on each team. When the balance is there and the extra people aren't disruptive to the team as a whole, it can be quite an effective approach to growing your team.

Shadowing helps people feel more comfortable in their roles by learning what is appropriate social behavior in their new context. So it should reduce anxiety, in theory. Another technique is to encourage the new hire to not only learn "how things are done here," but also to share who they are as a unique individual, as described next.

ENCOURAGE NEW HIRES TO SHARE ABOUT THEMSELVES

When you onboard new people into your company and your team, you are naturally starting a process in which the new employee is learning how things work at the company so they can feel like they belong and fit in. New hires might be going through an onboarding process at the corporate level, the department level, and finally at the proximal team or group level.

This process of learning the ropes at the company has been called *enculturation, organizational assimilation*, and even *absorption*.[16] I think those terms are

---

16 Cable et al., "Breaking Them In," 2–3.

understandable because when we hire new people, we want to get them up to speed so that they can be productive in how we work in our company as soon as possible. We want them to know and understand the culture they are joining so they can become part of it. And that's how it's been historically with onboarding—the organization is more in the active state and the newcomer is in the more passive state, as the recipient of the knowledge given to them by the organization.[17]

But there's been a paradigm shift in this process from top-down to bottom-up. It's a shift from being a passive recipient to an active participant. This shift has been a sign of the times not only in software development with the advent of the Agile movement, as described in the Manifesto for Agile Software Development (*http://agilemanifesto.org*) in 2001, but also in education. Back in the 1970s, for instance, Brazilian educator Paulo Freire wrote about liberating passive students from the "banking method of education" where students were passive recipients of knowledge instead of active creators of their realities.[18] When applied to onboarding, the newcomer is less of a passive recipient of information, and more of an active, engaged participant capable of shaping and impacting the organization they are joining.

Studies done in call centers, like the one by Cable, Gino, and Staats, cited in Daniel Coyle's book *The Culture Code*, have found great success in approaching onboarding as more of a two-way street. In their study, they found that when you encourage new hires to deliberately express their personal identities and authentic best selves, the result is higher employee retention and higher customer satisfaction.[19]

I don't work with or hire call center employees. However, what I have learned through the years is that when you encourage people to share their skills, interests outside of work, and learning goals, you can efficiently help a team realize the common ground that it has together. Knowing common ground usually leads to team activities in the community: potluck lunches for those who are foodies, hiking outside of work for the hikers, and video game playing outside of work for the gamers. People start to form relationships with one another. People start knowing and caring about one another and that helps when we are

---

17 Anderson and Thomas, "Work Group Socialization," 5–6, quoting Schein, "Organizational Socialization."

18 Freire, *Pedagogy of the Oppressed*, 53.

19 Coyle, *The Culture Code*, 37–39.

collaborating and building products together. Teams become tighter knit. Belonging is increased. Team members who have high-quality relationships with one another tend to have greater psychological safety and associated learning behaviors, such as the ability to frequently seek new information, speak up to test the validity of work assumptions, and devote time to figure out ways to improve work processes.[20]

I've tried to deliberately cultivate these relationships in the teams that I have coached since 2007. I think we can try to create the conditions for camaraderie to emerge. Here are a couple of ways that I like to do this.

Market of Skills, an activity I learned from Lyssa Adkins in her book *Coaching Agile Teams*, is by far my favorite activity to do when teams form, reteam, or have significant changes like the addition of new hires. In my version of this one-to-two-hour activity, each person makes a poster sharing the following about themselves: the skills they bring to the team, their hobbies and interests outside of work, what they want to learn in the next few months, and what they offer to teach each other. After they do that, each person presents their poster, and the participants listen for what they have in common. They might snap their fingers when they share an interest with the presenter, or write kudos, encouragement, and other general feedback on sticky notes that are added to their teammates' posters. For instructions on how to do this activity in person or virtually, see "Team Calibration Sessions" on page 198.

Another activity you can do to get even deeper sharing is to talk as a team about *peak experiences*. These are experiences that we consider defining moments in our lives. When coaching teams in Santa Barbara, California, where there is ample hiking and scenery, I would organize team hikes before work. We would hike up a mountain together in pairs and share our peak moments with each other. Then when we reached the top of the mountain we would share an abridged version of our partner's peak experience and as a group write down the values that are present in these stories. We would then decide which values we wanted to represent our team going forward. See "Team Calibration Sessions" on page 198 for instructions on how to do this activity. You don't need to hike up a mountain to do this exercise. You can do it in a conference room, or by using an online videoconferencing tool with a breakout-room feature.

Onboarding is really a two-way street. We teach the new hire about the company, and we learn about the new hire so that we can build on our culture. I

---

20 Edmondson, "Psychological Safety," cited in Carmeli et al., "Learning Behaviors," 81.

think that's what all this is about. You might notice, however, that team members might start to say things like, "How do we maintain our culture?" or "It feels so different now than it used to." As we add people, we add new personalities, differences, and chemistry from the people who have joined. The organization also tends to add new processes to keep track of the data about all of the people. It might start to feel more process heavy. In short, our culture changes. To dig into this further, see "What It Means When You're Asked, "How Do We Maintain Our Culture?"" on page 87.

When your company has a deliberate goal to grow, like AppFolio did in those days, you might get better at hiring and instead of having people trickle in one by one, you suddenly have a batch of new hires. This requires different strategies and, I think, is a natural progression from the one-by-one pattern, or a scaled version of it. Bootcamps are useful in this situation.

FORM BOOTCAMPS AND HELP NEW HIRES FORM NETWORKS

For a new person joining your organization, it can be particularly daunting at the start, especially if they don't know anyone else at the company yet. People want to be accepted by their peers, to be happy, and to make a difference in their jobs. Senior software engineer Bryce Boe from AppFolio puts it like this: "We want to give new hires a safe environment on an equal playing field so they feel comfortable and basically develop confidence and they know what they're doing so when they go and join a team, they'll speak up. They don't feel like they're the new person that can't get a word in or feel like maybe their opinions are not valid."[21]

At AppFolio, we first integrated new engineers by directly assigning them to teams on which there was a person assigned to be their mentor, or "first pair." This worked really well for years and helped to ease the transition of a new team member. We coupled that with a bunch of different technical talks to introduce our system as well. However, according to Bryce, about eight years down the line the company discovered that there was a "lack of consistency in training and in onboarding new engineers." The early teams were trained in Lean concepts, test-driven development, and other best practices for building solid, clean code. Some of this got watered down over the years like a game of telephone. Bryce explained, "We want their code to be maintainable. That's a lot of what the focus is on. That means they write atomic commits. Each pull request that they submit should really only focus on delivering one feature...Each commit itself should

---

21 Bryce Boe, in an interview with the author, December 2016.

deliver some sort of end-to-end value within the theme of the story itself. We help them to structure their code in such a way that is delivering end-to-end value."

Bryce took on the challenge of solving this consistency problem at the company. He did what many of us would do at the onset: he Googled information related to onboarding, and he found examples of what other tech companies were doing. He then discussed these findings with others in engineering management, and they decided to start the Ropes program, which is AppFolio's bootcamp-type program to incubate new hires for a time before they land on their destination teams, as demonstrated in Figure 5-3.

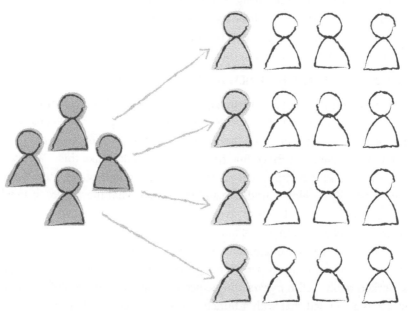

Figure 5-3. New hires are first together and then are dispersed to their teams

It works like this: A group of new hires starts around the same time frame. They are put on a small team together with one engineering mentor for all of them. In this group, they get up to speed like they would with an individual mentor, but in a more centralized and consistent fashion. If they need to learn Ruby on Rails and other internal tools, they do that with self-paced materials. Then they work as a team to build a project and in the process they become, according to Bryce, "basically masters of using the Git tool and working with GitHub in that process. They get exposure to thinking about what should a story encompass, how we can get it out there and iterate on it and improve it. It's not just following directions, but kind of taking a vague description of what should be done and then making it something useful, providing value to their customers." They also discuss the test pyramid (*https://martinfowler.com/bliki/TestPyra mid.html*) and learn that most of the tests should be written at the unit level—really, really specific, low-level tests.

After Bryce and his team reflected on the Ropes program, it became clear that they could improve it. In particular, they found a way to help new hires build larger networks across their engineering organization, as shown in Figure 5-4.

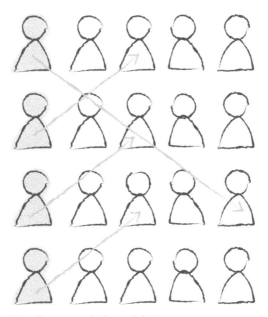

Figure 5-4. Help new hires form networks beyond their teams

Pair programming is a staple in AppFolio's environment and was built into this part of the Ropes program. Bryce described the process as follows:

An individual going through it each week has two, two-hour pairing sessions. We try to do that with as many different people as we can. The last two people that went through it had at least 20 pairing sessions. Most of those were with different engineers. We have almost all of our senior level and above, including architects, participating in these pairing sessions. That way a new hire gets to pair with, let's say, 20 different people during their period that they've worked. Now they have insight into what people are doing on different teams. Pairing is on their Ropes project, not on whatever that individual who's pairing with them is working on. But they can ask questions about that, so they get to learn a little bit about what people are doing at AppFolio, but more, they have this network that many new hires would not have gotten previously.[22]

This social network is incredibly useful, because they have already broken the ice with many other engineers. So later, when they have a question about how something was designed or architected, or they want input on their own designs, they can leverage this network to come up with a better outcome. Bryce imagines that it goes like this for the new hire: "Well I've paired with Jim and I know that he's an awesome person, so I'm just going to hit him up on Slack and be like, *Hey, can I ask you a question about this?* Whereas maybe before—even when I started this was kind of true—there were certain people that I felt weren't as approachable, because I didn't already have some sort of communication established with them."

It takes about four hours of time in all from a mentor's schedule to pair with the new people. This is less of an impact to their day-to-day work lives than the previous mentoring model. It has lessened the "mentor fatigue" that many felt, especially when teams were doubling in size. This approach is paying off. According to Bryce, new engineers are now reaching out more and asking for help across the organization when they encounter a challenge or curiosity.

After a number of weeks, the new engineers get to experience what it's like working on a few teams. Based on their experiences pairing with people on different teams, they get to indicate three teams that they would like to work with for the next phase of their onboarding. Once they select their three teams, they work for two days on each team for a total of about six days. These "host teams" have autonomy to integrate their potential new team member however they see fit.

After that point, the new hire indicates their preferred teams to join, and the managers work out the final assignment based on mutual selection between the new hire and the teams. Interestingly, what this company has learned is that certain teams get higher selection rates than others. This leads me to the following questions: What is it that makes every new hire want to work with a particular team? Is the chemistry incredible? Are the people more approachable? Is the

---

22 Bryce Boe, in an interview with the author, December 2016.

work more compelling than other opportunities? We won't learn the answers to these questions in this book; however, it is an area worthy of exploration.

This practice was in its infancy when I interviewed Bryce Boe. Because this process is propelled by retrospectives, I'm sure AppFolio has tweaked how it does this based on feedback from new hires and engineering teams that have participated in the experiment since then. Retrospectives are the heart of how you evolve and shift your organization and are a key to dynamic reteaming, as described in Chapter 14.

Up until now I have detailed a wide variety of practices for enabling the onboarding, or one-by-one addition of people into your company. The other side of the one-by-one pattern is when people leave your company. When people leave our teams, our teams are transforming and changing as well. It's a crucial part of the one-by-one pattern.

When People Leave, You Have a New Team

It takes the addition or removal of only one person to have a new team system. When a team member departs, it impacts the team. And, there are all kinds of emotions possible when people leave our teams and companies. If the person leaving was an undesirable jerk, causing harm and negativity, we are probably glad they are leaving. Conversely, if the person was well-liked and helped our team thrive in social and productive ways, their departure could bring us down tremendously and cause us to feel quite awful. When people leave our teams we need to talk about it and acknowledge the situation, and determine if any reteaming needs to happen as a result. This is part of dealing with the transition.

People either leave involuntarily or voluntarily. Sometimes it's sudden. Other times, people have some overlap time of varying lengths.

I don't think we always really know if someone was fired or if they left because they wanted to. Sometimes you can get pushed out of a company, but there is a facade like you chose to leave. Let's explore this flip side of the one-by-one pattern—when people leave—first starting with firing, and then with leaving in general.

FIRING PEOPLE—WHEN YOU RETEAM SOMEONE OUT

When people get fired suddenly, it can be quite awkward to communicate about it. People in the office might see this person, with box in hand, getting escorted out of a building. The person who has been fired can experience shock, anger, and despair. Any sort of goodbyes can be highly charged and emotional. Many times, the people witnessing the departure might not know what to do. They might have empathy, relief, or fear of losing their own jobs.

I remember a coworker getting fired years ago in quite a dramatic way. The managers had discussed firing the person and planned to do it on a Friday at the end of the day. They had HR ready to go with exit papers. They went over to the person's desk, fearful that he would "make a scene," and then let him get a few of his belongings together before escorting him out. He didn't have enough time to get all of his personal items together. And he didn't make a scene, like they had feared. A colleague coordinated with him after the fact to box up his remaining items.

When managers plan to fire a person who they fear might be disruptive, they sometimes identify different people who are close to this person to talk with in advance, in order to sense their potential reaction to the situation. In other words, they try to give certain people a heads-up. When this happens, word typically gets out in the trenches that someone is going to be fired, and it can spread fear and ambiguity. I'm not sure it is a good idea. It can feel rather cold or harsh when these things go down, and they can go down in a messy way.

HR departments typically have policies and rules for how to fire people. And I think in many cases companies act in particular ways to protect themselves from liability. It's beyond the scope of this book to dig much more into which practices are best for letting people go. It feels like a landmine. Work with your HR or People department to better understand the rules for your company.

What I will say, however, is that managers who band together to plan how to fire people should later reflect on how it went, so that the next time it can go a bit better. Put the process of letting people go under continuous improvement. It is something that will likely keep happening at your company. It's not easy to fire someone. Managers can be unskillful about this since they might not do it very often. Approach letting people go with kindness and consideration for the person affected. And have retrospectives about the topic.

Besides getting fired, sometimes people choose to leave.

WHEN PEOPLE LEAVE OF THEIR OWN ACCORD

I talked with a colleague who preferred to remain anonymous about the first four teams at his company. They were each tightly bound to four different product offerings. When new people joined, they would get spread out to the four existing teams. That worked for some time. Some of the teams started to get "big," which in his view was about 15 people on each team. They had legacy ways of working—

some variant of Scrum is what they were practicing.[23] There was a reluctance to change and evolve their Scrum processes, and people didn't even want to consider breaking up those teams into smaller teams. He said that they had operated that way for years, and that there was a lot of scrutiny for any type of change—mostly led by the opinions of two very experienced developers. Those two developers were very challenging and dominant. One day they both suddenly left the company. It was a big shock for people, and their departure was very hard for some of the engineers. Yet others experienced a sense of relief. They were able to shed their existing dogmas and iterate on their ways of working. The dominant voices against the iterative change that they wanted (and needed) were now gone. The anonymous colleague told me, "For us who were trying to try out new things, it was a relief, but for the developers in those teams that were technically reliant on them, it was a shock. And for the product manager, that was a shock as well." Gradually, the teams adjusted to their absence.

If we think about our current teams, we can protect our companies by building in redundancy. What I mean by this is that we can incorporate practices like pair programming, mob programming, test automation, and the like, which can help us be more prepared for the inevitable departure of team members. People don't stay at companies forever. We can plan for this strategically in how we work, and how we build our teams. It's a natural part of team evolution for people to leave our teams, as explored in Chapter 1. And when they do leave, we can deliberately acknowledge the situation and soften the blow of their transition out. So how do we acknowledge departures? How do we handle them? Let's explore.

SAYING GOODBYE—DO WE ANNOUNCE DEPARTURES?

If we are in a small company, like a startup in one big open room, it's quite obvious when someone leaves the company either voluntarily or otherwise because their desk becomes empty and they no longer show up. Other times if we are more distributed—like a company that has multiple office buildings or locations—there are other ways that we notice that people have left.

If the person has a visible leadership role in the company, their departure is usually announced, and the plan to find their successor is mentioned. The most awkward departure of a leader in a company I have worked for was a VP who, after announcing his departure, still came into the office daily for about six

---

23 Scrum is a framework for team collaboration on complex products. See *The Scrum Guide* (*https://www.scrum.org/resources/scrum-guide*) for details.

months while the company was searching for his replacement. Other times when I have witnessed the replacement of a leader, the original leader was still on the payroll but was nowhere to be seen. I think I prefer the latter because if the leader is being asked to leave, and everyone knows that, it's just awkward when they're still around.

Leadership groups need to align on how they will communicate departures in general. I've seen this happen at more than one company—when managers start announcing multiple departures it makes people uncomfortable. If quite a few people leave in close succession, with vague reasons, other people might feel like that company is "not the place to be." As Brené Brown notes in her book *Dare to Lead*, in the absence of information we just make up stories.[24] Who knows where our minds might go if we hear that people are leaving every week? Is the company going under? Is some big change coming that we won't like?

Besides announcing, I've seen companies post the departures on an intranet page. So it's not in your face every day, but if you are curious to know if someone has left or not, you can go find that information. Sometimes, though, our tooling might hint that someone has left before we even have time to check that intranet page. I've noticed that, with chat tools and with wiki tools, the person who has left is marked as "deactivated" within the tool.

Other times we discover that someone has left because we find out on social media like LinkedIn, where people prominently list where they work. We might notice that someone is now at a different company.

I like using LinkedIn's messaging tool to say goodbye to people who have left the company that I am currently at. If I worked with them in any way, I like to have closure and at least acknowledge their departure. Being able to say goodbye is one thing. Another thing is dealing with the fact that people have left the team for whatever reason, the subject of the next section.

PROCESSING THE FACT THAT SOMEONE LEFT THE TEAM

When someone leaves our immediate team, we need to talk about it and name it. We need to figure out what we will do in the absence of this person. Hopefully, as emphasized many times throughout this book, we have built in redundancy of their role so that someone else on the team, or nearby, knows what they were doing before they left, so carrying on their work will not be that challenging.

---

24 Brown, *Dare to Lead*, 247.

People add their own unique personalities to the social dynamic of the team. When some people leave, there can be such a void, especially if the person was well-liked or even eccentric. I remember when an engineer named Tim left App-Folio—without him, we had a lot less juggling going on in the office on a daily basis. Tim juggled while he was decoding complex challenges in his brain. He would take breaks and juggle. One day he even juggled knives as a stunt, before we had a formal human resources department. Tim's absence resulted in less juggling, and to me that was sad. We pressed on nonetheless.

One tactic I've brought to teams came out of discussion with my colleague Paul Tevis when we were coaching together at AppFolio. We would do an activity that asked teams to answer these questions on a whiteboard: What did the person who is leaving the company do beyond their formal job description? What were their inner roles?[25] For Tim, one of the things we'd write down was juggling. And the list would go on. After listing the inner roles, we would discuss which of these things should "live on" in the team going forward. Maybe we would choose to continue our periodic juggling in the name of Tim? Whatever the team decided here would be added to the team agreements (or just noted in our heads).

I was with a team in the past year who lost a product manager to another company. We got together and made a list of the things that this product manager did beyond his defined organizational role. One thing that we unearthed was that when the team accomplished a milestone, the product manager would take the members to the oceanside cliffs near our office and encourage everyone to scream cheers of victory. This was obviously not part of his formal job description. But it was a clear inner role he had on this team. The team decided that someone else would carry on that tradition.

Digging into inner roles like this is one way that a team can process the loss of a team member and really celebrate and continue the behaviors that impacted the team in a positive way. People do leave, whether we like it or not. The fact is, leaving teams is part of the natural evolution of people in our teams.

---

25 *Outer* and *inner roles* are concepts from Organization and Relationship System Coaching (ORSC) by Center for Right Relationship Global (*http://crrglobal.com*). I'm trained in its methodology and find the techniques highly applicable to dynamically changing teams.

THE EVOLUTION OF PEOPLE IN OUR TEAMS

We join companies and we leave companies. We go through a natural process of birth, adolescence, maturity, and creative destruction as individuals, as teams, as companies, and beyond, as shown in Figure 5-5, reprinted here from Chapter 1.

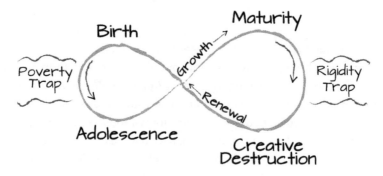

Figure 5-5. An ecocycle based on the adaptive cycle by Gunderson and Holling, Panarchy; and Keith McCandless et al., Liberating Structures

When we leave a team for whatever reason, we are essentially going through creative destruction and then starting anew somewhere else. I like to encourage people to think about where they are on the dynamic reteaming ecocycle. Are they in the birth phase? Are they ready for a change and stuck in a rigidity trap?

Sometimes we leave the company due to life circumstances. Maybe we are moving to a new city. Maybe our partner has an opportunity somewhere else, and we decide to leave the company to support them. Maybe we get a new opportunity that's just too good to pass up, and it's better for our career growth to leave the company. When these things happen, it can be bittersweet for those left behind. We are happy for our friend who has something new and exciting, but we might also be sad if we enjoyed working with them.

We can get stuck in rigidity traps and stagnate in jobs and stay longer than maybe is good for us. People who are highly paid might even have what are called *golden handcuffs,* which means they're paid so well that they feel like they can't leave their job. So they stay where it's comfortable, feel like they're on the top of their game, and just ride it out. People make their own decisions, and I respect that. I just feel sad when people choose to halt their growth in a sense by overstaying at a company for reasons like these.

Coaching helps when people are stuck in rigidity traps (or in poverty traps, when they can't quite get it together and succeed in what they just started doing).

Coaches help people cross edges and make life shifts through creative destruction. Coaching also helps if you are shifted unwillingly through creative destruction, like by getting fired unexpectedly.

We've covered a lot of ground here, exploring both growth via the one-by-one pattern and attrition via the one-by-one pattern. Here are some pitfalls with this pattern.

Pitfalls of the One-by-One Pattern

Reflecting back on this chapter and on my experiences helping fast-growing companies scale, the following are what stands out as the downsides, or pitfalls of the one-by-one pattern.

YOU REALIZE YOU HAVE AN IMBALANCE OF JUNIORS TO SENIORS

If you are not mindful of the level of engineer you are bringing into your organization, and you are not stopping to assess where you are at and what your ratios are, you might find yourself surrounded by staff who are relatively inexperienced. I saw this play out at two of the startups I've written about in this book. Both had to take a distinct step back at one point and shift their hiring toward more senior-level staff and place less emphasis on juniors for a while. It's almost like it snuck up on the leaders at the two companies.

More senior people who have worked at multiple companies bring industry patterns with them that they can apply when faced with similar challenges at your company. Engineers hired right out of college or after an internship bring fresh perspectives as well as their own budding expertise. You can't get industry experience as deep in college or right out of it. Years of experience are valuable, especially when the stakes are high and you're going after a tremendous opportunity to make a difference in the world. A healthy mix of levels is what I would go after. If you don't, it could also lead to the next pitfall, which is mentor fatigue.

MENTOR FATIGUE

When you onboard new hires, it's great to set up a mentoring situation for them. It helps bring them up to speed, and it provides a leadership opportunity for the mentors. If you have a shortage of mentors, though, people will likely become tired of mentoring—especially if they are doing it continuously. And, not all of us want to be mentors, just like not all of us want to be managers. Sometimes we just want to focus on our work as an individual contributor. And sometimes we want to be with our peers and be mentored by someone who we feel is more experienced than we are. So what do you do when you're the only senior person on the particular team and you need to grow? I remember our years of mentoring at AppFolio. At one point we had the realization that you didn't have to be super senior to help bring someone else aboard. We widened the definition of who could become a mentor. If you had been at the company for three months, then you could be a mentor. We also batched new hires together and had them share a mentor. There are patches like these that you can apply if you get into this bind. But maybe if you're reading this and your company is small, you can keep this in mind.

NOT VISIONING OUT CAREER PATHS FROM THE BEGINNING

At some point in the growth of every startup I have been at, some people start asking about career paths, and some express the desire to become a manager. Maybe people point out that there are too many people reporting to the original leader, and they want more attention. Others want a promotion and to start and manage their own group of engineers. Promotions are given out that are probably premature. Pay raises might be given out liberally, too.

With more and more people hired, we reach a point where we need to get more formal with all of this. People compare salaries privately and bring up inequities to leadership. Some notice that a senior hired in has a lower salary than someone more junior. Or the other way around. Then you need to stop and think about what your engineering leveling guide or career ladder must look like, and how that will align with pay. The particulars of that are beyond the scope of this book. But what I can say is this: plan a scalable approach to all of this while you are small. Talk to your colleagues at other companies and see what you can learn from their approaches. Don't leave this until the pressure is on, after "too much growth." Otherwise it's just harder to deal with dissatisfaction in this arena.

It is my hope that awareness of these pitfalls can help you if you are at a company that is scaling with the one-by-one pattern. This is a common, and quite rich, dynamic reteaming pattern if you take the time to notice it. It can literally fly by you if you don't pay attention.

In this chapter we've explored many facets of the one-by-one pattern of dynamic reteaming. We went over a variety of practices related to people joining teams. We covered a bit less about people leaving teams, but explored it nonetheless. In Chapter 8 you can read more stories about people leaving teams, including stories of poorly done layoffs.

A consequence of the one-by-one addition of people to teams is that some teams will grow larger. This can result in the next pattern of dynamic reteaming, which is called grow and split.

6

Grow-and-Split Pattern

A natural consequence of a lot of one-by-one reteaming is the grow-and-split pattern. The more people you add to existing teams, the bigger those teams get. At times with growth like this, you might experience some drag in the system. Things feel like they are taking longer than they used to because there are so many more people. Decision making might be stalled, and you might need to apply some new tactics to move forward. Then the grow-and-split pattern kicks in, to structurally split the large team into two or more smaller teams, as shown in Figure 6-1.

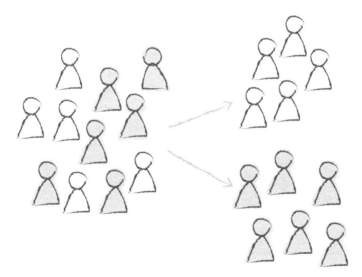

Figure 6-1. Grow-and-split pattern

It could also be the case that you feel that the dynamics present on the existing team need to be shifted. Maybe the team has hit a stagnation or a rigidity trap, as we learned about in Chapter 1. Things aren't working like they used to, it feels like the energy is not there, and you decide that, in theory at least, you might want to rejigger the team energy by splitting up the team.

So how do you know when to split a team? Let's look at some signals that tell you when your team might be too big.

Signs That You Might Want to Split Your Team

I've noticed four key signs that lead up to teams splitting: meetings get longer, decision making is harder, the work diverges, and it's harder to keep track of who is actually on the team. Sometimes these indicators brew for a while before someone decides to take action. The more this happens in a context, the more people wake up to the concept of morphing larger teams into smaller ones.

ARE YOUR MEETINGS GETTING LONGER?

Grow and split is a pattern that many startups face early in their history, and it's a memorable occasion when the first split happens. Comron Sattari, who was a software engineer at AppFolio during the early years, recalls:

> When we were a really small startup early on, there were only four engineers, or five engineers. The communication was easy, the standups were short, and things like that. But when we got to be 12, 16, 20 people, all of the sudden we couldn't do standups in 15 minutes anymore. The team communication was a lot of overhead. You were working on so many disparate things that you would switch to pair with someone else and would be a week behind, because you hadn't worked with them in over a week. So they didn't know what you were working on, or you didn't know what they were working on. There was a lot of ramp-up that had to happen when the team got big.[1]

This was really the inception of having different feature teams at AppFolio, as he recalled, "We split into two, then three teams. Each of the teams was four or five engineers. I think at that point we had QA float around and help us, but eventually we had one QA person per team...those teams were given specific

---

[1] Comron Sattari, in an interview with the author, March 2016.

sections of the upcoming backlog, of the upcoming product plan. Instead of saying, *OK team of 20 people, let's do features one, two, three, four, and five, it was a team of four people, let's do feature one."*

The downside was less pair programming variety for the engineers. As Comron put it, "All of a sudden you're not working with the 10 other people on your engineering team." That feels different and makes less possibility to learn from other people like you did before. Small teams are not the universal panacea for effectiveness. This particular team solved that by enacting a regular switching pattern a bit later in its development. See Chapter 9.

Besides the feel of longer meetings and overhead to keep up on what is going on, another signal that tells you the grow-and-split pattern has kicked in relates to decision making.

IS DECISION MAKING BECOMING MORE DIFFICULT?

If your team is used to making decisions by consensus, as you add more and more people to your team, it will definitely become more challenging to do that. As Paige Garnick, an engineering manager from Procore Technologies told me, "We could be in a retro, and we'd want to try something new, and a majority of the people would say yes, but then there would be three or four people who would say no, and when you have three or four people who say no, the debate can last a long time. It was really hard to make decisions just for improving our processes."[2]

When teams get big and they're still together, in order to make decisions they might choose to apply a myriad of facilitation techniques to get through it. Creative facilitation can be applied to help larger teams work.[3]

In addition to decision making becoming more challenging when your team grows large, another challenge is that the work can become unrelated, and team members diverge into different directions.

---

2 Paige Garnick, in an interview with the author, January 2020.

3 If you need ideas on how to better facilitate decision making, consult the book *A Facilitator's Guide to Participatory Decision-Making* by Sam Kaner. In addition, to get better discussions to happen in larger teams, consult *The Surprising Power of Liberating Structures* by Keith McCandless and Henri Lipmanowicz.

HAS THE WORK OF THE TEAM BECOME UNRELATED?

When teams get larger, it feels like you have more capacity to get additional work done. This is probably why you grew bigger in the first place—you thought that if you hire more people, you can accomplish more.

When teams get too big, you might notice subgroups forming within teams, working on items that don't necessarily pertain to the whole team at large. In her team, which grew to more than 10 people, Paige talked about the organic ways the team would try to manage its work. She said, "There were like two or maybe three projects going on at a time. And there would be eight to ten people that were working on it; they would split into groups of two or three focusing on the different things." This was a natural divergence of the team. This splitting in order to handle divergent work is a tactic I've seen with teams that grow big, diverge into these "strike teams," get the unrelated work done, and then return back to the larger team.

Moreover, in distributed teams, when the team grows, you might have the additional challenge of remembering who is on the team.

ARE YOU FORGETTING WHO IS ON YOUR DISTRIBUTED TEAM?

Imagine everyone on a phone call with videos turned off. Even though everyone is likely on the call, you might have pockets of silence. You might notice less participation from some of the people on team during your team meetings. They were likely more included and engaged before the team grew so big.

Agile coach Mark Kilby, who works with purely distributed teams at a DevOps tooling company, experienced this situation and said, "If you've got team members forgetting who else is in the meeting, that's usually a signal right there, or if you realize that you haven't really heard from a team member in the last two or three standups, it's maybe a signal that the team is too big. I want to make sure everyone has a chance to have their voice in conversations."[4] I can relate to what Mark is saying from my experiences in teams that have grown big. During meetings, it's not uncommon for only a few people to speak, and everyone else remains silent. If the team is distributed, the problem is just compounded and you can't necessarily "see" the people unless you're all connected with video.

The first step in splitting your team is realizing the challenges described previously and coming to the conclusion that splitting the team is a valid option to consider. Executing the split is another story.

---

4 Mark Kilby, in an interview with the author, October 2016.

You've Decided to Split, Here's How to Do It

Don't just declare a split without consulting the team. Have respect for the people. Splitting a team without its involvement can cause a lot of resentment. Instead, coach the team to drive its own reteaming.

INCLUDE THE TEAM IN THE DECISION

So how do you go about splitting a team so you're not just executing a top-down change without the team's buy-in? Bring the team along, like Kristian Lindwall did at Spotify. He told me a story about a team split at his company.

He chose to bring up the split with one team by saying, "I've started noticing some changes and how involved people are in our standups in the morning. It seems like you guys are essentially forming subteams in the team. It seems like we are wasting some people's time in our common meetings and stuff. Do you agree? Have you seen this? How do you feel about this?"[5]

Just asking a powerful question to teams about their structure can get the gears turning so they become participants in solving their problems and not just the recipients of a team change conceived by someone else.

Furthermore, socializing the idea that it's OK to talk about changing our teams is another way you can create a culture that acknowledges that team change is normal, and that it's just another lever to pull during the pursuit of effectiveness. I like to encourage teams to talk about their structure during regular retrospective meetings. In this way they can come up with ideas of how to shift their structure to better work together.

At any rate, once you've decided that, yes, we will split the team, there are many considerations to keep in mind. Splitting can be emotional and highly charged, as detailed in "The Emotional Challenge of Splitting Teams" on page 80. You need to proceed with caution. The "easiest" splits in my experience are the ones that were determined by the team itself. But sometimes that's not the case, and someone from outside the team tries to influence it. Here are some guidelines.

ARTICULATE WHY YOU ARE SPLITTING THE TEAM

Why are you splitting the team? Being able to articulate the reason is important. Those around the team will want to know why this is happening. It might be because new work is coming in, and you have decided to have one team continue

---

5 Kristian Lindwall, in an interview with the author, September 2016.

on existing work and the other pursue the new work. It could also be that the team just feels too big. Things are taking too long and you have decided you want to split the team in order to be more effective in how you go about work. Whatever the reason, get your "elevator pitch" together and align on it as a team so that everyone can socialize the idea inside and outside of the team.

FIGURE OUT THE MISSIONS OF THE NEW TEAMS

Teams need a reason to exist, and that is typically connected to the work they are doing as a team. You can articulate their focus using mission statements. The mission is the "North Star goal." Mission statements explain the *why* of the mission—one or two sentences describing why it's important. When talking about Spotify teams, Kristian Lindwall shared some examples from his company, which makes software related to music playback. One of the features of its software is for users to put songs into playlists. He said, "One mission could have been *Create a rewarding experience for the user to shape their Spotify identity through playlists.*" A different example is from the Holistic Experience team, whose mission was to "Empower other squads to shift into a higher quality, coherent user experience."

It's important to partner with other team members to create the missions. Kristian described this:

> I was coaching the team, and there was also the product owner who was driving the whole area. So we had a couple of conversations and the product owner in this situation, then drafted a few suggestions for missions that this broader mission could be split into. We then brought in the whole team—everyone—to look at those. Some were challenged and changed heavily, and others were just refined. We ended up with three that would kind of still solve the bigger problem, the bigger mission, and in this case we then said, "Okay, so these are the missions, now we need to figure out how to split this team into this."[6]

You might be figuring out which people will go onto each team in the course of having discussions about the missions. So how do you assign people to work on these missions?

---

6 Kristian Lindwall, in an interview with the author, September 2016.

DETERMINE WHO WILL GO ON EACH TEAM

In the case of the Spotify example, what happened next was a brainstorming session in front of a whiteboard to encourage people to choose their own teams. Kristian said, "We just crafted the missions, drew circles on a whiteboard with the new teams, and put everyone's face as an avatar up on the board and said, 'So in a couple of days, let's try to have these teams.' And we started out by people just putting their face where they wanted to be. People started talking to each other. We were there to support the conversations, and, yes, after a couple of days we had a new team structure."

I think it's a good idea to give the people some choice in which team they will move into, like this example shows. Taking the situation to the team for problem solving can be very powerful. They've likely solved harder problems than team composition before.

I've also witnessed managers figuring out who will go on each team, and then working out the team assignments via one-on-ones with team members, and then all together in a group to make it official. There are different degrees of openness used to approach team change, as described in Chapter 3.

Once you've figured out who is going on each team, it's a good idea to figure out the physical implications of this change, such as where the new teams are going to sit—that is, assuming that they are in the same location.

COME UP WITH A NEW SEATING PLAN FOR THE RESULTING TEAMS

Teams that are colocated should sit in the same area. They can have their own team space that, ideally, they can customize to express who they are as a team system. Once you decide to split teams, you need to figure out these logistics, and work with the appropriate people in your company to make these physical changes a reality.

You might not have the luxury in your setting to actually sit together in your team. If that is the case, some teams set up separate "team rooms" where they can go and have their meetings and events, and then they go back to their desks, wherever they may be. I've found that being not only colocated but also coseated—that is, sitting in the same area—is much more encouraging for collaboration.

None of this matters if your teams are distributed. If they are, there are tools and systems that you will need to update with your team split, as described later. See "Not Involving Your Facilities and Technology Groups Early Enough" on page 80.

Claiming who you are as a team system is something that I love to encourage teams to figure out, and we will explore this in the next section.

FIGURE OUT THE TEAM NAMES

Naming your team is an expression of team identity and ownership. I've seen teams that are named after the tools that they create or the components that they build, and I've seen completely made-up, silly names dreamed up by the team members.

At AppFolio, it was a trend for years for the teams to name themselves. There was a trend to name the teams a combination of music band names and nerdy concepts. For instance, the first two teams were named Diff Leppard and Hex Pistols. The third team was called the Fu Fighters. Years later, teams branched out to movie names like Saving Private Repo, Ace of Rebase, or whatever else they wanted.

As the years went on, these team names lived on, too. People would move into these teams and out of these teams. Work would be assigned to the teams, changing based on company priority as the years went on. When the company grew, new people would be added to teams using the one-by-one pattern, as described in Chapter 5.

Typically, when the changes to the team were one by one, the teams would keep their existing team names. When the changes were larger or involved splitting to create more than one team, the result was two team names. One might have kept the original name while the other received a new one. Following that name change, the team would let other teams know.

TELL OTHERS ABOUT THE RESULTING TEAM ASSIGNMENT

The membership on each of the resulting teams after the split should be made clear to everyone, using the communication channels that exist in your company. Meaning, you should make it explicit and write out who is on each team to clear up any potential confusion about team composition. You could even draw a *before and after* picture on a whiteboard to depict who is on each of the two teams (or more if you're splitting beyond that). See Chapter 12 for a visual of what a before and after picture might look like. Besides telling others about the reteaming, you can choose a date on the calendar to start up the new teams, with a formal kickoff event.

FORMALLY KICK OFF THE NEW TEAMS

I like having team calibration sessions to get the new teams going. In these events—which could occur in as little as two hours, in my experience—you can discuss how you want to work together as a new team, talk about the mission and content of your work, and define what success and excellence looks like from the standpoint of how you work together as a team. There is a lot that can be considered for a team calibration, and it really depends on how much time you want to devote to it. For ideas, see "Team Calibration Sessions" on page 198.

I've witnessed many teams growing and splitting in different companies through the years. When you split a team, you are disrupting the team dynamic with the hope that it will result in a better situation. The best splits I've seen have been decided by the people in the team, usually after having many discussions about the possibility. But splitting teams is not an instant panacea for all of your team challenges. There are some difficulties that may come up.

Pitfalls of the Grow-and-Split Pattern

Sometimes when you split, if you're not careful, you might trade one set of problems for another. Here are some pitfalls that have been challenging for the teams, and some ways you might mitigate them.

SHARED PEOPLE ACROSS TEAMS

I often see teams that split and then share specialist roles like product manager, UX designer, and quality assurance engineer. This is a shift that takes a great deal of consideration because if you do have shared team members, they need to attend twice as many meetings (most likely), and that can be very challenging. The more shared people, the more it might feel like you're just one big team, which defeats the purpose of the team split.

I've also seen teams that acknowledge this, and then get the approval to hire people to fill the slots on the resulting teams. It can sometimes take months to hire. If you do this, align with the team on how you will cope with this situation, and try to work across roles in order to move the work forward. The alternative is staying as a larger team until the hiring is complete and then splitting.

In addition to the pitfall of having shared people across teams, splitting in half might result in dependencies across the team, which bring another set of challenges.

DEALING WITH DEPENDENCIES BETWEEN TEAMS AS A RESULT OF THE SPLIT

Ideally, the work of the resulting teams is separate, and each of the teams can operate autonomously without having to consult excessively with another team. If the work is shared between the two teams, which is typical if you're dealing with a monolith where all the code is together in the same codebase, you need to work out some way to keep the information flowing between the two teams so a change in one team doesn't break code for the other team. There are different approaches to managing this type of situation, and people have written books covering just this. I will give a few pointers here.

First, you might consider applying ideas inspired by the Large-Scale Scrum (LeSS) Framework. In particular, there are planning sessions, retrospectives, and sprint reviews for each team individually and then across the teams. For example, in the case of one team that splits in half with a lot of dependencies, what might result is planning individually for both teams, and then an overall planning where point people from each team get together and share what is going on. The same can happen with retrospectives, and with sprint reviews, where you demonstrate the working software created in the iteration. This is a very simple application of the concept that is worked out in depth in the book *Large-Scale Scrum.*[7]

Second, a different approach is to follow the lead of Pivotal Software and AppFolio and apply the switching pattern, where team members pair across team boundaries to take care of dependencies (see Chapter 9). With this approach, which necessarily is coupled with writing test-driven, self-testing code, code ownership is more distributed and shared, and we work across boundaries to get things done. There is so much that I like about this approach because it also focuses deliberately on code quality.

Third, I've seen other companies rely on specific people to manage the cross-team dependencies. I've personally hired, managed, and grown technical project management groups as dependency managers across a multitude of teams. That can work, too, if the technical project managers have the mindset of being servant leaders aimed at helping the teams succeed. It really depends on hiring, training, and ongoing feedback to ensure that the technical project managers

---

7 I don't mean to trivialize LeSS with my application described here because it has a lot more depth. The book *Large-Scale Scrum: More with LeSS*, by Craig Larman and Bas Vodde, has an interesting strategy for managing multiple teams and the dependencies that are present, and is worth a read. Their workshops are also very inspiring.

remain productive and successful. I've also witnessed managers serving in the role, acting kind of like "glue" between teams.

Carefully consider whether it's actually a good idea to split a team if it results in shared work between the two teams. It might be less overhead and easier for the people if you keep them together due to the intertwined work.

If you do keep them together, you could lean into the art of facilitation to help a large team become more effective. Consider applying the facilitation patterns from Liberating Structures, (*http://www.liberatingstructures.com*) which are designed to bring out full participation inside your teams. Another resource to dig into is the *Facilitator's Guide to Participatory Decision-Making*, by Sam Kaner, for ideas on how to get better at building consensus and agreement on teams but also how to include others in decision making.[8]

One message I want you to get from this book is that we don't change teams for the sake of changing teams, and we should not take it lightly or flippantly. You need to apply critical thinking and envision how things might play out after you reteam. Study and apply the planning techniques in Chapter 12.

Besides dependencies as a pitfall to splitting teams, there are other things to consider, such as how you time the team split.

DRAGGING OUT THE SPLIT

Teams that decide to split sometimes make the agreement but then stagnate on that decision for a while. Maybe it's because they do not choose a point person to be the "lead" of the split. Or maybe it's because they are too busy doing their day-to-day work, and this idea of splitting takes effort and they haven't yet devoted the time to it.

To all of this I say the following: Don't let the team split drag on forever. Choose a date on the calendar for doing the split. Celebrate and have a party around the time that you change desks. Do it virtually if you are distributed. Get creative. Bring in a cake or some food to help commemorate the split and celebrate the end of the large team, if you are colocated. If you turn this into an event, it pushes it forward and makes it happen. I can't emphasize this enough. Make it a point in time in which the change is acknowledged and felt to be real. Have all the logistics in place so that the team can really begin as a new team at that point. The teams can also use that time to come up with their team names that you can announce to the rest of the teams and department after the event.

---

8 See McCandless et al., Liberating Structures, and Kaner, *Facilitator's Guide*.

I also like to encourage teams to create a schedule with milestones for the split. Especially if you have to coordinate with other groups to make your split happen, which is often the case in larger buildings with facilities and IT departments, as described in the next section. Don't forget to line up these groups so that your split is not stalled.

NOT INVOLVING YOUR FACILITIES AND TECHNOLOGY GROUPS EARLY ENOUGH

Another pitfall to splitting your team is not involving others at the right time. So when you need them, they are not available. You don't want delays when you choose to transform your teams. Instead, plan it in.

Why do we involve these groups? Well, we want to make sure any of your tooling is updated in advance of your team split event. Some teams need to update or create a new project in their work-tracking tool (like Jira). Other teams need to update tools (like GitHub). Maybe you need a new channel in your chat program (like Slack). New calendars or email addresses might need to be created for the teams. The smaller your company, the more likely you have direct access and control to manage the internal systems that your teams need. But as you grow larger, all of these things become more formal and are controlled by someone else.

I encourage you to determine the facilities implications for your team split in addition to the IT things, if you work in a colocated environment. Are your desks easily movable and reconfigurable? Do you need to schedule a desk move or reconfiguration with your facilities and IT groups? That could take some time, so plan for it.

In addition to these pitfalls, another that you might not think about in advance is the emotional impact and challenge of splitting teams.

THE EMOTIONAL CHALLENGE OF SPLITTING TEAMS

It's not always easy to split into different teams, and for at least one engineer I talked with, there was a feeling of sadness about not being able to work with the same people in quite the same way as before. At AppFolio, the office at the time was one large room. The engineers would still see each other within the physical space of the same room after the first team split in half, but that was not the same as working together on the code. It was a loss. Coming from a humanistic stance, as coaches, managers, and caring teammates we can pay attention to how people are feeling when teams split, giving extra time to listen and encouraging people to talk about what's going on so that we can figure out the best way to support them.

It can be quite scary and emotional to split up a team, especially when it is the first team at the company, like the previous story from AppFolio. A similar sentiment happened, as recounted by Rachel Davies, a coach and development lead at Unruly, a London-based company that is in the digital advertising space. She told me about how their original team split into two teams. It was a highly significant event for the colocated team. Its identity was strong, as demonstrated by this story:

> The large team decided that it had grown to a size where they might benefit from splitting. So they did split. But it was much more of a socially considered split, and what was interesting was they had a big retrospective about all their worries about splitting [...] one of the team members even made a cake, and it was like a **Lord of the Rings** cake; it was a chocolate volcano with Lego figures on it, and it was **the breaking of this fellowship**. So they obviously felt emotional about breaking. Because a lot of the people had joined the company very early on in their career and then they had been there for quite a long time and they felt like, "Oh now we are splitting."

Rachel explained that this split felt even more emotional and scary to the team because when many of these developers joined the company, the development team had been led by the CTO. This split also marked the time that the CTO went away from the team to work more closely with the business and to help foster the development of its new analytics product. So it went beyond being "just a team split." It really represented a broader organizational change that impacted the people.

As it turned out later, the split put the team in a better place. As Rachel said, "There was a big surprise because they were much happier...we could get loads more done, and the standup was quicker." Although the teams were worried about the change going into this, they were able to get more done with a narrower focus after the split. This split worked out so well that less than nine months later, one of the teams split in two again, in order to enable some specific, focused feature development work on their initial product. Team splitting was starting to become a pattern for Unruly.

Paige Garnick shared with me that when you feel such ownership and attachment to your code, it's really hard to let it go. And that can slow down when a team splits. She said this when thinking of her experience: "The split took longer than we wanted it to because of that issue of letting go of code, you know, personal attachment."[9] The strength of code ownership can be an inhibitor of reteaming and is one of the constraints detailed later in Chapter 11.

In addition to team splits as described thus far, the grow-and-split pattern of dynamic reteaming can happen at levels beyond the cross-functional software team. It can happen at the tribe, or team-of-teams level, as stories in the next section describe.

Larger-Scale Splits

As I mentioned in "Panarchy" on page 7, team changes happen at different levels in organizations. It's not just at the lowest team level. It can happen across multiple teams. It can happen in department, division, and company levels. Here are a some stories of these kinds of team splits.

GROW AND SPLIT AT THE TRIBE LEVEL

AppFolio consisted of cross-functional teams within its research and development (R&D) organization. They were grouped together, often around three to five teams each, into structures that they called *colleges*, which I will refer to as *tribes* in this book. This is similar to the structural concept of squads and tribes popularized by the company Spotify years ago.[10]

Tribes would sit together in the same region of the building, separated into different team areas. Engineers in each tribe were managed by one engineering tribe director, or a hands-on tech lead within the tribe, if it was a larger size. Other roles like QA engineer, UX designer, agile coach, or product manager had a different reporting structure, but sat in the same area with their teams.

The work that was done by the teams in the tribes, at least at the writing of this book, was pulled into the teams by choice from themed backlogs. This work used to be pushed out to the teams, but after feedback from the engineers that they wanted more choice, the organization made a shift to more of a pull system.

---

9 Paige Garnick, in an interview with the author, January 2020.

10 For background on this concept, see Spotify Engineering Culture videos at its website (*https:// labs.spotify.com/2014/03/27/spotify-engineering-culture-part-1*). It is quite common to tell people not to copy the Spotify model in cut-and-paste style when transforming organizations. We did not cut and paste at AppFolio from an existing structure into that structure, but we grew into it, starting with our first team of 10, after applying what I now call the one-by-one and grow-and-split patterns. That is a key difference, and that resulting tribe and squad structure suited us quite well.

Having collective code ownership gave this organization and the people in it flexibility on what they worked on, and didn't corner them to working in only one area of the app.

As the company got bigger, it had a deliberate way to grow new tribes. As the teams multiplied, engineers were promoted to be tribe directors. When hiring someone from the outside to be a director, which would also happen, that person would first join an existing tribe and be part of a team as regular code contributor, as shown in Figure 6-2.

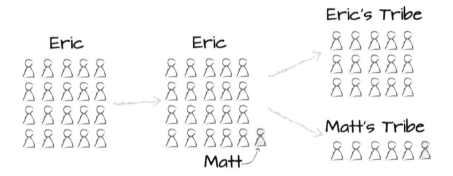

Figure 6-2. Grow and split at the tribe level

The existing tribe director was their mentor, teaching them the ins and outs of what it meant to be a director at this company. The new director would pair program with other team members on the regular work of the team. Team members knew that this new director was on their way to becoming the director of a new tribe. It could take several months for this to happen. This in-the-trenches experience helps the engineering directors build credibility and gain essential domain knowledge with the products as well as learn the characteristics of successful management in this context.

This also reduces the risk of bringing an outsider into a leadership role that might not be the right fit after getting to know them. Having a gradual entry in this way helps to manage that risk by making the person's sphere of potential impact smaller until they get up to speed.

When up to speed, that director and their team break away to spawn a new, separate tribe. To grow this tribe, new people will be added, or people from another part of the engineering team will join. How is that done? It could be by using the grow-and-split pattern or by seeding the new team with members of the tribe's original team so that the mentorship system can be present, as detailed in Chapter 5.

Tribes facilitate localized community and culture building. Having social events is a part of AppFolio's culture, and it was not uncommon for each tribe to have a certain amount of money allocated for each team (and each tribe) to do team-building activities, including team dinners, short local excursions, wine tasting, or even events like Segway tours in their city of Santa Barbara.

This tribe structure helps you feel like you are at a smaller company even as your company grows in size. It's a proactive way to combat Dunbar's number, which is the theory that you can only successfully maintain relationships with around 150 people.[11] People get to know others in their tribes, which facilitates future reteaming within their tribes. If you subscribe to the "forming, storming, norming, performing" philosophy of team development from Bruce Tuckman,[12] in many ways, planned socialization at the tribe level proactively starts up some of that before the people change and are part of their new teams. It's like priming for reteaming.

Besides growing and splitting at the tribe level with the onboarding of a new leader, as we just explored, there are other ways that larger-scale splits happen in our companies in order to attain particular goals. Next is a story from Greenhouse Software, where the company reteamed for a different type of goal—to realign its code ownership.

Grow and Split to Drive Code Ownership

At Greenhouse Software in New York, I spoke with Mike Boufford, CTO, as well as Andrew Lister, who is their senior director of engineering. They told me stories of how Greenhouse grew and scaled. At one point, when their team grew to about 60 engineers, they realized that they needed to reorganize so that they had more specific code ownership. Until that point, everyone would work on every part of the codebase, and so the owner of any area of code was really just "the last person who touched it." As a result, there were many areas that didn't have clear owners. Mike said, "We started realizing that everyone was kind of working on

---

11 Dunbar, "Coevolution of Neocortical Size," 686.

12 Tuckman, "Developmental Sequence in Small Groups," 6.

everything, and we hadn't done a good job of carving up the work into bits and pieces that allowed for clear lines of ownership and accountability."[13]

As their codebase grew, and as they added people—they went from 40 engineers to 60 in one year—the onboarding cognitive load grew as well. People felt like they needed to learn *everything* in order to be ramped up. The time needed to onboard new engineers grew with the size of their codebase, so they knew they'd run into challenges during the next phase of growth.

Furthermore, at Greenhouse they believe that engineers should be able to rotate from one squad to another—to work with different people, to keep up social connections, and to feel refreshed. The problem with their current structure was that, since every team would work on every part of the codebase, when someone changed teams it felt to engineers that they were expressing a preference for one manager over another, rather than one area of the codebase over another. This issue was compounded by the fact that the teams were named after their managers. Mike described this as feeling like "emotional friction to changing teams." They really wanted to break out of this pattern as well.

So they decided that they needed some kind of reteaming to solve problems like these. They envisioned a reorg. It happened in the way that many reteamings happen. Someone thinks about it and writes down some ideas. In this case, that is what Andy did. He wrote up a document and proposed what their new structure might look like—centered around customer domains and personas, each team ideally having a dedicated product manager, designer, engineering manager, quality assurance engineer, data scientist, and software engineers. He and Mike discussed, and then they met with their product leadership, who really liked the idea as well. With buy-in from key stakeholders, they went back to their organization with their proposal. Andy told me, "We had one-on-ones with all the members of the teams, started shopping the idea around, and went through all the engineering managers. I went through every single person on the team and just showed them the idea. We tried and encouraged people to move teams. In having these domains now, people could actually start to focus on different areas."[14] In the end they just picked a day—which was the start of 2019—on which they shifted to their new structure.

13 Mike Boufford, in an interview with the author, January 2020.

14 Andrew Lister, in an interview with the author, January 2020.

They have been in their new, customer domain–focused organizational structure for about a year. They're glad they shifted and have reaped some benefits. A few benefits in particular stood out in our interview.

Now that the engineers have greater levels of code ownership of specific areas, they have noticed that people are starting to see opportunities for how to evolve their architecture. Andy said, "People are actually now saying things like, *Okay, could this become a separate service? Maybe it should become a separate library? or a gem?*" Evidence of Conway's law (*http://melconway.com/Home/Committees_Paper.html*) at work.[15]

In addition to this ownership and a more focused view of the codebase, their new structure has also helped engineering leaders to connect the work of the engineers to the amount of dollars they wanted to invest into each problem area. They felt that this would help them to explain their resource allocation and spending, as we all must do in our organizations at some point. It felt like their new structure had a closer connection to that spend. As Mike put it, "Team organization is our most effective lever in figuring out how to allocate spend efficiently across the group."

And finally, when people ask to switch teams, they no longer have the stigma of "wanting to leave their manager." This ability to change teams is what Mike calls a "secret weapon in retention." He said, "After a few years at any job, people just want something to feel different; they get an itch for change, and this strategy helps to address that need. It's not that a person considering other opportunities is necessarily unhappy with their job. We all want to just feel movement and growth in our lives."

After a lot of movement and growth, not only as individuals, but also as companies, things start to feel different. Reteaming after reteaming occurs as we scale, and it can be even more pronounced during hypergrowth phases where hiring is rampant. The culture shifts and evolves, and people start to notice that. It can become uncomfortable. Let's take a deeper look into this in the next section.

---

15 Conway's law states: "Any organization that designs a system (defined broadly) will produce a design whose structure is a copy of the organization's communication structure."

What It Means When You're Asked, "How Do We Maintain Our Culture?"

Thus far, we've explored reteaming patterns related to growth, including the one-by-one pattern and the grow-and-split pattern. After some time has passed and your company has grown in these ways, things start to feel different and the people around you might ask, "How do we maintain our culture?" I feel like it's almost a trick question when this is asked, because it means that your culture has already shifted into something else.

When I joined one of the startups I was at, I found myself in the position of advising and coaching a handful of engineers who were early employees at the company. There were about eight hundred employees at the time and probably two hundred in engineering. These early hires were concerned that the company was changing—they could see it and feel it with all of the new hires around them. At that time, we were all in one large open office with the capacity to hold around three hundred people. You would walk in our development area and come across so many people you didn't know. It became hard to remember and match names with faces. It's like you're living in an example of Dunbar's number—where so many new people have been hired to such a degree that you don't have the ability to have relationships with all of them—there are just so many more people.

This growth continued for years. Some might call it the hypergrowth phase—applying the term that, to my knowledge, originated in a *Harvard Business Review* article by Alexander V. Izosimov, CEO of the telecommunications company VimpelCom, in which he wrote about the growth of cell phone markets.[16] I'm applying it here to label the time at the company when you're hiring like crazy. You have a mandate to grow. You have all of these open positions. It's a very distinct time in the growth of a company. There is a lot of reteaming that is happening—mostly the one-by-one pattern and the grow-and-split pattern, in my experience. Splits and reorgs happen at higher levels than the teams as well. All of this going on all around you feels very dynamic and changeable—hence, dynamic reteaming.

Yet while all this is happening some things feel like they are getting slower. Decision making might take longer due to having more people. You feel less nimble than you did during startup days. More process is developed. How you

---

16 Izosimov, "Managing Hypergrowth."

did it before is different now. Maybe there was more freedom and autonomy before, but now it's changing. You need to use software that you didn't use before. Things are "rolled out" across the company. There's a greater need to track employee data since there are so many more employees. I've been at three startups that grew, and at all three I was there on the day employee badges were given out with everyone's name and photo, and they started locking the doors because of security concerns. You just don't know everyone anymore. It's a visceral experience. It's a milestone. It's another signal that the company has grown.

Furthermore, during this type of culture change, power is shifted around. All three startups I've been at were founded by technical people. Engineering always felt like the center or hub of the company. We had the funding, and we seemed to have the power. With time, in my experience, this shifts out, and things are driven by outside forces like finance and HR. When these things happen it feels quite different, again, because it is. We have new rules to follow that are given to us from outside our department. People try to standardize human systems, like performance management practices and career ladders, across all different departments. The freedom to do things as you want in your own department is now part of a wider discussion. Resource allocation is discussed. Work gets capitalized or expensed. You have all-hands talks about the ratio of revenue to expenses. The hiring slows to help you get to a better ratio. Hypergrowth takes a new form—a new stage of being efficient and "doing more with what we have."

All of this change is not for everyone. When startups grow and shift forward into larger companies, people start leaving. Some of the early employees might feel like the company has changed too much for them, so they need to go find another job or start something themselves. When this happens I think it's a good sign. People self-select out. If they do not, and they don't like the buildup of process around them, they might add drag to the system, doing things that are counterproductive to what the company must become. So we send them off in a positive light—we thank them in public for their contribution and wish them well.

In her book, *Powerful*, Patty McCord, who served as chief talent officer at Netflix, talks about hiring people for the future company you want to have. She says, "Identify the problem you want to solve, the time frame in which you want to solve it, the kinds of people who will be successful at that, and what they need to know how to do, then ask yourself, *What do we need to do to be ready and able, and whom do we need to bring in?"*[17] I think that there's a lot of truth to this perspective. Your current team might not have the skills, the interest, and the gumption to do the work of the future state of the company. Some of them might, though, and re-roleing into something else still might work. You need to take this human by human to see what they are doing now, what their future goals are, and what they want to grow into. You need to decide whether you want to support them on that journey and provide opportunities or whether someone else might be better suited for that role. You need to look out for the business entity while at the same time considering the humans that are already there. It's not always easy.

People might experience a false sense of loyalty at companies and feel invincible. Just because you were there at the beginning doesn't mean you have the skill set to help the company to thrive at scale. This is where tough decisions come in, to do what's best for the company and where it is growing.

When you're at a startup and you're in love with it, it's hard to see it grow and change. But it's what it must do if the goal is to develop a large, global company that is out to change the world. You need to hire in people who are along for that ride. Nostalgia for the past startup days is a trap that I've fallen into, at least in my second startup. You need people who can propel the thing forward.

So, when people ask, "How do we maintain our culture?" you need to pay attention to them. Meet with them. Listen. Maybe they are ready to move on. Or maybe they are ready for a new role that they see as beneficial to helping the company morph—because it has changed, and it will continue to change. That's the nature of the beast.

Dynamic reteaming is driven by growth, and it's also driven by the desire to work on new things, in new teams. In the next chapter, we will take a look at the isolation pattern, which is typically driven by new areas of work.

---

17 McCord, *Powerful*, 78.

7

Isolation Pattern

Thus far we have explored reteaming patterns related to company growth. Another reason that companies reteam is due to the work. That is, new work they are going to embark on might be best attacked by changing the team, or starting a brand-new team. This is home to the isolation pattern of reteaming (as well as the merging pattern, which is discussed in the next chapter).

When you have a bold, new idea to go after, and you need intense focus, you might consider forming a team to the side and letting the members run with it via the isolation pattern. This pattern works equally well when you're dealing with an unexpected emergency and you need focus. I experienced this viscerally when the first startup I was a part of made a do-or-die pivot to reorient the company for success. I started this book with that story, in the preface, and have expanded upon it in this chapter.

Beyond new work and emergencies, I've noticed that as companies get bigger, processes and procedures get more formalized. And, if you're not careful, things could start to take a lot longer and really feel burdensome to the people. This is akin to a rigidity trap, or period of stagnation, as described in Chapter 1. Processes can feel quite heavy when you want to move fast. You can rejigger that dynamic by applying the isolation pattern.

The isolation pattern of dynamic reteaming is when you take a team, put it off to the side, and give the team members explicit freedom to work in a different way than they had been previously. You keep the existing teams moving like they were, but you catalyze a new team that is distinctly separate, like in Figure 7-1.

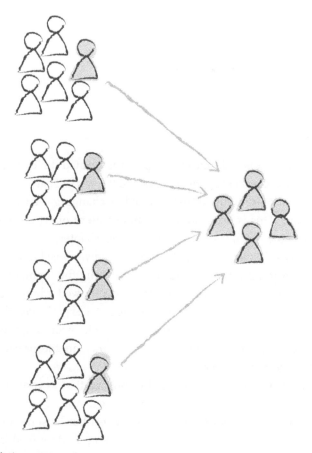

Figure 7-1. Isolation pattern

Throughout this chapter, I'll share stories that bring this pattern to life, followed by some general recommendations for what to do when you want to apply the isolation pattern. Let's get started, then, with the story of Expertcity, where I first experienced the isolation pattern in action.

Isolation to Pivot the Company from Failure

At Expertcity, we built an online marketplace for technical support. We also envisioned ourselves becoming the "eBay for services." This idea was attractive enough to raise more than 30 million dollars to start the company, but the product failed. Cofounder Klaus Schauser, at Catalyst for Thought, spoke about it like this: "We found that people loved the screen-sharing software, but no one wanted to pay for tech support...the $10 million lesson? Do market validation!"[1]

The company pivoted after doing this market validation to reduce risk on its next product. After that, the reteaming started. To work on the new product idea, several engineers were pulled off of existing teams and were moved to another area of the office. I was able to be on this team as a writer. The rest of the engineering teams were told that we would be working on something different, that they should leave us alone, and that we would not be using the regular process. This put our team in a special, intentional, beneficial silo.

We were tasked with developing a product that would let anyone access and operate their computer from a distance. The product was named GoToMyPC.

We had complete process freedom in the initial stages of this product. We were liberated from the Waterfall way of working that the other teams at the company were using. We didn't need pixel-perfect mock-ups of web pages, and we didn't have to write a specification describing what we were attempting to build. The engineers created the baseline artwork with the thought that later someone else would reskin the web pages, which made everything go so much faster. We didn't have to estimate how long we thought it would take to do the work. We just got to do stuff.

That liberating pivot led to a new path for the company. We later went on to invent products that became very popular at the writing of this book, called GoToMeeting and GoToWebinar.

Besides using isolation reteaming to pivot and find a new path for a struggling startup, you can also apply the isolation pattern to start up new products in your company. Here's what we did at AppFolio to birth SecureDocs, which is now a separate company in Santa Barbara, California.

Isolation for New Product Development

Fast-forward nearly 10 years later. At AppFolio, we used the isolation technique to create our second product, which was a secure online data room for mergers and acquisitions, called SecureDocs. I interviewed Comron Sattari about this. He recalled:

---

1 Turner, "Catalyst SYNC."

We had a goal which was outside the day-to-day of the engineering team. It was kind of a blue-sky project. We were building this whole new product. We did market validation. We experimented a ton...and on that team, not only were we completely separate but we totally changed the process. Instead of sprint planning and Scrum and two-week or four-week sprints...we said listen, we can't predict what we will be doing two days from now, sprint planning doesn't work in that world, stories go from being 8 points to 1 point overnight because we learned something brand new...and so it doesn't necessarily work planning that far out in the future, so we switched to more of a flow-based process where we had a backlog, we kept it in priority order, and we just took stuff off the top and we just constantly iterated.

He added, "We couldn't necessarily commit even one week at a time, so we went down to basically one-hour sprints. And, we would take a story off the list and we would learn something by doing that story...and so it was just a completely different process than the rest of the team. [...] We didn't necessarily know how it was going to work, and so splitting it off to a separate team that had its own feedback loop outside the bigger team allowed us to experiment more."[2]

SecureDocs became a separate company that exists today. Comron became the cofounder and architect at that company. This is an example that dispels the myth that in order to succeed you need to have stable teams that don't change their composition. In both of these cases, if we had remained on unchanged, "stable" teams, who knows? We could have had quite a different result. I doubt either case would have been as fast to release as they were. There is a power in dynamic reteaming.

I'm proud of SecureDocs and the successful company that it has become. It was fun to witness its roots while it incubated within AppFolio. At Citrix, a division within it called Citrix Online started up new products using methods similar to the isolation pattern, as described in the following story.

---

2 Comron Sattari, in an interview with the author, March 2016.

Isolation to Spawn New Innovations in an Enterprise

In 2015, Carey Caulfield, my friend and the principal product manager at Citrix Online, led a team that had created an in-app communication tool that helped to validate the acquisition of a company called Grasshopper, which provided a similar service.

At the time, the company had a relatively new CEO who encouraged Carey and a few others to form a team with the mission "to innovate and disrupt GoToMeeting," the company's flagship product. It was time for her new team to work differently. They applied techniques from the book *The Lean Startup* by Eric Ries.[3]

At the beginning of this new team, they were in the same desks as on their previous teams. "We did end up moving later," Carey said, "and that really helped us."[4] They moved into a garage-like area that they wound up calling the *Startup Garage*. When you have a change of location after reteaming, it feels like a new experience. It matters. When you're distributed, having new chat channels for only your new team also feels different.

The team had the privacy from others, and that helped it innovate. "No one was really watching what we were doing. Now we just started to do what we wanted," Carey said.

The team members also had process freedom and were encouraged by their CEO to use third-party tools if they wanted to. "We didn't have to do things the same way anymore. We didn't have to talk to operations. We didn't have to get permission from the UX team. It was like an unraveling, sort of shedding of skin of all this baggage we'd had for years."

After some time, the team pivoted and created a product called Convoi, which enabled users to have second phone lines. The product took off. The executive team moved forward with an acquisition of Grasshopper, which offered a similar product to Convoi, and was more established in the marketplace. In essence, Carey's team helped to validate the acquisition of this company. This ultimately led to the dissolution of Carey's team as Grasshopper merged into Citrix Online.

---

3 See Ries, *The Lean Startup*.

4 Carey Caulfield, in an interview with the author, April 2017.

After her team was folded into Grasshopper, the spirit of the team changed. As she put it, "We weren't innovating anymore. We weren't allowed to develop anymore. We were just migrating customers." They also had to move out of their garage and back in with the main engineering team. After a while, the team dissolved. That was sad for the team. They had been on this incredible ride that wound up coming to this end. There is a love-and-loss quality to some dynamic reteaming. Teams don't always live on and expand, and at times our thrilling rides come to an end.

Besides isolating teams for the purpose of innovation and new product development, the pattern can be used as a strategy when you are dealing with an unexpected technical situation.

Isolation for Solving Technical Emergencies

Very early on at AppFolio, before officially releasing our first product, Property Manager, we were testing internally and determined that the product wasn't fast enough to release to customers. We decided to tackle that problem, and that is where the isolation reteaming came in.

An assortment of senior engineers were called to leave their regular teams, and "lived" in a conference room for a week or so, trying to improve the speed of everything, according to Comron Sattari, who was part of that team. He shared:

> We needed to improve speed by 2x, or something like that. We spent a lot of time doing a lot of experiments. There was very little structure. There were three or four of us, and we were all exploring different avenues. Then we started actually seeing commonalities, and then we would find a bug or problem, and we would all focus on it and fix it. Then we would move on to the next exploration and try to figure out what's going on. Over the course of, I don't know it wasn't that long, two weeks maybe, we accomplished the goal. We dissolved the little team, and went back to our normal activities.[5]

Comron and I spent a while talking about this team. He told me that it didn't feel like doing this emergency work would fit within the regular teams that they had in place, which is why they reteamed off to the side. The structure of the regular product development teams worked for building new features into their

---

5 Comron Sattari, in an interview with the author, March 2016.

existing software platform. But this emergency work felt different. They needed freedom to work differently, and they needed the freedom to not have to convince their existing team that they needed to do that. So they reteamed using what I now call the isolation pattern. Comron explained, "Sometimes you have problems that don't necessarily fit the processes you have, and you got to change the process a little. It's easier to do that in a small team than to do it in the context of a bigger team when you have to explain what you're doing, and you don't necessarily fit into the daily routine that everyone else has."

This idea challenges the notion of doing *spikes* within regular sprint work. A spike is a special research story that comes up from time to time in teams. For example, if the team doesn't know how it would attempt to build something requested by a product owner, the story in the backlog is considered a *spike* so that the team can timebox a certain amount of days or hours to do this research. It's really a mismatch for the other type of work going on in a sprint, which is typically feature development that is more "known." This type of work needs different feedback loops, and doing these things within two-week sprints, for example, can feel like a big drag or a mismatched cadence. In a two-week sprint you have daily standups. With unknown work, you might need hourly standups. It's challenging to do within the other cadence and existing rules.

Comron contrasted this, in the case of this performance team:

> We had a very specific goal [to improve performance] but it wasn't a product manager saying, **Hey we need to implement feature X, Y, and Z,** where there is a known end goal and we can use the process that we have to get there. We can do sprint planning, break down stories, and estimate them. [...] For this tiger team for speed, the end goal was nebulous—it was to make it faster. We didn't know what that was going to take. We didn't know what tools we were going to need. We ended up calling in consultants. We had conference calls with 10 people on them talking to experts. On Monday, we didn't know what we necessarily were going to be doing on Tuesday or Wednesday.

Having this type of work planted into a team with a different type of work cadence, such as maintenance work slogged forward during two-week sprints, is inappropriate. As Comron mentioned, since this work was unknown, they needed faster feedback loops in order to explore and discover what needed to be done. After a couple of weeks this short-lived team accomplished its mission, and its team members were folded back into the regular teams. It was liberating to this team to be free from the chains of the existing process. This is a huge benefit of the isolation pattern.

The isolation pattern can also be applied in contexts with a greater number of teams to accomplish a shared goal, like in the following story about solving performance issues across a large monolith.

Scaling the Isolation Pattern

When you have a crisis and you have 50 teams, it's most likely insufficient to create an isolated team off to the side to solve all of your problems. You might need a different structure to coordinate the work across multiple squads. I call this structure *hub and spoke*, invoking the image of a bicycle wheel that has a center, with spokes connecting to the tire or edges of the wheel, as shown in Figure 7-2.

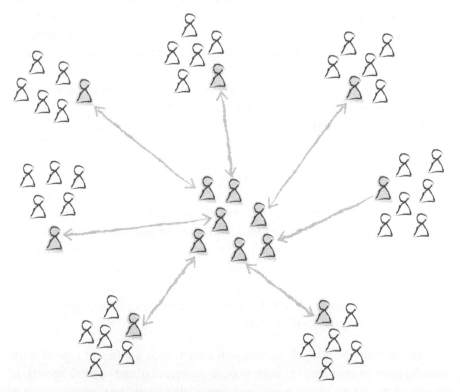

Figure 7-2. Scaling the isolation pattern with hub and spoke

The people in this story organized into a pattern where they would come to the center of their workspace for their daily standups and go back out to the periphery of the building to share information with the multiple teams that they were a part of.

This particular team of 50 was facing performance issues as well, and the leadership decided to deploy a "stop the line" type of command to get all of the people refocused over to working on performance issues as a collective whole. This edict was shared across our chat tool, via email, and via multiple engineering directors. Here's what we did.

At first, it was kind of disorganized, and people started working on and talking about the different efforts that they were attempting in order to solve the performance issues that they could see. There were other people who wanted to help; however, they did not know how. To solve this problem, several key tactics emerged:

- Clear dashboards that tracked the progress of the efforts
- Clear definitions of what success looked like
- Key point people identified for each squad or cluster of squads who could dispatch work to the squads and people who were ready to help
- A daily standup for the key people (open to anyone interested)
- A regular cadence of status updates to the R&D organization at large
- A self-selected leader who stepped up and was the visible face of the endeavor
- Leadership meetings between engineering and product teams to communicate on and be on the same page with priority questions

After some time, the work that had been done was enough to declare the emergency over. We wound up with better dashboards, the ability to organize during a crisis, and a community of practice to monitor and strategize on performance-related efforts going forward. This was emergent organizational design, and it was highly effective for us. Think of applying the isolation pattern of dynamic reteaming the next time you face a crisis.

We've gone over a handful of stories that demonstrate the power of the isolation pattern. Following are some general recommendations for the pattern, as well as pitfalls to avoid.

General Recommendations for the Isolation Pattern

Thinking back on these stories and the experiences that I have had with the isolation pattern through the years, I have some recommendations for success in applying this pattern deliberately, starting with who you put on the team.

INVITE ENTREPRENEURIAL PEOPLE TO JOIN THE TEAM

It helps to have people on isolated teams who do not, by default, need to be led by others. On an isolated team catalyzing innovations or new work, you might hit roadblocks. You might have to work differently. You might have to do things beyond your traditional job role. Having a personality that enables you to do what it takes to move things forward is key. And it doesn't have to be a team comprised of only senior engineers. I've seen isolated teams of interns catalyzing incredibly insightful value with a good mentor at the helm. Now, if it's a "do or die" situation for the company, I would definitely handpick the people for this team, and give it all you've got.

TELL THE TEAM THAT IT CAN WORK HOW IT CHOOSES

Proclaiming to the team that it has freedom to determine how to organize is an incredible thing to do, especially if it is used to working in a rigid process. If the people on the isolated team are not passionate in this area, they can always try the baseline process they used in their last team. I think the key here is to treat people like professionals and give them freedom. If that doesn't work, you can always try to influence them later.

MOVE THE TEAM TO ITS OWN SPACE

When working in a physical office, it feels very different when you move locations in or out of your office. It can feel like a completely new job. Move your isolated teams and let them start fresh somewhere.

TELL OTHER TEAMS TO LEAVE THEM ALONE

Especially if your team needs great focus, tell the other teams not to interfere with your isolated team. Whoever is managing the isolated team can serve as a buffer if people come and bother this team. If you're the manager, then tell this team to send people to you with questions.

DETERMINE WHETHER THE TEAM WILL LIVE ON, OR FOLD BACK INTO OTHER TEAMS

Once the team has accomplished its goal, you need to determine what happens. If the team has catalyzed a new product that will live on, maybe the people on it are considered the founding members, and you grow other teams around them. If they have worked on a short-term emergency, they probably just go back to their other teams.

Besides these recommendations, there are also some gotchas for the isolation pattern, which I describe next.

Pitfalls of the Isolation Pattern

I see three main pitfalls for the isolation pattern, and they relate to elitism, lack of foresight into who might maintain the code created in an isolated team, and the loss of engagement after an experience in an isolated team comes to an end. These pitfalls are described in this section.

ELITISM

I think that sometimes isolated teams like these can be viewed as having greater privilege than ordinary teams. They probably have a flashier profile, the people are usually hand-selected to join the teams, and they are typically empowered to do things however they want. They could develop an attitude themselves about their special status and appear to be arrogant. Some isolated teams solve gnarly problems and are viewed as heroes, and maybe they were for the technical feats they accomplished. They get reputations of being superstars.

But not all teams have the freedom to operate like this. So it could cause an us-versus-them situation with other teams. Jealousy could occur. To mitigate elitism, you need to pay attention to the other teams as well as the isolated teams. Be sure to recognize other teams for the great work that they are doing as well.

WHAT ABOUT MAINTENANCE OF THE CODE?

If a team is created off to the side and then disbanded, and the people are folded back into other teams, you need to figure out who is going to maintain the code that was created on the isolated team. Come up with a strategy for how you will maintain the code that was created, and get the buy-in from any other teams that might inherit the code so that this isn't a point of friction later on.

I witnessed an isolated team form, create a feature that was highly sought-after for some sales team members, and then disband. The code it created was quick, and saved the day. But the team also tarnished some of its relationships with engineers who were shepherds of the code it changed. In other words, the team left a mess and then went on to other teams. This caused friction at that particular company. Imagine instead if the isolated team had first made some lightweight agreements with the teams that normally worked on and owned that code. Some up-front alignment on what it was about to do would avoid catching the other teams by surprise, and it might help create more harmonious conditions later.

THE THRILLING RIDE THAT COMES TO AN END

Most isolated teams that I have come into contact with have disbanded in the end and have been folded back into other teams. This contrast can be very striking if you have a lot of freedom on an isolated team, and then have to go back to join a team that has a tightly controlled process. Watch for that. Carefully consider the assignments given after someone leaves an isolated team. Healthy one-on-one conversations between team members and their managers can help here.

This chapter has looked at teams that have re-formed around work areas using the isolation pattern. The pattern is a good one to apply when you need to pivot your work, as we saw in the Expertcity story; when you need to deal with an emergency situation, such as a performance crisis; and when you want to create brand-new innovations within a company.

The isolation pattern is also about recognizing that our teams might fall into rigidity traps in terms of process. We very well might get into a groove of working one way, and then, when faced with new challenges that are unlike our normal work, find it very refreshing to have the permission and freedom to innovate and work in smaller feedback loops, as was the case in the SecureDocs story.

This wisdom goes against the grain of ideas of standardizing and holding people to all follow the same process all of the time. Personally, I think it's delightful to diverge, and even more delightful to witness the energy that emerges when we give our teams the freedom to work differently.

Another pattern that is connected to reteaming because of the work is the merging pattern, described in the next chapter.

8

Merging Pattern

Another pattern often driven by the work at hand is the merging pattern. The merging pattern is just like it sounds: it's when two or more teams or entities combine together, as shown in Figure 8-1.

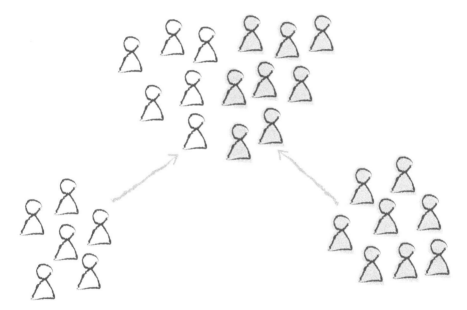

Figure 8-1. Merging pattern

So why merge teams, especially considering the benefits that smaller teams yield, which we went over in Chapter 6?

Well, maybe you want to combine teams in order to harvest their collective intelligence to tackle a specific challenge. Or, maybe you feel that having one team per work area is confining, and you desire more fluidity in your work allocation by reteaming within a larger team. Even beyond that, maybe your company wants to acquire another company so that you combine forces and can more quickly offer a feature set that could save your company years of development time. These are some of the scenarios in which the merging pattern comes into play.

This section has stories from the team level, the tribe level, and the company level to explore this pattern, starting with a story from New Zealand. Pitfalls from this pattern are also discussed, related to some very challenging mergers.

Merging Teams to Enable Pair Programming Variety

At the division of Trade Me where delivery manager William Them worked, they experimented with self-selected teams when working on a project to make their web frontend *responsive*, or able to be viewed on multiple devices and screen sizes.[1]

Here is how the experiment came about. In his tribe, William had roughly eight squads. In his part of the almost 250-person product development organization, it was conventional that squads would remain relatively static and, accordingly, work would be assigned to them. When a squad finished its work, the management would look at the next highest priority work to be done, and it would be assigned to that "freed up" squad. This left the managers wondering if the most highly motivated engineers were able to work on the epics that were most interesting and suitable to them. Matching people up with work was really just the luck of the draw, or a timing issue. So, as a manager of some of these squads, William decided to do an experiment and merge together three squads of about 15 people total—engineers, analysts, QA, UX—and try out a new way of working, via regular dynamic reteaming, as shown in Figure 8-2.

---

1 William Them, in an interview with the author, November 2016.

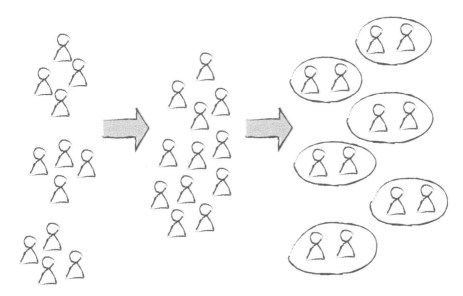

Figure 8-2. Merge squads, then engage in self-selected pairing

They chose to experiment like this because the work is relatively known. They are basically porting their existing frontend feature set to Angular to make it responsive in various screen sizes. This is the merging pattern in action.

To get started, they put the names of the features or epics that the team would be making responsive up on a wall. Each team member put their name on a sticky note, and put it on the feature that they wanted to work on in the coming weeks. William didn't set rules in terms of how many developers, UX designers, QA engineers, and so on, for each team, and instead he trusted the team members to work it out themselves. This repeated self-selected team exercise took about 20 minutes each time. When a team was about one to two weeks away from finishing its particular epic, that was the signal to kick off a new reteaming event. Each of the "in progress" and new epics were put on the wall. Each person was able to put their name on a sticky note and then place their note on the epic that they wanted to work on for the next few weeks. This was a continual process that had been going on for about six months at the time I interviewed William.

The power of this self-selected reteaming is that whenever new work entered the picture, there was the opportunity to best match up the people with the work. Putting the decision of "what work goes to which engineers" into the hands of the engineers minimizes the command-and-control nature of the work assignment. This, in theory, brings more potential fulfillment to the people. In addition, people can self-select into the work that they were doing already, which should meet the needs of the people who want to stay with a certain work topic or with certain team members for a longer time frame.

Notice that due to the merging of the teams, the company now had a much larger team than before. With this, Trade Me had a deliberate reteaming pattern—in this case pairing and switching pairs. In other words, the company put in a structure to help the people organize and reorganize when work was completed. This appears to have mitigated the challenges that teams face when dealing with larger team sizes, as described in Chapter 6. Remember this: when you have larger teams, you need facilitation structures to keep the teams from degrading in how they organize and how they communicate.

Not all merging happens at the team level. Let's explore an example at the team-of-teams, or tribe level.

Merging Tribes Together to Form Alliances

Kristian Lindwall told me that at Spotify, at one point in their development, they were starting to see *mission pollution*. What that meant was that the company had too many missions—in other words, too many work focuses in play at the same time. Some were overlapping. Some squads had the same overarching missions. It was clear that the squads needed to "reset" the missions to make them clearer across the large group of people. Furthermore, he said that on a higher level, they had outgrown the organizational structure that they had. The size of the tribes was getting too big. They were also getting too many tribes. Each tribe lead was reporting to the CTO. That was also becoming a problem. And there were tribes that had adjacent missions or similar missions that did talk to each other a lot, so it would be better for them to sit more closely together in the organization. So the squads decided that they needed to reteam and cluster the tribes together.

In Kristian's words: "So we did reform on a higher level. Tribes got merged, and we formed the concept of *alliances,* which is a grouping of tribes. This was also an approach to solve the issue of scaling...that we had probably grown too big for the structure we had."[2] A tribe is a kind of incubator for squads and the grouping of squads. An alliance is the same for tribes. So tribes that had similar missions ended up being grouped into an alliance.

---

2 Kristian Lindwall, in an interview with the author, September 2016.

Kristian described to me how Spotify went about reorganizing the people involved in this situation. At the time, there were probably around two hundred people working in his part of the org, which consisted of the client infrastructure teams and some closely related tribes. They decided to "do a bit of a reboot to see *What missions make sense? What teams make sense? What doesn't? Where should we merge? Where shouldn't we?* So I gave a lot of thought to how we could do this in a way that's fully transparent and inclusive. It was crucial to us that people would be able to heavily influence or control where they end up, including who they work with, what teams we have, what missions we have, and so on...which is a bit of a tricky thing to do with two hundred people."

How they went about this "reboot" is interesting because the intention comes from a very humanistic stance that strives to give choice to the people involved, instead of just placing them onto teams and letting the people know about it later. Lindwall said they initiated the conversation with people who were close to the mission, such as product owners, leads, and some engineers. Early on, it was mostly people in more formal leadership positions (although he would involve more engineers earlier if doing this again). This group was about 40 people. They did a series of facilitated exercises to discover what the high-level missions were, and how they could break them down into a new tribe structure. In other words, to "take the overall mission of all of these groups of people and the work that they were doing and make it a bit crisper." They did a couple of ideation workshops and came out with a few suggestions for a tribe structure that was brought to the wider group of two hundred people for facilitated input sessions.

Next, they did the same exercise with squads and squad missions. And, in between those sessions, they had a lot of conversations within the bigger squads and via one-on-ones with people.

How did the people ultimately get on the teams? According to Kristian, it happened like this: "We ended up with 4 tribes and something like 15 squads. We had a massive whiteboard where we drew up all these four tribes with a suggestion for squads along with some constraints on sizes of the squads and with the missions for everything. We then talked to everyone and said, 'Okay, so this is what we want to do now... This board will be up for a week. We want to organize ourselves into these tribes and squads, and this is for all of us to solve.'" They had daily standups by this board. Each afternoon they also had a *fika*—a Swedish term that means "coffee break"—where they staffed the whiteboard with people that could talk about the proposed structure. People had avatars representing themselves, which they could move around the tribe and squad structure to represent where they would like to go. The people were supported by one-on-ones with their existing tribe leads and manager so they could talk privately about their concerns.

As it turned out, some of the existing squads and missions remained, and they were present on the boards with avatars for current team members there already. Kristian recounted, "So a lot of the teams remained fairly intact, but maybe one or two people seized the opportunity to go after something new and interesting to them."

Before this reorg happened, and they were discussing the approach, Kristian told me that there were some concerns about the approach. People were wondering if it was going to work. But Kristian and some others who were supporting this approach thought like this: "Hey, you know these people are solving hard problems every day, and they are all very smart people. So figuring out how to reorganize themselves is just another problem to solve. They will figure it out and we'll be there to help out. We might run into some problems along the way, but that's what we do every day. We'll solve those as well."

After two or three days they did have one squad in particular that was blank—no one wanted to be there. And so they started talking to some people about it and learned that this mission itself "was not interesting or compelling for people." So they said, "Okay, let's just wipe that team."

Kristian said:

> We also had teams that felt a little bit too big and some that felt a little bit too small. And there were some chats with people like, you know, bit of selling maybe, but largely...I would say no one was forced to go somewhere they didn't want to go. Some teams ended up being a little bit smaller than we hoped for, and some a little bit bigger. But looking at the big picture, we said that was probably fine. And as we hire and grow, things are going to change anyway. People will quit or join, and, well, that will sort itself out.

I really like how the people are included in this reteaming, and that the organizers of the reteaming allowed time for people to stew over the future structure and have the needed conversations with their managers about where they might wind up. There is a lot of trust, care, and respect for people in this reteaming story.

Beyond the tribe level, as this story described, merging is most often heard of when it relates to one company acquiring another company, the subject of the next section.

Merging at the Company Level

Back in 1999, I joined Expertcity as the 15th employee. I really felt like we were changing the world with the screen-sharing software that our team had invented. It was exciting to be a part of a company that was revolutionizing global communication technology. There was a special energy to our first team. The excitement for what we were building was contagious. We worked hard. I remember working well into the night on many days, and many of us also worked Sundays. I remember feeling that I would be left out if I wasn't around. The work was really fun and highly engaging.

After four years, in 2003, we got notification that we had been acquired by Citrix. At my level—I think I was a technical project manager at the time—I remember finding out about this merger along with everyone else during a company announcement. This announcement was disappointing to many of us because we had the hope of becoming a public company and riding that "going public" wave that many of us had never experienced before. And, let's be honest, we wanted the cash from such an event. Although our stock wound up being worth a nice sum of money, it was disappointing for many people who had worked so hard for not such a huge payout that was notorious in this dot-com era.

How the merger went down must have been different depending on the vantage point of people's positions within the company. I was in engineering. I remember that we were left alone to continue our work, and we were not disrupted or asked to reteam, at least in my sphere. We continued to focus on and invent GoToMeeting. It was almost like the isolation pattern. Our leadership knew how to buffer us from whatever was going on. I believe it was different for other departments like human resources and accounting, and there was a period of *finding synergies*, as they called it. The duplicate roles between the companies were worked out, and some people wound up reporting over to the new "mother ship," which many of us called "Big C." If people were asked to leave at this time, it was not advertised.

I don't really remember meeting many people from the "new" company besides the CEO, who paid us a visit and gave an all-hands talk. I felt like we were a separate division, and we were. We were given the name Citrix Online, which cemented this new identity. I think that worked out well for a while, at least for me.

Besides the financial disappointment, I didn't feel that bad until after more than a year, when one of our key founders left, and then other key technical leaders started leaving as well. That was the beginning of the end for me there, especially after the engineers I loved working with from early days went to another local startup, Appflio, which I later joined.

I've been on both sides of mergers. In this Expertcity story, I was part of the company being acquired. In the subsequent experiences in my career, I was part of the companies on the acquiring side. I'll share a story about that next.

When I was at the second startup that I joined, AppFolio, after some time we acquired a company called MyCase. This was a company that created software for law firms. AppFolio's mission, as articulated at the time, was to create workflow software for a variety of vertical industries using a shared platform. We started out by creating software for property management companies, and then through this acquisition of MyCase, we were able to say that we were in two verticals, this new one being law. So this was a reteaming for the work-type situation. Our portfolio was expanded, and we were able to say that we were a multivertical company sooner than we would have if we had built this vertical ourselves. The culture of the company meshed very well with ours, too, and I remember how our teams combined.

Through this merging of our companies, we acquired a presence in San Diego, as that's where the MyCase office was. We had new team members and new leaders from MyCase who joined us. I remember that we decided to first keep all of the law software down in San Diego. Gradually over the years AppFolio built out that office to also contain teams from the property management vertical. But we socialized together and even had tech retreats together, such as a trip to Big Sur, California. This helped to blend our cultures and encourage us to become *one team*.

Some of the founders and other leaders of the startup that we acquired left the company after more than a year as well. I think that's a common pattern after merging happens. Key leaders from the company being acquired inevitably leave and move on to something else. Maybe that's not always the case, but I've seen it firsthand at least five times in my career.

I've been through some mergers that felt positive to me, and other ones that felt like my heart was being ripped out. Mergers, like some other examples of dynamic reteaming, aren't always the bright and cheerful organizational changes they might appear to be. Sometimes they hurt like hell.

That brings us to the pitfalls of the merging pattern. You can experience pitfalls on the team-merge level as well as the company-merge level. Both levels will be explored in the following section.

Pitfalls of the Merging Pattern at the Team Level

When teams merge, they combine together, so you're naturally left with a larger team. This can pose some challenges if you are not familiar with managing large team dynamics. The first pitfall relates to a lack of calibration.

WHEN YOU DON'T CALIBRATE THE NEW, LARGER TEAM

The first pitfall of merged teams is when you do not calibrate the new, larger team. It's critical to calibrate so people will understand how their new team system will function. You need to calibrate on the people and roles, the work and the workflow. Use some of the activities described in "Team Calibration Sessions" on page 198 to come up with your plan.

Furthermore, if you don't talk about the new, combined team structure, there is likely a greater transition time over to the "new team." There could be fear around the teams combining. People might wonder how they will work together with people in the same role that they have. What will the overlap look like? Will there be duplication of efforts? Or will their roles actually be reduced? I find that when teams merge—for example, when three teams merge—the merged team is usually left with only one product manager, rather than including all three. This is an important change to discuss. If you don't talk about it but instead leave it to chance, it's just messy and can lead to upset and frustrated feelings. I go into the concept of transition more deeply in Chapter 13.

Again, what you need to do when teams merge is to proactively run a calibration session with the new, larger team. Moreover, you can deliberately discuss how you will collaborate together as the larger team system. Will you pair program and switch pairs, as described earlier in this chapter with our Trade Me story? Will you form subteams that expand and contract around opportunities? Will you work in a solo fashion and pass the baton to other team members? You can experiment and try things in order to pursue effectiveness. The point here is to talk about how you're going to collaborate and get started. Then reflect on your team structure during a retrospective from there on out.

Meetings are another topic to revisit when teams merge, which brings us to the next pitfall.

WHEN YOU DON'T RESET OR FACILITATE YOUR NEW, LARGER MEETINGS

When your teams merge together, they each bring with them a collection of "legacy" meetings that would take place within the precombined teams. Another pitfall of the merging pattern is when you don't take a look at your meetings and adjust them for your new team system.

You need to get together and decide what to *start doing, stop doing,* and *keep doing,* in terms of the meetings that you have. Maybe you delete all the legacy meetings and start over with what makes sense for this new team system. Talk about it and see what is needed with your new, larger team.

Moreover, since your meetings may now be larger, you need to have a plan so you don't devolve into the default structure in which a large percentage of the people in the meeting are passive, and only a few people are talking or engaged. This is where facilitation techniques for having effective meetings come into play. It's more than having a meeting agenda and sticking to it. That's not enough. And it's not enough to just agree on an outcome for a meeting. I would challenge you to figure out how to bring some aliveness into your meetings so that they are inclusive and encourage all voices to be heard.

Throughout this book I've mentioned Liberating Structures as my go-to set of facilitation techniques. The beauty of these techniques is that they scale, and they are open source. You can apply these techniques in any of your meetings to include people in the conversation. They can be used virtually or in person.[3] Create a facilitation plan that is interactive to serve as the default for each of your meetings, or prepare for them to be awkward.

On a related note, when your teams merge, you will also want to reset on your communication channels, such as the team's chat channels and email distribution, or whatever communication mechanisms exist. Figure out these logistics head-on, and then when you have an official date to "combine," you're ready to go.

Another pitfall when your teams merge is not aligning on decision making.

---

3 Visit the Liberating Structures website (*https://liberatingstructures.com*) and join their Slack community.

WHEN YOU DON'T FIGURE OUT HOW YOU WILL MAKE DECISIONS AS A LARGER TEAM

If everyone in your larger team defaults to consensus as the decision-making style, and you're in a meeting where only two people talk and everyone else is silent, it's incredibly awkward and frustrating. When a decision point comes up, some people try to get around this by saying that if you don't speak your decision, then "silence is consent." But to me that doesn't feel right. It feels forced. It doesn't have to be that way.

Instead, what you want to do is to get really clear on how you will make decisions. Get clear on which decisions are made by any specific roles. You can make a list of each role, and the types of decisions they make. You can make a list of the decisions that you want to make by consensus in your squad. You can also determine what to do if you can't make a decision, or when you need to escalate to someone outside of the team for a decision.

One technique that I like to teach squads is the *fist of five* technique for polling for consensus. The following is how I teach this technique to teams, and I think it really helps, especially when you're dealing with larger, merged teams. This technique is referenced with a more extended description in Jean Tabaka's book, *Collaboration Explained*, and she credits the method to her colleague Janet Danforth.[4]

Fist of Five

Using your hand, show how you feel about this idea using five to one fingers, according to this protocol:

- 5 - I wildly support this idea.
- 4 - I support this idea.
- 3 - I don't feel strongly about this. I'll defer to the team.
- 2 - I need the following clarifications before I can support this (then go through the clarification needed).
- 1 - I don't support this.

---

4 Tabaka, *Collaboration Explained*, 80.

> After voting the first time, maybe it's clear that you will move for-
> ward with the idea, or abandon it. If you have any twos, you will want to
> discuss the clarifications needed, and then do another fist of five vote,
> and so on.

The importance of doing a fist of five is that it shows you the sentiment about an idea you are deciding on. If everyone gives the idea a three, for example, maybe you don't want to pursue that idea.

Typically, if the decision is not obvious after polling for consensus like this, I will then do a *majority rules* vote in the team. The actual voting on ideas is sepa-rate from polling for consensus if you dig deeper into this stuff. Majority rules, or when the majority of people vote in favor of an idea, is how you can close on deci-sions. This is a nuance. I find that in practice, just polling for consensus helps teams make decisions that are good enough to enable them to move on.

Besides these team-level pitfalls, I also find that there are pitfalls when com-panies merge together. It can get quite complicated when companies merge because it usually impacts a lot of people, most of the decision making is abstrac-ted, and it's not clear who is actually making all of the decisions that are forced upon you. These are mostly top-down decisions. I really believe that people have positive intentions and want to do the best for their companies. The pitfalls with company mergers are the fallout of human emotion and unclear communication, as the following heart-wrenching stories illustrate.

Pitfalls of the Merging Pattern at the Company Level

When companies come together and merge, at times people are asked to leave. It can be really heartbreaking when this happens, and it can feel like decisions are obscured. It's unclear who is making the decisions, everything can go down quite dramatically, and it all feels rather heartless.

The cascade of information from the top of a company downward, especially in the charged time of a company merger, can fall into failure traps. We think we are clear and getting our points across, but we are not. This failure of communi-cation can spread fear and chaos, as these stories illustrate. First is a story about drawing out the layoffs, next is a story about ambiguity and layoffs, and last is a story about chaotic takeovers. These are indeed scenarios that we don't want to duplicate; however, I think we can draw lessons from them, as I've annotated throughout the rest of this chapter.

DRAWING OUT THE LAYOFFS

"They should just rip off the Band-Aid! Why do we have to wait until next week to see what happens to our department?" A friend and coworker at a client assignment said this to me as the company went through a takeover by one of its competitors. She added, "I haven't been able to do any real work for the last two weeks."

While posters appeared in the kitchen welcoming us to the "new company," there was still signage of the old company all over the office and outside multiple buildings. A change of identity was forced upon us, and, as a consultant with engineering teams "on the ground," I was right in the middle of this tectonic shift with everyone else.

We watched the webinars, we received the emails with video messaging in them, and we integrated our email and IT programs into those of the new company. On our desks, we found swag branded with the logo of the company taking us over, welcoming us into our new company. The new leadership regime was announced via email with glossy headshots; only one was from "our company," and that person was labeled *interim*.

Next came the process of *finding synergies*. Who has duplicate roles? Who is going to report to whom? Are we going to be reorganized by products? By components? We were in limbo. When two companies come together to form one "new" company, the whole organizational structure needs to be thought through and redesigned. This is a key part of the merging pattern. As a result of this particular merger, the company became three times the size of the acquiring company. So we were waiting to find out the fate of our coworkers and wondering whether particular office locations were going to close or remain open.

So what's a team to do? We tried to press forward and focus on finishing our current sprint and planning our next one. The mood was tense and brooding, amplified by the dimly lit facility we were in. It was a good time to take some days off or work from home as a coping mechanism. Many team members did just that. Others altogether avoided discussing the topic at hand, and forged ahead on the old plans that could have changed dramatically in the next week. It's all they had.

The discussions about the "elephant in the room" happened at lunch and during one-on-ones: "I don't know if my boss is going to be here." "Should I really push that issue with Joe? Maybe he will be gone next week." "Will I have a new manager?" "The way I heard we are reorging is the same structure that we reorged out of last year." The more people I talked with, the more I realized that some people were privy to more information than others. But even who had what info was mysterious.

It's hard to focus on doing any real work when you don't know if you're going to have a job the next week. In this situation, the layoffs took place over two weeks. If your department was part of week two, then you had more time in the hellish unknown. According to Stephen Heidari-Robinson and Suzanne Heywood in their *Harvard Business Review* article, "The psychological impact of uncertainty during a reorg can be even more distressing than an actual layoff. The longer that badly planned reorgs drag on, the more the misery endures and the longer it takes to see the business results the reorg was intended to bring about."[5]

Drawing out this type of news is really hard for the people involved. Maybe there are rationalizations that are made about this: "We don't have the staff to simultaneously lay off people in all departments at once. This week we will address Sales, Marketing, and Service, and next week Engineering and Product Development." As reasonable as that might look on paper, the fallout on the ground is quite the opposite if you're in the teams that have delayed layoffs.

Being on the ground in this situation as a consultant was a different experience for me because I didn't have the same kind of fear. I had my own work and multiple clients. However, I could feel the fear in my body from others, as people vented to me during our one-on-one meetings, and I could feel the fear during our faux grooming and planning meetings.

When you are with people who are going through a traumatic experience, it feels quite different than if you're just reading about the company's layoffs on social media. There is more empathy when you are in it on the ground with people. You can almost see the pain through observing their body language and facial expressions, and when you see them whispering to each other in small groups. Simon Sinek writes about this in his book *Leaders Eat Last*.[6] Through this experience, I felt this firsthand.

So how can this type of situation be approached more humanistically? Laying off people promptly is probably the more humane way to go. Environments of fear (as well as joy) are contagious. People can't get any real work done—or it is

---

5 Heidari-Robinson and Heywood, "Assessment," 1.

6 Sinek, *Leaders Eat Last*, 96.

incredibly challenging to do so—when they don't know if they're going to be escorted out of the building the next week. You need to just rip off the bandage.

And if you're going through a situation like this, you might get some insight into what is going on by talking with your manager. See what your manager knows because it may be helpful to you to understand the context of your department. Blowing off steam about the situation at an offsite lunch with coworkers could also help, if talking things out is your thing. Some people don't like to process events like this quite so publicly, and so venting might not be appealing.

Having a plan B or seeking other opportunities is a completely appropriate thing to do in this type of situation. Maybe now is a good time for you to make a change and switch jobs. If you've been at the company for years, however, you might consider waiting it out to take advantage of a severance package. Who knows—maybe that would be better for you to consider.

Ambiguity flourishes in times of change, and even if we're trying to be as clear as possible when structuring larger reteamings, it can cut into our hearts, as this next story did for me.

AMBIGUITY AROUND LAYOFFS

"It's my last day," Carlos told me in the parking lot, right after showing me his Chevy Volt, the type of car I was about to lease. He had tears welling up in his eyes.

"Were you laid off?"

"Yes," he said.

It's the beginning of a horrific week, I thought to myself. Oh my god. This is getting so personal.

"What kind of severance package did you get?" I asked him, hoping that they at least had given him a generous send-off. "I hope they gave you a good package—you've been here for so long."

It had been about 15 years since he started at the company, maybe longer. He was a key architect. His visa was sponsored. He was more than well-respected by his peers. He had kids in high school and college. He was a fixture at this company.

His kind eyes flickered and looked away. "I don't know yet. I'm supposed to find out today."

I was stunned. He was a very senior engineer. As we both walked back inside, the excitement of the car moved to the wayside.

I had a feeling that the upcoming week was going to be tough. I walked back to my desk and couldn't help but talk to Joe, the engineer at the desk next to me.

He was one of the many whom I was happy to reunite with for this short-term, local gig at a client site I knew and loved.

"They must be trying to get rid of the high salaries," Joe said. He looked at me with sad, empathetic eyes as I told him the story from the parking lot.

I walked to another part of the office and saw a program manager. She saw the look on my face. "Yeah, I heard about Carlos, too."

I went back to my desk and started to get our task board ready for standup. Brent, an engineering manager, walked by. I noticed and went over to him. "I can't believe that Carlos is being laid off."

He looked at me with surprise. "What?"

"Yeah, he told me today is his last day. He's waiting to find out about his severance."

Brent appeared more and more animated and concerned.

"Are you his manager?" I asked.

"No, I'm his manager's manager," he said back to me. "I'll be back!"

Brent rushed off. No, actually, Brent bolted! He was trying to go and clear up the situation because Carlos wasn't being laid off. It was a big misunderstanding.

About 30 minutes later Carlos came to my desk. "I'm not getting laid off," he said. "I thought I was, but it's not the case."

"I'm so glad you're safe, Carlos," I said. "This has been quite a week."

When your company has a lot of ambiguity around layoffs or any other big change and you're swirling in despair, I think the best thing you can do is talk with your manager. It's their job to support you. Have a discussion about your job and the safety of it. You manager is probably more tapped into what is going on in the organization than you are. Managers must field questions in times of uncertainty and cascade information to their reports so they can make sense of the changes.

When we lack information, we tend to make it up. Brené Brown has a very nice treatment of this topic in her book *Dare to Lead*. She references the research that she did for her book *Rising Strong*, and notes that the most resilient research participants in her study would use some form of these sentences: "The story I'm telling myself... , The story I make up... , I make up that... ," and so on.[7] So think about that if you're processing partial information, whether during a takeover or merging situation or during another situation where there is a great deal of uncertainty. What stories are you making up?

---

7 Brown, *Dare to Lead*, 247.

Drawn-out layoffs, ambiguity around who is getting laid off, and the general loss of coworkers is the darker side of the merging pattern, as we will see in the following story. It can feel chaotic, uncertain, and just physically awful.

CHAOTIC TAKEOVERS

I arrived in the San Francisco office expecting the worst. At the standup the previous Friday, one of the engineers had proclaimed, "No we didn't get to the code review yet. They were too busy firing most of our office." I was consulting at this company that was in the middle of the takeover described in the past two stories. We were just acquired by a competitor.

It was a sad and painful time. Five percent of the global workforce had been laid off days before. This San Francisco office was hit the hardest. As I walked into the office I saw many empty desks. As one of my team members put it, "They fired everyone around my desk. I'm the only one left."

I had worked at this office for the past three months, coaching two teams. Each of these two teams had members in the San Francisco office, as well as another remote office, so I traveled back and forth between the offices to get to know the different team members.

The previous time I had worked from the San Francisco office, there had been a baby shower in the kitchen for a well-liked coworker. "You should try the biryani," Nimita, an engineer, had told me. I was excited to have met her for the first time that visit. On this visit, however, we would be saying goodbye. She had just gotten laid off, in addition to another member of my team—both were highly talented mobile developers who were still expected to be in the office for another couple of months for "knowledge transfer."

Indeed, the mood was the polar opposite during this visit. The people from the party were gone. The happy times had passed. The space felt very different. Actually, at one point during the day, I felt like I was being beaten over the head with who knows what. The energy of the place was beyond what I had ever felt in a workplace. As a coach in that environment, I knew the people needed me. So I was there with them. I rolled with it.

As the week progressed, more and more visitors arrived at the office. They were all from one of the European divisions of the new company. Despite all of the layoffs, the company was also going through a reorganization.

My team was impacted by that. We lost our product owner and also our UX designer. We heard that we were going to get a new product owner from this European office. I was excited to meet him that week to get started. After all, we had had a new, different product owner a few weeks before that. We were essentially about to meet our third product owner in the past three months. That was quite the dynamic reteaming that we didn't desire or like as a team. It felt like a revolving door. Yes, it was highly disruptive.

Many of the visitors were in a large conference room all day. We heard that our product owner was in there. So I went ahead and found out his name and sent him an email, since even though he was physically in the building, he was unavailable. I wrote, "We'd love for you to meet the team." He told me that he would be in meetings most of the time.

A couple of the other team members met the product owner by chance. But we had no formal get-together with our new team member. He was too busy, and then he hopped on a plane and left the country. "We'll have to adjust some of our meeting times now that our product owner is in Europe, and the rest of us are in California," the program manager said to me as she, too, left to go back to Southern California. And that was it.

This was a bizarre and "distant" reteaming to say the least. And, it was more than a missed opportunity to get to know each other as people. Before I knew what had even happened, it was like the people had slipped through my fingers and dispersed across the globe. First impressions are important. And this one was more impersonal than I could have imagined. We were starting out our new team with an already damaged interpersonal dynamic.

If you find yourself in a chaotic takeover like this and you feel physically crappy, I have two words for you to consider: vacation time. If you have vacation days that you can use, this seems like a great time to use them and get out of the office. You could also take a mental health day and call in sick. Getting some distance by working remotely might be better for your health.

If you can't possibly get away from the office during a time like this, you might try to distract yourself in order to cope. Maybe you can work in a conference room, or outside near the office. Maybe you can go for some one-on-one walks with some colleagues. For some of us, talking things out when they get difficult is helpful. For others, maybe being quiet and alone is better. If you're in a situation like this, I feel for you. For me, changing consulting assignments was the ultimate solution.

In this chapter we have gone over how at the team level you can combine forces between teams to bring greater collaboration opportunities. You can also join groups of teams together to reorient them toward work missions. These are fairly contained and smaller entity transformations that to me seem easier to get your head around in comparison to the higher-level merging of companies, which is a much bigger deal.

This chapter detailed what can go wrong or get messy when individual teams combine. These mergers of sorts are lower risk than merging at the higher level of panarchy, the company level. I don't claim to have all of the answers about company mergers, as I've experienced them at a certain level of abstraction up to director level in the three software companies I consulted with or worked at full time. But I have experienced mergers as a human, and I will say that being successful with them takes great care and attention for the people. So how do you do mergers better than the horrors that I have described here? There's another book that remains to be written on that.

Until then, let's burn some sage and switch to a new topic, something lighter and driven by learning and fulfillment. Onward to the switching pattern!

9

Switching Pattern

There's nothing worse than being stuck on a boring team assignment, where you feel like every day is a complete drag, and you feel like you're stagnating. It doesn't have to be like that. Engagement at work can happen when you are intellectually stimulated and are able to continually learn in your job. Sometimes that can mean finding a new team situation where you are with completely different people, working on completely different things to refresh your focus. Just having the opportunity to switch teams can bring companies tremendous retention possibilities.

Besides that, switching can help us to build a more sustainable and resilient company. If only one person maintains a critical system and then leaves, you could experience tremendous setbacks. So why not mitigate that by building in some proactive switching? Don't fall into the "we must have stable teams" dogma that can lead you into these traps.

The pages that follow dig into the switching pattern, where one person leaves a team and then joins a team, as depicted in Figure 9-1.

Figure 9-1. The switching pattern

Switching is also when people switch pairs within a team when pair programming, as the next two stories illustrate.

Switching Pairs Within a Team

Pair programming is a classic method of spreading knowledge around a team. It's when two software engineers work with one monitor on the same code, at the same time, with one or more keyboards. Combined with the switching pattern, it's an awesome way to spread knowledge and learning around a team, as described in the following stories.

Richard Sheridan, reflecting back on his pre–Menlo Innovations days, told me about how he discovered *Extreme Programming Explained* by Kent Beck.[1] As a programmer himself, Richard was struck by something in Kent's book. "It's when Kent said, *Think back like I did. When were you the most productive?* I was the most productive when I worked closely with another person." Richard reflected back to when he was a programmer and remembered when he paired with another person...that they were able to be productive together and that they had safety together to not make a big mistake.[2] He and James Goebel (who would later become his Menlo Innovations cofounder) decided to propose an experiment with their software engineers to try out extreme programming as a way to learn Java.

This was back in 1999. They wanted to spread the knowledge of Java around the team, which at the time was about 14 developers, and only 3 had knowledge of Java. They paired in order to spread the learning as quickly as possible.

As their experiment started to progress, they started what he called *dynamic re-pairing*. To his surprise, "there was actually a productivity to it that we hadn't expected, and we just started tracking for that.... We paired people for two weeks at a time, and then we just let them sort of dynamically re-pair."

After a while, they noticed that "cliques were starting to form." To mitigate that, they started to assign the pairs. They framed it as an experiment: "We started orchestrating the pairs, almost like a *square dance* because we wanted to make sure, again, that everybody gets a chance to pair with everybody." People liked that because it took away the social pressure of trying to figure out who they

---

1 Beck, *Extreme Programming*.

2 Richard Sheridan, in an interview with the author, October 2016.

were going to pair with. If you were picked last for a pair it could get very awkward.

The side effect of this pairing system was that people formed new friendships. As Richard said, "Some of them, they have worked with for a decade or more, but they never worked with them quite like they had in this circumstance. So suddenly there was this new energy about getting to know people in the team, and believe me, these were introverted engineers, right? So this was not their natural inclination."

After interviewing Richard, I reviewed his book, *Joy, Inc.* He recounts this story there, too. What strikes me from the book is the following passage. Richard wrote about what the atmosphere was like on this team during this experiment: "I couldn't believe what I saw immediately in this new space: energy, noise, collaboration, progress, work, learning, and fun. In a word, joy. (Although I wouldn't think of it in those terms until years later)."[3]

This switch from solo programming to pair programming was a huge, animated contrast. Moreover, the switching of the pairs in particular brought additional fulfillment to the people who were present in that space. When you switch pairs, or teams for that matter, you are exposed to new people and new ideas. You just learn more. That feels good to us as humans.

When I was at AppFolio, especially in the early years, we always kept an anchor when we switched pairs. An anchor is a concept we learned from Pivotal Software, who trained us way back when. One engineer would stay with the work, while another engineer would rotate in. That's not the only way to apply the switching pattern to pair programming, as this next story, also from Menlo Innovations, illustrates.

Switching Pairs Out Completely for Problem Solving

Another benefit to switching pairs was revealed in a story Richard told me was a "magical moment" for him. It was about two engineers who paired on a bug for two weeks but couldn't figure it out. When you're in a situation like that, you feel like you have so much time invested that you might be hesitant to switch out (or split up) the pair. But Richard's cofounder, James, suggested that they try an experiment. They didn't just switch in one person in the pair; instead, they reassigned the bug to two different people entirely. The two people switched in were

---

3 Sheridan, *Joy, Inc.*, 25.

one experienced developer and one junior developer—and those two people wound up solving the bug in an hour.

"The whole idea of keeping the same people doing the same thing over and over again, which is this fundamental belief from productivity and efficiency and all that sort of thing, is a false premise," according to Richard. He talked about the pattern he saw when a pair cycled off of some work and a new pair cycled into it: "The people who supposedly didn't know as much [...] were better contributors than the long-standing team members." In addition, those long-standing team members were excited about having a chance. In his words, "What you saw in them was excitement. You saw human energy. They're thinking, *Oh, I get to learn something new. I'm not doing the same thing over and over and over again.*"

The huge insight for Richard is best articulated in his words: "It challenged my thinking as a manager, as a director, as a vice president. And, things I thought were true probably weren't. [...] James and I at that moment were forever changed, and we've never varied."[4]

As I alluded to earlier in this chapter, in my experience at AppFolio it was very rare (at least in the first nine years, from my vantage point) to entirely switch out one pair for another. It was more common for us to keep part of the pair on the story, and switch out one person. So we had the continuity of the original person and the addition of the new "brain" to the mix. Learning this story from Richard really shifted my thinking. There are so many different ways to work. In his book, he talked about the shift from "less *I* to more *we.*" In his words, "If a pair was silently stuck at their computer, staring motionless at the screen, another pair would arrive and ask, *What's going on?* It felt safe and nurturing, rather than competitive and tense."[5] This is a strong sense of "whole team."

Switching pairs within a team is one way that the switching pattern shows up in organizations. But that's not the only level. Sometimes we switch one person from one team to another with the deliberate goal of sharing knowledge, as the next story illustrates.

---

4 Richard Sheridan, in an interview with the author, October 2016.

5 Sheridan, *Joy, Inc.*, 31.

Switching Teams to Share Knowledge and Support a Feature

In the nine years that I was at AppFolio, we had feature teams that had collective code ownership, and we had full stack Ruby on Rails developers. For years, any team could work on any area of the codebase. Collective code ownership was valued. Over time, however, some teams organically became specialized—specifically the teams that dealt with complex commerce systems. To get things done quickly, as was desired at times for this area of work, that team became a logjam of sorts. We made the deliberate decision to spread the knowledge of this business domain to another team.

Because we still had the strong pair programming ethic, we spread the knowledge across teams via pairing. A developer from the initial commerce team went and spent time with the new team, which was going to be getting commerce-related work in the future. This developer stayed over there for a few sprints and then left to go back to his initial commerce team. Having that developer leave his home team to go over to another team for the short term might have felt painful for the initial team for a bit, but in the big picture it wasn't that long for him to be away. And, since the teams were colocated, it didn't feel like he was physically going too far away, as the teams were seated near each other.

This same type of situation happened when training AppFolio's tech support team on how to use some key commerce features. After the initial team built certain systems, it started to field the escalated customer service–related requests for the rest of the company. This wound up getting in the way of developing new features. It reached a point where it made sense to the people involved to transfer knowledge and responsibility to another team. So one developer from the commerce team went and paired for a while with the tech support team to teach it how to field the related questions in order to support the commerce feature. When the tech support team and the developer felt that enough knowledge was shared, and that the tech support team could be on its own with the customer service requests, the developer left the team and returned to his original team.

I think that switching people across teams for temporary periods of time and then sending them back to their home team is an overlooked strategy for tackling dependencies. That comes up in the next story, as well as the idea of switching at a regular cadence, deliberately, to spread knowledge proactively.

Deliberate Switching at a Cadence to Share Knowledge

Switching teams to spread knowledge deliberately is also commonplace at Pivotal Software, where the company automates the deployment of "platform as a service" as its business. In fact, it's built into the organizational strategy, as relayed to me by Evan Willey, director of program management. Using a home-grown tool called Allocations, created while consultants at the other division of their business were on the bench and not on client engagements, engineering managers and leads keep track of their 50+ teams and are able to understand and see who is on which team "now," and for how long. Evan described Allocations as their "meta-level team creation activity that we do and team engineer rotation tool that we use."[6]

Evan said, "Our engineering directors and leadership look at Allocations twice a week in set rituals." They make decisions about who should remain on teams, and who might move to other teams. He explained the context like this:

> Let's see how we can kind of rejigger the overall makeup of the team. It's fairly incremental. It changes week over week. It depends on factors like where the backlog is going, how critical is that team's feature set, but also, are there engineers on the team who've been there for over nine months who are getting due to rotate out to another team? They'll keep an eye on those factors as well to make sure that we're not ending up with silos of information that are growing because somebody's been on a team for two to three years and just becomes the holder of all knowledge.

Their organizational structure and code organization is designed to match their reteaming. Each team at Pivotal is fairly atomic, and in Evan's words, "We really try to maintain as much contract-based, API-based separation of concerns between teams as much as we can. We try not to share codebases between teams. All the Git repos for a particular team's feature are wholly owned by that team, and if another team is going to make an addition or change to that codebase, they'll either do it with a pull request or through cross-team pairing—where we would kind of send one half of a pair over to the dependency holding team and one half of that team's pair back to the upstream team to work on that feature."

---

6 Evan Willey, in an interview with the author, February 2017.

Pivotal Software has two levels of deliberate reteaming to spread knowledge. Through its strong pair programming culture, within-team switching is highly encouraged. Pairs are like microteams within teams. Two people are continuously integrating ideas. And then the pairs switch, and knowledge is spread around within the team. "If you don't have pair rotation within a team, it can get kind of stagnant, and eventually it gets a little frustrating for the folks that are on that team, so we try to keep that from happening," said Evan. I asked Evan to describe the concept of "stagnation" further. (This is a word that came up across many of my reteaming interviews.) He said he was referring to the collaboration: "You don't get the variety of interactions that you would if you were more frequently rotating within the team."

Pair switching is so important in the "Pivotal process" that it's tied to a role. The "anchor" role on the company's teams is the developer responsible for the delivery health of their team. This person is also responsible for making sure that their pair rotation within the team is taking place successfully. They are also making sure that the retrospectives take place and that standups are healthy.

The second level of reteaming is cross-team. If one team has a dependency with another team, Evan told me that "those teams may arrange to swap pairs, and somebody might go from one team to another team for a few days or a week to get the feature done." This is a very functional reteaming with a clear goal.

Besides cross-team switching for getting dependencies completed, they also switch teams to proactively share knowledge. According to Evan, "knowledge sharing generally happens through the ongoing rotation of engineers through all the teams so that they get a variety of different kinds of teams to work with."

By working with different people on different subject matter, we can learn new things from each other and make the knowledge stickier in our companies. This helps us to deliberately sustain the knowledge. It's good risk management. It's quite the opposite of the *Tower of Knowledge* anti-pattern described by Richard Sheridan in Chapter 10. "We like to build that generalism amongst the entire engineering staff," Evan told me. "We really believe in generalism and that it leads to empathy. So we aren't creating *my team versus that team* because I might be on that team for a month. It helps us outsmart the *Mythical Man-Month* a little bit as well.[7] So that if we have a critical project or if we get in the middle of a release and there's a feature that becomes a long pull, and it's falling behind and

---

7 See Brooks, *Mythical Man-Month*. In his book, Brooks asserts that "adding manpower to a late software project makes it later." He calls this Brooks's Law.

it's the thing we said is a *must have* for the release, we do have the option to make the team that's working on that feature stronger." Because the team switching happens, it takes less time and effort to switch over and help out another team: "We already have a larger pool of folks that already have familiarity in that team's domain and feature."

This reteaming is quite contrary to the now-seemingly antiquated, canonical software organizational advice that encourages us to keep our teams stable or "the same" as a strategy. I'm blown away, frankly, by this deliberate generalism. It's almost as if they are creating microorganisms that move around within the team and across teams. This brings up visuals of building an organization that really *moves*. It's antistagnation. It's alive.

There are other reasons why we might encourage the switching pattern across our teams, and they're human ones, discussed next.

Rotating Developers for Friendship and Pairing

I was working once with three teams at AppFolio. The developers pair programmed. When we made the switch from one team to two teams using the grow-and-split pattern discussed earlier in this book, and then added a few team members to form three teams, some of the developers were sad that they could no longer pair program with their friends who were now on "other teams."

So we started a regular rotation of one engineer from team to team, as shown in Figure 9-2, in order to address that concern and to provide more fulfillment to these engineers. That was pretty dynamic in that context.

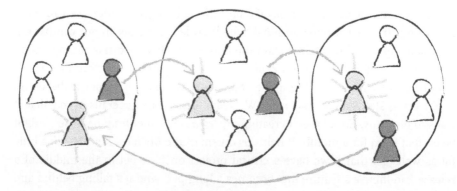

Figure 9-2. Rotation of engineers between teams

Comron Sattari reminisced with me about this. In his words: "So eventually you want to rotate people out. But you don't want to rotate everyone out at once. So what we ended up doing, I think every six weeks or every couple of sprints we would rotate one person out. So three of the team members stayed the same, and we'd take one person from another team and would rotate people out. Eventually the teams would get all mixed up and you'd get that bigger team mentality because you're working with everybody but you've got more focus on the smaller team."[8]

He elaborated on what this was like for him: "It was really good because you had that momentum with your team. You knew what everyone was working on. We'd sit right next to each other. Communication was super easy. But then every few weeks you get new blood, new ideas, new faces, and they are people you see every day in the office, obviously. I was on a team, I really liked working with Donnie, but Donnie was on another team. But I knew in a couple weeks he might be on my team and we could do something new together."

There isn't a one-size-fits-all cadence to use for team rotation. Start somewhere, visualize your reteaming, align on why you're doing it, and reflect at a regular cadence to grow and evolve to the best situation for your team. And better yet, listen to your developers. See what they need. I love how AppFolio adjusted with the hope of bringing fulfillment to these engineers.

Fulfillment at work is one of the keys to engagement and retention. When we are able to pursue our learning goals within the companies we are working at, it's like we've struck gold because we'll probably look forward to coming to work each day. This brings us to the next section about switching.

Switching for Personal Growth and Learning

It's nice when people aren't stuck in one team forever and when we view people with a growth mindset as opposed to a fixed one.[9] We can learn and grow and change in our lives. It's more engaging when we are learning and interacting with different people.

At Jama Software in Portland, Oregon, where at the writing of this book they had around 35 engineers, Cristian Fuentes, an engineering manager, has seen the company grow from about 9 people to 140 people. Cristian told me about

---

8 Comron Sattari, in an interview with the author, March 2016.

9 Dweck, *Mindset*.

how their team members self-select onto different teams depending on work needs and personal interests. People have the opportunity to leave the team they are on now and switch to a different team that matches what they want to learn. He said, "If a team member has been working on an API-type of project [...] and they want to learn frontend, for example, they move to one of the teams working on frontend-type features for their own career growth." When you find the right fit, and you are enjoying your team, you might not change teams. In his words, "Right now we're at a point where there's certain teams or team members that have really enjoyed working together—so they stuck together. There are other team members that still move around teams."[10]

At AppFolio, we were organized with feature teams that could really work on any part of our property management application. We had a few more specialized teams when I was there, one that built and maintained the data centers that housed our software, a handful of other teams that focused on noncustomer visible infrastructure projects for customers and others in the engineering team, and a tech support team. I worked with all of these teams throughout the years in an agile coaching capacity.

From time to time, engineers would rotate in and out of infrastructure teams. One engineer told me that working in those teams, as opposed to feature teams, provided different, larger, more systemic problems to solve. And, the product managers were other engineers. That was very motivating to him.

People in our tech support team would leave their team and go work on feature teams from time to time. There, they would gain specialized knowledge of the features they would support when they returned back to their tech support team. There was at least one instance where a tech support engineer left their team and then stayed over in a feature team. It's nice that the company was flexible to allow for this personal growth and choice.

Enabling switching can be considered a strategic advantage. Mike Boufford, CTO at Greenhouse, views it as a "secret weapon." When people have been working somewhere for a while, they might just get the itch for change. So when you rotate them to a different team "their itch has been scratched." He said, "I actually think it's like a secret weapon in retention to give people the opportunity to move between teams and change their environment a bit."[11]

---

10 Cristian Fuentes, in an interview with the author, April 2017.

11 Mike Boufford, in an interview with the author, January 2020.

We've gone over several different facets of the switching pattern. We've seen how it applies when switching pairs within teams as well as across teams. You can apply the switching pattern for knowledge sharing, and to encourage the fulfillment and learning of your people. It also has the potential to enable awesome transformative learning for people to reinvent themselves at work. Sounds good, right? There are also pitfalls to this pattern.

Pitfalls of the Switching Pattern

Keeping the people and their personal development in mind is one aspect of switching. There can be threats to this, which lead us to sometimes want to restrict switching because we want to keep the best people on our teams. Additionally, if there is very low knowledge redundancy on our team, switching can be quite painful, so we might desire to avoid it. Furthermore, if we have single specialist roles on our teams, and when they're the only ones on our teams, it's probably more challenging to embark on switching. Let's explore these three pitfalls, starting with the desire to hoard good team members.

THE DESIRE TO HOARD GOOD TEAM MEMBERS

When you get "good people" on your teams, it's natural not to want them to go to other teams. However, this can get in the way of switching for the pursuit of learning and fulfillment, or what could be the best for the team member at hand. This came up in conversations I had with Rachel Davies. She told me about managers who had control over reteaming, and during reteaming situations, would keep their "stars" but share out the less competent engineers.

As she put it, "Sometimes people don't want to let a good person go. So when the decision about team rotation is with the team leads, then it's easy to kind of go, *Oh yeah, you can have this person who's not very good but this precious person who's fantastic I wanna keep them*. But that's not good for the person."[12]

You can think of reteaming methods on a scale of transparency. On one end you have manager-decided reteaming, and on the opposite spectrum you have team member–decided reteaming. The greater the visibility you have on your reteaming, the more freedom your team members have to control their own destinies.

---

12 Rachel Davies, in an interview with the author, December 2016.

Manager-driven reteaming can be more of a closed and guarded system, and team member–driven reteaming can be a more open and liberating system that provides people with greater autonomy.

If this is an issue in your organization, you can work with leadership to give feedback to the manager who is doing the hoarding. Sometimes all it takes is giving feedback to help someone see things differently. The book *Crucial Conversations* even has syntax you can apply to give feedback that might be triggering for the person receiving it. Another book to consult for inspiration is *Radical Candor*.[13]

Cultivating a community of managers who have shared goals to help the whole department succeed is another idea to go after. You can have an offsite meeting with managers and, with some coaching, have a session to create a shared vision and values for how you want engineering management to be at your company. In that context, you can lay the groundwork for helping engineers follow their career goals by reteaming.

Another thing you can do is strengthen the individual development plans for your software engineers. An individual development plan, or IDP as it is sometimes called, is a document where engineers can detail their career goals for the upcoming two quarters, for example. If the engineer's learning goals suggest that reteaming might help that engineer achieve their goals, you can use that in your discussions about team change. You need to strike a balance and find the place on the Venn diagram that represents what the individual wants and what the company needs.

Helping people follow their learning paths may lead them to switching to another team. After they have switched, sometimes the team members are missed and it's hard for the people on the original team if they haven't prepared for this change.

IT CAN BE CHALLENGING WHEN A TEAM MEMBER IS "ON LOAN" TO ANOTHER TEAM

When you're on a team with someone, and then they switch to another team (or leave, for that matter), you might miss them and really feel the pain of their loss. Maybe you liked having them around—they could be a person that you really enjoyed collaborating with day to day. Or maybe their contributions were so great when they were with the team, and now that they're gone (even if only

---

temporarily) it is hard to get by. This is all interesting information to take in. If it is highly difficult to have this team member leave in terms of the work that needs to move on in their absence, maybe you need to focus on more pairing or knowledge sharing within your team so that people can practice healthier switching in the future. We can build up our companies to be more resilient so that when we want to switch team members out for whatever reason, we can still continue on as the original team. Prepare as if everyone will leave your team at some point, because they will, as you might recall from Chapter 1. Strategize on how your teams can be resilient.

WITH TEAMS COMPRISED OF SINGLE-SPECIALIST ROLES, YOUR SWITCHING IS LIMITED

If your team is comprised of named roles—such as one frontend engineer, one backend engineer, one iOS engineer, one Android engineer, a quality assurance engineer, a user experience engineer, and a product manager, for example— switching out any of those roles leaves you with a loss, unless someone comes into the team to fill the single specialist "slot." You've built such a specialized team that it is not as resilient as it could be if you were to have a setup as is suggested in Scrum, with "development team members," who are people who can really work together across roles to move the work forward. If you have two of each role on the team, maybe there is more wiggle room for switching. But is it realistic to think our companies would fund "Noah's ark"? I'm not sure—but if they did, you'd probably have a team that grows too big that you'd want to split anyway. Single specialist roles could be one of the root causes of teams that grow too big. If you are in specialist world, however, you might consider having developer "exchanges" where you get one frontend engineer, for example, who is interested in what you are doing, in exchange for sending yours over to the other team.

This chapter covered the switching pattern and some pitfalls with it. Switching is very much a human-driven reteaming pattern, and you might think that it is quite similar to the one-by-one pattern because it also involves moving one person into a team or out of a team. These are separate patterns because the one-by-one pattern is very strongly tied to growth and attrition. The switching pattern is very strongly tied to the pursuit of learning, knowledge sharing, developing a resilient and sustainable company, and the quest for fulfillment.

All five of these dynamic reteaming patterns—one by one, grow and split, isolation, merging, and switching—define dynamic reteaming. The fact is, these patterns are likely to be happening simultaneously at our companies, and at different levels—the company level, department level, tribe level, team level, and individual level. This is the panarchy concept discussed in Chapter 1. When we realize that all of this is going on at once, and to different degrees at different companies, maybe dynamic reteaming as a concept is a bit easier to grasp.

Despite that, reteaming is not easy to experience at times. Depending on what you are trying to do pattern-wise and how you go about it, it can be very challenging. It is either going to happen to you naturally through the course of time and then you have to deal with it, or you will decide to deliberately catalyze changes along the lines of the five patterns described in this book, and then you have to deal with the consequences of that. You don't get anything for free here. You need to think deliberately, reflect, and act accordingly while applying critical thinking. You can't just "install" dynamic reteaming.

This brings us to the anti-patterns to reteaming. Many were expressed in each of the pattern chapters as pitfalls. But there are more. What follows are identified changes that I wouldn't seek to repeat. And I'm sure there are more out there in the world that remain to be harvested. I'd like to think that all these anti-patterns emerge out of positive intention. We are trying to help our companies succeed, yet sometimes things can just, well, go wrong. We can learn from anti-patterns. Let's explore.

10

Anti-Patterns

Reteaming does not solve every problem, and it can be done poorly. If you decide you want your teams to be more collaborative and to spread information within the team, and then you force them all to pair program because you read that it's a good idea, you will probably have a lot of unhappy developers who think that you don't trust them and that you've taken away all of their freedom. I lived that scenario at a company. A similar situation is recounted in one of the following anti-pattern sections about trying to reteam in order to share best practices. This is just one example, but my point is that you need to exert great care when practicing dynamic reteaming—especially when you're doing a larger-scale reteaming that will change an existing dynamic. See Chapter 12 for what to consider when planning a large reteaming initiative.

It is less risky to do a reteaming on the edges, which is when you apply the one-by-one or switching pattern, for example, and you aren't disrupting the entire dynamic as dramatically as if you were to, let's say, split a team in half or take four team members out and put only two back.

I'm not trying to paint a picture in this book that all of this is easy or that dynamic reteaming will solve all of your problems. It depends on what you are trying to do. You can't make guacamole out of an unripe avocado—sometimes teams and organizations aren't ready for change. And then sometimes it just happens, like someone leaves and you don't want them to, or your company gets taken over by a competitor, or the entire earth is taken over by a virus and everything shifts, as we are experiencing at the writing of this book with COVID-19. This is all the concept of creative destruction, illustrated in Chapter 1. When this plays out, it helps to have prepared for it in some way or another. This book is your guide.

Digging into anti-patterns further, here are some stories that share the darker side of reteaming, or what makes some people fear reteaming. If all that you experience is the negative side of reteaming, you might preach team stability and miss out on the benefits of reteaming when it's done well. It's all a matter of perception. As your career continues while working in different contexts, you collect patterns for how things go down, and your perspective is broadened. Let's get started with the first anti-pattern.

Reteaming to Spread "High Performance"

If a team has great chemistry and high performance, the team members are engaged. They are delivering incredible value at a good cadence while delighting customers. Keep them together until the people are ready for a change. Then, when you do change the teams, you might just do it "at the edges of the teams." Jon Walker, CTO and cofounder of AppFolio, learned this lesson in that company's early days. He had the desire to spread out the high performance of one team across multiple teams.

He said, "I remember specifically a team that had a lot of really experienced people, and we got a bunch of new people in, and I broke up that team. I regretted it afterwards. It was a highly functional team. They were doing great work. They were excited about what they were doing. Then we split them up, and we ended up with three pretty good teams when we had one great team. Maybe we would have had pretty good teams anyways without doing that."[1] Jon was trying to "load balance" the seniority across the teams. It made sense to him theoretically, but it came at the expense of team chemistry.

A story related to this idea of spreading out the high performance among teams came up in another interview with Damon Valenzona. Damon is an engineering director in a different location of the company, who told me about a "team shuffle" that they did with the intention to spread out best practices among five to six teams. The idea was to have a better balance of junior and senior team members across all teams, so juniors could witness what it was like to be a senior team member. It's hard to explain on paper the difference between software engineer levels like these: software engineer, senior software engineer, staff software engineer, principal software engineer. Sometimes by being around people at these levels you can learn the behaviors that are valued as a way to understand how you can "level up."

---

1 Jon Walker, in an interview with the author, February 2016.

For this "shuffle," which was really a *reorg* explained more lightly, they had kept about two team members the same across the different teams for continuity of work context. But, the rest of the team members changed, which included on average a product manager, QA engineer, UX designer, and three software engineers.

The result of this shuffle was similar to the case of Jon's reorg mentioned previously, and the chemistry of the teams suffered. I spoke with Damon three months after the shuffle, and he said, "One of the goals that we didn't even come close on was to make all the teams more efficient. Shuffling is a way to share best practices, but it takes a lot of storming on the team to get to norming, and those don't kind of come to fruition pretty quickly. So, I think a lot about team efficiency is the chemistry in a team and not necessarily the best practices. I think it's easier to share practices across teams. It's harder to get good chemistry on a team."[2]

He went on to share his learning from this situation: "I think our assumption was a little wrong that we take an engineer from our effective team that will share the best practices, because I don't really think the best practices are the most important thing." Instead, to him, high performance is more closely related to having a good dynamic on a team, as opposed to how it goes about doing the work. In his words, "What I found is that really what you're trying to do is create that good dynamic on the team and not necessarily the practices, because the practices can be different, and that's okay. But when you shuffle, you basically mix up all the dynamics and then have to figure out a way to work well together again."

The learning here is that when you reteam the dynamics "extensively" across multiple teams, it's going to take time for the teams to get into a flow again, and you don't know what the chemistry is going to be like for a while—especially if the people don't choose their own teams. It's less risky to make minor changes in team compositions.

Jon, who played college basketball at Westmont, a private college in Southern California, compared it to sports teams: "If you hear professional athletes, like if a team wins a championship, and they've got a bunch of players who can be together for a while, they're like, *We're trying to win as many championships as possible and keep this team together.*" Further, he talks about adding in people gradually: "If you're almost winning a championship, try to add little new pieces. If

---

2 Damon Valenzona, in an interview with the author, October 2016.

they're far away from winning a championship then totally break up the team and start over again." We gradually added people to teams for years at AppFolio as a growth strategy. This reteaming at the edges brought in new perspectives and was less disruptive to teams as a whole.

When the chemistry is working, and the teams are delighting customers, you might think twice when attempting to reteam to spread the high performance.

The examples shared here involved busting up entire teams in order to spread out the high performance (or in one case the seniority). Trying more of a "reteaming at the edges" approach is something to experiment with. When one person comes in or out of a team it's less disruptive than completely disbanding teams.

If you have a team that you consider to be doing very well, encourage the members to do a "tech talk" to share the ways that they are working with other teams in your context. Great companies I've worked at have encouraged engineers to do weekly tech talks that last no more than an hour. And if it's during lunch, you can get food for everyone as a draw—but that's not even necessary.

You could also encourage teams with practices you want to spread to write blog posts for the company. I pair with engineers at Procore more and more often to catalyze blog posts. Maybe hearing from peers will influence others to try things out.

Team coaching is another avenue to explore. Teams need to own their improvement efforts so that they care about them. We may read that the best way to work is via pair programming, for example, but you can't just force teams to do that or you will create other problems. Encourage teams to reflect on how they are working and to determine an experiment to run in order to become more effective. For example, when I coach teams to have greater workflow effectiveness, I first get them to visualize their workflow on a physical board. Then we discuss where the bottlenecks are in their workflow. Where does work get stuck and can't move forward? Where are the delays? Then teams come up with experiments to try in order to unclog their workflow. We follow up on that in a future coaching session. This, in conjunction with a conversation of what excellence means to the team, is a start.

One of the classic anti-patterns I've seen is one that I lived through quite viscerally at Expertcity. There, we had component-based teams, and I was a technical project manager. Let's explore the percentage anti-pattern.

The Percentage Anti-Pattern

For eight years I worked in a Waterfall environment. First, I was part of a web development team as an individual contributor, and then I became a technical project manager.

We were organized into component teams. People working within each component were assigned to projects. In many cases, we were assigned to a product line, and to multiple projects within the product line. People were assigned to focus a certain percentage of their time on each project. In practice, that can prove to be very difficult. How can a person really allocate 10% to project A, 20% to project B, 40% to project C, and so on? In this context, as a project manager, if I was not overseeing all of the projects assigned to this person, I could fall into the trap of trying to pressure this person to get the work done for me instead of for the other project manager. As new work would come up in this context, people might get assigned to new project teams. This is the type of change that is very overwhelming to individual contributors.

It's hard for humans to program themselves for availability like that. It's better for machines. This is an example of how, if we're not careful with how we organize our teams, the people can get objectified.

This also challenges team effectiveness. Richard Hackman's definition of effective teams includes the following components:[3]

Client satisfaction
   The work meets the quality, quantity, and timeliness of the people who receive the work of the team

Team viability
   The team works together in a way that increases their ability to work together interdependently again in the future

Member growth and fulfillment
   The team experience contributes to the growth and personal well-being of team members.

Clearly when people are working simultaneously on multiple teams, they are spread thin, which threatens the quality of their work and their team's viability.

---

3 Hackman, *Leading Teams*, 23–29.

So what can we do when we encounter the percentage anti-pattern? Just say no. It's a skill to push back when people start to overload you. I think it takes courage to do this. If you are a leader in a context like this, you can demonstrate that the company values saying no. Let people see you do that. Socialize how you do that. That gives others permission to do it.

I value working at a sustainable pace and having a life outside of work. If you're working in a context that is overloading you, and you can't have any sort of balance, it's worth some deep thought to explore whether this company is the right fit for you.

The other thought I have about this relates to your energy and passion to try to change things at your company. If you're in a system where the percentage anti-pattern is present, maybe you have the energy to help catalyze a reteaming event to change how work is allocated. Maybe you do, since you are reading this book. If that is true, study and apply the material presented in Chapter 12.

Besides the percentage anti-pattern, I've also seen that it can be a bad idea to reteam to spread best practices or when there is the desire to "standardize" everything.

Disrupting a Productive Team to Conform to a Standard or Best Practice

With the best intent, managers and directors want to help teams succeed and become more productive. They might even get together and talk process and how to help their teams become better at what they do. They might judge teams and try to apply consistency metrics on them related to size. They might write down beliefs like, "We believe that the best team composition has four software engineers, one quality assurance engineer, a UX designer, and a product manager."

It gets written in handbooks. It gets shared during team meetings as a cascading message. I was at a company once that decided to go look at all its teams and then investigate the larger teams to see if they should conform to the best practice of "team size." Some of the teams split in half and viewed this exploration as an edict. One team, at the urging of its engineering director, came to me and discussed its particular situation and what to do.

This particular team had grown to be 16 members. Their manager, who preferred to remain anonymous, told me, "We were doing really well. And every week it seemed like we were shipping all these features, and that's probably the main reason why we've been hesitant to split, since we don't want to rock the boat. I think that we have resources in every area we need. It seems like we have good product direction. There is a sense of urgency that I think has been echoed from the top."

I asked her why, then, would they consider splitting, and she said, "I think the number one reason is that the product management team noticed that we look big. And probably engineering noticed it too. And feeling like we're violating a best practice." She continued later, "There isn't really a problem we're trying to solve other than we look big. It's the joke on the engineering floor that we have this massive standup every morning."

I dug into how this team was operating, and she told me that one way they stay productive in standup is by talking about the work on a visual board kept in priority order, as opposed to defaulting to the standard Scrum questions of what I did yesterday toward the sprint goal, what I will do today toward the sprint goal, and what are the blocking issues toward our sprint goal.[4] They had ways in which they navigated the communication and facilitation of being a large team. They owned multiple tools in their software. They found a rhythm of navigating their size and tool ownership. They were doing really well.

In the end this team did not split. It stayed big and continued to work together as they were before. The team members spoke with the management, showed their results, and moved forward.

If you are faced with a situation like this one, where an outside force is judging your team based on a physical characteristic like your team size, without even investigating your team's performance, take the time to educate them on why you're badass and shift their perspective. Talk with the manager of your team for support if they are not involved already. You can first approach it with a question. You can lead with something like this: "I'm curious why you think shifting our team size would help us be more productive." And then share the frequency of your delivery and feedback from your customers on how they love what you've built.

In my years of working, people would sometimes say, *you need to pick your battles.* I think there is a lot of truth to that. Pushing back on decisions that appear foolish or nonproductive is sometimes necessary. This is where stepping into your leadership comes in. Analyze the requests of your team. Consider the pros and cons. Make informed decisions about your team structure, just like you do when you're building software.

---

4 Schwaber and Sutherland, *The Scrum Guide*.

Another anti-pattern is when people are suddenly gone from your team, due to some decision made by someone higher up on the food chain, with short notice. Welcome to the mysterious world of reteaming by abstraction.

Reteaming by Abstraction with Poor Communication

While getting onboarded at a large client, I worked with nearly 30 team members. As a consultant there, I decided to do an initial assessment of how the people were doing on the team by visiting with each team member individually.

After a week or so, I had made my way almost halfway through the list of people that I had gathered. The company was going through a lot of different changes. In fact, it was in the process of being acquired by one of its competitors. Some team members told me that people were "dropping like flies," and there was a lot of attrition. People were afraid. They didn't know if they were going to have a job in a month. Nevertheless, the company brought me on board to help a group of its engineering teams be more effective during this uncertain time.

In one standup I attended, we suddenly learned that our QA engineer was no more. He got reallocated to a "higher priority" project. He was just gone. *Poof.* And he didn't even say goodbye. This person was on my get-to-know list, but suddenly my list had become shorter, due to whatever "resource allocation" procedure was happening from a distance at the cusp of a new quarter.

The abrupt exit struck a chord with me in terms of how impersonally it was handled. It was really just a matter of fact. It hurt the team. Team members struggled as time moved forward because they lost their quality assurance person. They now had to work differently to deal with this change, and it wasn't easy or expected.

It was almost as if the company was a threat to its own teams. This was a very large company—its employees numbered in the thousands. Managers kept spreadsheets listing which "resources" were targeted to work on what each quarter. There was, at least at the management level, a keen awareness of the cost of team members for each project, and at some abstract level (at least to me), people could get "reallocated" to other projects that were a higher priority to the company, at any time. This is really a threat to relationship building. I mean, if, conceivably at any time, a team member could be suddenly reassigned to another project, how much time do you want to invest building a relationship with them? Would it matter? This is the darker side of dynamic reteaming.

In speaking with engineers at this company, I learned that this sort of reteaming was nothing new. They were used to a great deal of changes "happening to them" throughout the years, especially near the beginning of a new quarter, when things were reassessed and projects moved up and down a priority list. As the company had many different office locations throughout the world, people would hear of changes via remote meetings or announcements made by people they didn't even know personally. Plaques showed up in the kitchen announcing upcoming "unfiltered" talks with leadership. It was eerie. Many of the old-timers at this company have endured and survived through multiple rounds of layoffs over the years. Why do they stay? The pay is really good, and the job has high flexibility. The products are compelling to them. They deal with the changes.

Reteaming by abstraction is when people are treated as, and are typically called, *resources*. They are moved around and manipulated on spreadsheets by management. In classic command-and-control fashion, someone changes a cell in the spreadsheet, and that initiates a change in real life that impacts actual people. It's almost like the Wizard of Oz behind a curtain, deciding the fate of team members, but maybe with a committee of other managers. It's unclear, though, because it is so far away. It's obscured. No one really knows what's happening or who initiated the reteaming—unless you're at a people-management level, or unless you go out of your way to find out what happened. When management is in another office, there's more mystery. This space, or distance, really disconnects the humans. The people in charge of the reteaming likely have good intentions for the company. But due to this disconnect, that message gets lost in the execution of the reteaming.

So what do we do organizationally when faced with reteaming by abstraction? It could be about the distance to decision making, and to the people making the decisions. I like this advice from Simon Sinek in his book, *Leaders Eat Last*. Sinek talks about abstraction and comes to the conclusion that working in smaller groups, such as those below Dunbar's number of 150, is the place to start.[5] When you work in smaller units within the company, the people are closer together—they know each other. Maybe it's easier to spread information when team changes are happening. In the software world, this could match up with working in tribe-like structures.

I think it's important to have feedback loops set up at different company levels. Not just between individual contributors and managers, but well beyond that. There are commercial tools like Peakon and Culture Amp that can be leveraged

---

5 Sinek, *Leaders Eat Last*, 115.

to tap into how the people are feeling on an ongoing basis. With Peakon you can set it up so people can share anonymous feedback, and leaders in turn can respond to it, while still holding the confidentiality.

Beyond people being yanked out of your team without an ounce of notice or advanced warning, there is another anti-pattern that is related to what we might perceive as toxic team members.

The Impact of Toxic Team Members

Keeping people on teams, and in your company for that matter, whom no one wants to work with and are a distraction from getting things done, is a situation to take very seriously. These are the human impediments in our workplaces that we need to pay attention to as managers and coworkers.

Think of the behavior you have seen in the past, when you were working with someone and their action or inaction caused severe obstacles to getting things done. Maybe they were arrogant or verbally abusive. Maybe they were insulting or abrasive. Maybe they were passive-aggressive and hoarded information. These types of behaviors threaten the safety of others on the team and in the workplace in general. Feeling safe is tied to high performance.[6] We need to address threats to safety as a priority.

This isn't a new concept. In 2012, Fitzpatrick and Collins-Sussman wrote an excellent chapter on this topic in their book *Team Geek*. Their discussion included separating the person from the toxic behavior at hand. Toxic behaviors are a threat to the attention and focus of your team. Toxic people usually lack HRT: humility, respect, and trust.[7] Toxic behaviors might include the following: not respecting other people's time, not having the ability to compromise or achieve consensus, being demanding or over-entitled, exuding hostile behavior, trolling, and having a high degree of perfectionism that gets in the way.[8] People can be misunderstood and really have good intentions. They might be acting in a way that is distressing to others; however, as my friend Chris Smith reminded me, "Few people are actually evil." It could be that something else is going on in their lives, and they are acting out at work because of that. We can apply ideas from Kim Scott's book *Radical Candor* here, and get curious. She suggests that we

---

6 Edmundson, *Teaming*, 129–131.

7 Fitzpatrick and Collins-Sussman, *Team Geek*, 89.

8 Fitzpatrick and Collins-Sussman, *Team Geek*, 85-101.

"Challenge directly, but care personally."[9] I think there is a lot of wisdom in that approach. We need to take the time to dig in and explore what is going on interpersonally and care about the people. People do get reputations, however, and that is something for all of us to keep in mind in our world of work.

Rachel Davies told me a story about people who didn't want to switch onto a particular team because the team had a loud person who was easily annoyed on it. She said, "They had this dominant character in that team. [...] He was quite loud and complaining, and then they had these introverted characters on their team as well. And people didn't want to rotate into that team because of that person." She went on, "Some people who preferred a more peaceful life, they said, *Well, I would quite like to work on the new product but I do not want to work with this guy, so I don't want to change teams.*"[10]

Later in our discussion she connected the concept of reteaming to the ability to "choose the culture you want" on a team. Rachel said, "It goes beyond, *Who do I want to work with? What area of the code do I want to work on? What coding language do I want to use?* and over to, *What kind of "mini culture" do I want for my day-to-day life?*" It's nice when we get to choose what we want. As Rachel described it, "some people didn't want to join the frontend team because it was too laid-back and they wanted to get more work done. And then other people wanted to join that team because it was laid-back." People, when given the choice of which team they work in, get to weigh all those types of things.

If you are not aware of the social dynamics present on your teams, like if you had no idea that this person was disruptive to team change, you could wind up with unhappy people. When companies reteam from afar (what I call reteaming by abstraction), the risk of having incompatible teams may be higher as a result. Allowing people to self-select their teams, or having enlightened managers who value considering social dynamics for team assignment, can help reduce your risk of getting teams with poor chemistry that threaten performance.

When there is someone on a team and the other people don't want to work with that person, especially if you pair program, it becomes quite noticeable. If the collaboration pattern is farther away, and there is more individual work and isolation, maybe it's less obvious. When we learn about things like this, we can get curious and try to understand what is going on.

---

9 Scott, *Radical Candor*, 9.

10 Rachel Davis, in an interview with the author, December 2016.

Giving the "toxic" team member feedback is key so that they have an opportunity to try and make a change. Maybe they are not aware that their behavior is creating such problems. People can be given the benefit of the doubt; with feedback, I believe they can have the opportunity to change and learn from mistakes. If this doesn't work, discussing how to deal with the situation with other managers or your human resources team is worth a try.

It can be really hard especially for new managers who encounter challenging team members. Coaching for managers is highly recommended. Manager communities can also support each other by sharing challenges and giving each other advice for how to face the challenges.[11]

Besides having a toxic team member, you might also encounter what you, or others, perceive to be a highly toxic team that no one wants to work with. Keeping that team together brings a host of challenges.

Keeping the Toxic Team Together

Like people, teams get reputations. I remember working with a particular team that was comprised of some rather quiet characters. They steadily did their work, heads down. They went trail running together, and they built incredible things. There was a major problem, however. The product managers were afraid of this team. It became such a problem that it started to create a rift between the engineering group and the product management group. Things had to change.

It was hard to get "in" with this group of engineers. The best way "in" was to do sports with them. The QA engineer who worked with this team was easily accepted because he did this. It was impressive how he got "in there" and built the relationship with the engineers. For a time, this QA engineer was essentially the interface between the team and "the outside world." This QA engineer was the translator between the quiet-yet-mighty team and the other personalities around the team—such as the product owner, the user experience person, and any other person who needed to interact with the team.

A product manager was in tears one day after a particularly brutal meeting with this team. The team members really didn't respect her because she didn't appear to know what she was doing, and she was unclear on what they were

---

11 A wonderful facilitation technique to try when fostering a community of managers is Troika Consulting, from Liberating Structures. In this technique, people get into groups of three, and through very creative rotation they take turns sharing challenges and giving advice to each other. The instructions for doing this exercise can be found on the Liberating Structures website (*http://www.liberatingstructures.com*).

building. The features they worked on were highly technical. They didn't really need her to build the system they were working on. She didn't have any control or influence. But, as custom had it, each team was assigned a product owner. She didn't feel successful. It wasn't working out very well for anyone.

So an agile coach was assigned to work with the teams to try to help out the situation. Activities were facilitated, and things got a bit better—or at least more out in the open. They had dialogue. They retrospected. They tried to improve the relationships and to repair the situation. It was the usual drill—almost like an organizational hack—a bandage or a softening of an abrasive situation without really addressing the root cause. The combination of the people on the team was toxic to the environment as a whole. It wasn't what was best for the organization or the people.

If you look at your teams and think, "Do I want the rest of my engineering organization to be like this team?" and your answer is clearly *no*, you might consider "reteaming the dynamic" of the team. In other words, you might choose changing up the team, or, if you're bold, you might choose to destroy the team. Split up the chemistry. Abolish the vibe. This can be culturally very difficult to do. It takes courage and care.

Just because a team came together and is producing value, doesn't mean it's in the company's best interest to perpetuate the vibe that the team emits. That's part of the problem with insisting that all teams remain *stable* or having the same team members as a default rule. Sometimes the chemistry can be off. We need to have the concept of reteaming "on the table" for consideration as a valid organizational pivot.

Sometimes the dynamic is such that if you let it become contagious, you can have worse problems. You can perpetuate toxicity. Instead, we need the polar opposite.

We want the "multiplier effect" when we have teams in which people are highly collaborative and cooperative with each other, and when the energy is high. It's fine to be a quiet team. That's not the issue. It's not that we need a team of extroverts. Rather, we want a collection of people who together are creating incredible things that delight customers continuously, and it's a very enjoyable experience for the humans present. The people are excited to come to work each day. People are excited to work with the teams. They feel safe expressing their ideas without fear of shaming or bullying.

A leader's job is to drive fear out of the workplace, according to Point 8 of "Deming's Lessons for Management."[12] That applies here. We need to get bold, step up, and have the courage to destroy teams that spread or represent fear in our environments.

This chapter has explored a variety of anti-patterns for dynamic reteaming. One thing in common across most of these anti-patterns is the mechanistic approach that has been employed. Sometimes, with managers off to the side, deciding on the team setup and change, the results can become not what we were going for. Maybe we are too far away from the work of the teams and the problems that we are trying to solve. We think we know best. We have the rank and paycheck as the manager, but it could be that we are "too far away."

This is where inclusion comes in—actually involving individual contributors in reteaming planning. Doing so can likely reduce our risk that a reteaming will go wrong. The people on the ground have the knowledge about the relationship systems that could be impacted. They might know who gets along with whom. If you are a manager or are higher up than that, you might have no awareness of the social dynamic, and hence you could place a couple of people on a team who are like oil and water. Nonetheless, there are ways to get better at reteaming.

We can learn a lot from looking at anti-patterns. They really illustrate the dark side of reteaming. On the flip side, the patterns are also instructive. I'm not trying to pretend here that reteaming is easy. You will learn a lot as your career progresses and reteaming happens to you. You will also learn a lot when you are in the position to catalyze reteaming. You can get better at this entire concept of dynamic reteaming. Let's go further into that; in the next part of the book we will go over a variety of tactics for how to get better at reteaming in your company.

---

12 Deming, *Out of the Crisis*, 59–62.

PART III

Tactics for Mastering Dynamic Reteaming

Thus far, I have shared five patterns of dynamic reteaming with advice and tactics woven throughout. I've also shared anti-patterns. This part of the book goes deeper into the specific practices you can leverage to catalyze dynamic reteaming with greater confidence. It also shares how to cope with unexpected dynamic reteaming. Here's how Part III is organized.

First, we get into the topic of designing your organization for dynamic reteaming. You don't have to be starting from scratch. This section includes information on how to evolve your organization. We revisit the dynamic reteaming ecocycle in order to bring alignment to how your team views the current state of the company.

Second, we dig into some of the organizational constraints and enablers to dynamic reteaming. Following that are strategies for priming your organization for future reteaming. This includes community building and aligning on roles— both are critical scaffolds to hold continuity in place as you grow forward into change.

Third, I include some planning tools for people who want to embark on deliberate dynamic reteaming that is larger than the single-team level. Embarking on these reteamings is risky and challenging. Reorganizing teams is not a trivial endeavor. It requires great care and preparation. I've included several questions for you to analyze as you think about what you're trying to do.

Following that, I include activities that you can do after your reteaming has taken place—it could be after an unexpected reteaming, or it could be after one that you deliberately catalyzed. Whether it's after a one by one, grow and split, isolation, merging, or switching reteaming, you can use similar tactics to help people transition over to the new team situation as well as to "speed up the gel" of relationship building and to set context on the work and aligning on the workflow. I call this set of practices *team calibrations*.

No matter what kind of reteaming happens in your organization, it's imperative that you learn your way forward through action and reflection. Therefore, this section concludes with some recommendations about having retrospectives to propel your organizational change. I'm hoping that all of these ideas will help you get better at reteaming so that your organization, and you, become more skillful and resilient.

11

Adapt Your Organization for Dynamic Reteaming

You can grow your organization with dynamic reteaming in mind so that you have a resilient and flexible structure, or you can adjust your existing organization to enable dynamic reteaming. In doing either, there are several factors to consider, and this chapter provides ideas for both vantage points.

First, we will go over tools that you can use to analyze your context and align on it with your colleagues so that you are coming from the same mental frame. This is where the ecocyle tool that we learned about in Chapter 1 comes into play.

Next, there are constraints and enablers for dynamic reteaming to take into account that either help or hinder it. We will explore these, starting with a deep dive into collaboration dynamics first, and then we will go over some other key variables that impact dynamic reteaming.

Finally, we will talk about how you can prime your organization for reteaming. That is, we will cover what you can do to cultivate connection and alignment in your organization so that when reteaming happens later it will be easier.

Let's get started then, with the ecocyle tool for analysis of your current work context.

Explore Where You Are on the Dynamic Reteaming Ecocycle

Have you ever been to a theme park and walked up to a poster of a map to see the *You Are Here* dot? We can do something similar to that with the ecocycle tool shown in Figure 11-1. It can be used to put our organization into a shared, visual context before even talking about reteaming. It is an alignment tool that I use strategically to start discussions about reteaming.

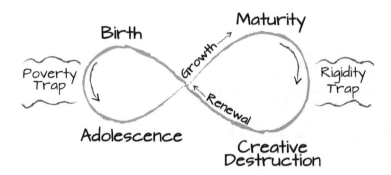

Figure 11-1. An ecocycle based on the adaptive cycle by Gunderson and Holling, Panarchy; *and McCandless et al.,* Liberating Structures

When showing this ecocycle to teams and groups, I like to introduce it first with the forestry example I wrote about in Chapter 1. Next I dive in and use the metaphor in the following ways.

Is the team or organization ripe for reteaming? If you suspect that a team is stagnating and that the people are ready for a big change, bring the ecocycle tool over and see where they would place themselves. Just draw it on a whiteboard, or show it via screen sharing if your team is distributed. Ask individuals where they would place their team on the ecocycle and why.

Ecocycle Sensemaking Activity

If your goal is to align on a shared vision of the evolution of your company, you can do a short activity like this for 30 minutes.

1. Draw a picture of the ecocycle, either on a whiteboard or in a shared virtual space. Ask people to draw their own ecocycle on their own paper.

2. Ask this question: Where is our team on this ecocycle? How do you know? Write down on your own what the evidence is.

3. Ask them to discuss with a partner what they wrote, and then ask the pairs to share out with the entire group.

4. Debrief the short exercise. See what the perceptions are in the team. Do they match? Where do they place themselves? Do they find that they are in a rigidity trap? Will people be open to the

idea of creative destruction and team reinvention? These are all possibilities that might make it easier to start a dialogue about reteaming.

I've also used the ecocycle with people who were in the same company going through a merger. I asked them to draw their own ecocycle and then to put an X representing where they thought their company is currently represented on the ecocycle. One person viewed their company in renewal, and the other viewed their company in creative destruction. One of these individuals was having a harder time than the other in coping with the merger. The other person was past a lot of the disruption of the merger, and had already started to move on and shift their perspective to renewal.

Talking about where we are at in our company, especially when going through a large shift, can help us make sense of what is going on around us so that we can process it and move on. Sometimes it helps to name what is going on and have a discussion about it. The ecocycle tool is something that I've found helps with this because it's a good discussion starter.

In addition to getting a shared understanding of where you are on the ecocycle, I like to encourage people to analyze the collaboration dynamics that are present in their current teams, in order to get an idea of what might hold back their reteaming (constraints) and what might make reteaming easier in their context (enablers).

Organizational Constraints and Enablers to Reteaming

There are several factors that influence dynamic reteaming. Some make it harder to reteam, and others make it easier to reteam.

If you are in a startup, and your goal is to optimize for fluidity and resiliency so that you build a sustainable, adaptive company, as described in Chapter 4, this is the section to explore to design your organization.

If you are in an existing company with a legacy structure, you can use this section to determine how you might change your organization in order to better enable dynamic reteaming.

Let's explore, starting with collaboration dynamics and then taking a deep dive into a variety of variables that impact reteaming.

COLLABORATION DYNAMICS THAT RESTRICT AND ENABLE RETEAMING

How team members collaborate with each other impacts the ease or difficulty of their reteaming. In essence, when there is information overlap between people on a team, it's theoretically easier to reteam. The more overlap you have, the easier it is to divert someone to a different team. This section talks about the ranges of this collaboration—from the extreme of coding alone, to the other extreme of coding in groups, and how these setups restrict or enable reteaming.

Coding alone restricts dynamic reteaming

Richard Sheridan, cofounder and chief storyteller at Menlo Innovations, and author of the best-selling book *Joy, Inc.: How We Built a Workplace People Love*, talked with me about his experience with what he calls the *Tower of Knowledge problem*. It's a problem that he encountered quite viscerally as a vice president of R&D prior to founding Menlo Innovations.

Here's how he described the Tower of Knowledge problem:

> *You know, the one guy, in this particular case in my team, who knew everything about a particular subsystem, and nobody else knew what he knew, and he couldn't take vacations. [...] He became very bitter, cantankerous, difficult to work with because he was always under pressure. He was always working lots of overtime. [...] When he did schedule vacations, we would typically send him out the door with his laptop, with a pager, with the phone number we could reach him on, so these vacations could never truly be vacations because if something broke in his area of code, we needed him.[1]*

Can you imagine this situation? It's like you're chained to your work. Multiply that across your organization, and you have a workforce that's destined for burnout.

You can't scale your company if it's comprised of a bunch of heroes, Richard told me, as they can only work 60–80 hours per week—and who would want to do that? It's not sustainable nor livable. It just doesn't work. We are not machines; we are humans and need better working conditions. Our goal is to cultivate a workplace where people are learning continually and are excited to come to work each day.

---

1 Richard Sheridan, in an interview with the author, October 2016.

In addition to that, the more people you have working individually, the less connection exists. The people become islands of specialization. The complexity of coordinating their work increases, which is more costly. Heroes work independently on a greater goal. Maybe later, out of necessity, this is facilitated by project managers as the communication interfaces between the people. I lived this scenario when project-managing component teams building GoToMeeting. Just getting a shared list of work between all of the individuals was challenging. The shift to Scrum at least brings cross-functional specialists together onto one team, and ensures you get a shared list of work, according to the rules of the game in *The Scrum Guide*. However, if your specialists continue to work "alone" together in the Scrum team you still have the following problems of coding alone.

Coding alone gives engineers less opportunity for switching to work on other subject matter because they hold so much responsibility that's not shared with others. After a while it can be like you're chained to that feature set you own. It's not the setup that I would recommend if you want to build a learning organization where people can reteam and expand their knowledge bases. It's too rigid.

And, inheriting the code of someone who was working alone for an extended piece of time is no picnic, especially if it's not equipped with tests or forethought for future developers.

Pair programming and mob programming add in redundancy, which makes it easier to switch teams when the time arises. Combine that with writing code with tests, and you enable greater agility and movement. Let's take a look.

Pair programming with test-driven development enables greater fluidity in teams

When I was talking with the cofounder and CTO of AppFolio, Jon Walker, he told me that he felt strongly that pair programming and test-driven development have helped reteaming at AppFolio succeed. Both practices facilitate someone new starting on the team, whether they're a new hire or switching teams, and they give developers freedom to work on different areas of the codebase without being trapped.

He said, "If you wanted to put in just one new person, they instantly get people up to speed quickly through pair programming. It's a really quick way to do that. Test-driven development also is a great safety net where people can go in and change code in an area they don't understand. Then they've got harnesses of tests. The test will fail if they've broken something. I think without those it would be a lot harder to reteam. I think that's why people don't do it frequently at other places."[2] Pair programming helps to ease the transition of engineers joining any team.

This goes beyond mentoring. As Jon put it, "when someone's mentoring you, they'll talk to you every once in a while; that's very different than having someone work with you every day doing pair programming."

Combine the pairing with self-testing code, and you can be freed from the chains of being the "knowledge source" on one area of code, as we saw in the previous Tower of Knowledge section. Jon said, "I think one of the big benefits that we've found in how we work is that developers tend not to get pigeonholed. It's largely because there are tests there, and anyone can work on any piece of code. So we resisted code ownership for a long time. We are starting to have little bits and parts of it, but even then it's a super light version of code ownership." If you're not bound to a section of the codebase as an individual developer, you can have greater ease at switching later.

Jon said it well: "One engineer leaves, and you're not lost with the only guy who knows how this *light bulb* works. But for programmers, there's huge benefits to it in that it doesn't become, *Jon's the only guy who can work on this light bulb, so every time we ever want to do anything to that light bulb it has to be Jon*. And Jon's like, *I don't want to work on that old light bulb that I wrote 20 years ago*."

Pair programming provides that cross-pollination of knowledge and a sense of shared memory of what is being worked on. And, when amped up with tests, it can really help raise the confidence of engineers who are making changes to the codebase due to the feedback they receive from the pass-or-fail tests. You can turn up the volume on the cross-pollination and shared memory or understanding of how the code works by mob programming.

Mob programming fosters even more fluid reteaming

Mob programming—programming in a group on one computer—is a movement that emerged in a team led by Woody Zuill at Hunter Industries in Southern California. It's a "continuous conversation," as described by Jason Kerney, a mob programming veteran from Hunter. He said, "Ideas are coming from a bunch of different points of view at a bunch of different times. It's all just coming in."[3] He explained a situation that drove his learning about the approach home.

---

2 Jon Walker, in an interview with the author, February 2016.

3 Jason Kerney, in an interview with the author, January 2017.

What actually happened to me is I left for a cup of coffee and got pinned down talking to this guy. It took, you know, 20 minutes to get out of that conversation. When I came back [to the mob] I realized that I could quickly pick up where I left off just because I could understand the different conversations and stuff that were going on. Because it's a continuous conversation. You walk away for 20 minutes from a good conversation and come back. You're not lost forever. It's maybe 10 minutes to get back in step, and then you're back in the conversation. It's all very much like that, and that was the big eye-opener for me.

When all the people are together, with one keyboard and screen, and are coding "live" with each other, people can move in and out of teams with greater ease. There is simply more knowledge redundancy among team members.

When you work in a mob there are certain interaction patterns. You have the driver and navigator and the rest of the mob. People cycle in and out of these roles at a regular cadence, sometimes facilitated by a mob-programming timer.[4] Because the communication pattern is known and relatively consistent across the mobs, switching from one team to another is easier to do, and it's easier to integrate people into teams.

If you break up the majority of the team, that's disruptive. If you follow the "trading places" practice, people can move in and out of mob programming teams without much disturbance to the team as a whole. See "Team Members Trade Places, Then Tell Managers" on page 28. Since all of the people are working on the same thing, there is a "group memory" and stream of thought. New people can join in. All of the details about what they are building do not leave inside the brain of the person who switched to another team. Hence, this collaboration structure is more redundant and fault tolerant.

If you work in a context with "towers of knowledge," and there is not much collaboration, pairing, or mob programming, what can you do? How do you evolve your teams over to working more collaboratively?

One idea to consider is to apply the isolation pattern, described in Chapter 7. Start a team off to the side. Invite people to join that team who want to work differently, in this case, more collaboratively. Joining this new team means that we

---

will pair program, for example. Hire in new engineers to that team and grow it bigger. Then split it, as described in Chapter 6. Now you have two teams that work like that. You can continue building from there by growing and splitting. Then, as time passes, have the teams that pair give lunch-and-learns sharing how they work. Who knows, maybe these practices will catch on in other teams.

There are other factors that impact the ease or difficulty of reteaming. We work in different contexts, with different people, different technologies, and so on. In the next section, we will go over several variables to explore this topic.

VARIABLES THAT IMPACT DYNAMIC RETEAMING

Every software development context is different. Companies have their own cultures and dynamics based on what's present and what's absent. Here is a discussion of the variables that impact how easy or difficult it is to reteam. The presence, absence, and quality of these conditions can be constraints to your reteaming, or they can be enablers.

Think deeply about your context in regard to each of the variables. Doing so will help you better apply the concepts from this book.

Context Analysis Activity

- Think of a reteaming initiative that you have experienced in the past. Which of the following variables came into play? What was their impact?

- Now think of a future reteaming initiative you can imagine happening in your context. Look through the following variables. Which do you need to consider in your reteaming strategy? How will you mitigate potential challenges?

Platform

When changing teams, will the person be working on the same platform (like iOS, Android, web), or will they be switching to a new one? If switching to a new one, there is a potential learning curve, and they will need to acquire new equipment to work in the new platform. At a company I worked at, I was involved in an effort to spread out mobile development teams to integrate them with web development teams so that features for our customers can be cocreated in a more synchronous manner rather than separately. After moving our first two iOS developers out to web teams, we initially ran into constraints related to testing and deployment that slowed us down. The quality assurance engineers resident on those new teams either needed new testing equipment or had to work out ways to pair with existing iOS testers in order to complete their work. Moreover, spreading the ability to deploy onto the iOS platform was a new area of learning for the newly minted cross-platform teams.

Changing teams is a forcing function to learning. You can make the learning easier if you plan for it and have institutional support for it. We built an engineering academy of engineers teaching other engineers to support the learning needs that arose from this reteaming. Woody Zuill, one of the mob programming founders, held workshops on working collaboratively for any interested team members across our organization. This exposure to a more collaborative way of working had positive impacts on these new teams, some of which immediately began working collaboratively across their platforms by implementing mob programming. This accelerated the learning.

Programming language

When changing teams, does it require the person to learn a new programming language? This impacts the ease and speed of the reteaming. Things change fast in the technology world. For many of us, it's obvious that we need to keep learning in order to stay relevant. If we're used to coding in one language for our entire careers and then we need to learn a new language, there is an obvious learning curve. In the mobile reteaming mentioned previously, having iOS engineers work on teams with web developers spurred learning Swift on the part of the web developers on the existing teams, and the iOS engineers started to learn to code using Ruby on Rails. Pairing and mob programming supported this learning. This learning will most definitely slow down the work in progress in the short term; however, if successful, the teams will be more adaptive and able to deliver on customer needs in multiple platforms more easily in the future.

I was with another team at a different company that was creating software in web, iOS, Android, and Windows platforms. They decided to *pause* or stop working on the Windows platform for business reasons. The developers on that team switched into iOS development. Some of these engineers had been in the software industry more than 20 years and had been coding in C++ all that time. When I heard that this was happening, I was worried for them and thought that it would be a negative experience because it was not their choice. As it turned out, it was quite refreshing for one of the engineers in particular. Sometimes change thrust upon us is received positively; however, doing that, in my opinion, is still quite risky.

Single specialist roles on teams versus full stack roles

If we are making the switch into a new team that works in a completely different way than we do, it will challenge and add drag to our reteaming. For instance, if we are coming from a team in which we occupy a role like backend developer, and we are working with other people in siloed roles like frontend developer, iOS developer, QA engineer, and the like, and then we are moving to a team in which we will now be a full stack engineer coding the frontend, backend, and anything in between, then it could be a more cumbersome and challenging change for us (especially if we don't like the idea). Moreover, if we now have to change our way of coding to ensure quality by writing more tests, for example, and not throw our code "over the wall" to a separate role who will quality check our work, that is another change that will make the reteaming more challenging.

Conversely, if we retain the single specialist roles on all of the teams, and we are just changing teams and retaining our single specialist role, it will be easier because there is that parity across both of the teams. It is the same if we have full stack generalists on our current team and we switch to another team that is comprised of full stack generalists.

There is definitely a balance needed in terms of having generalists and specialists. It's up to the company to determine the right balance to fit its needs. It could be that an environment dominated by generalists could use a healthy sprinkling of specialists across the teams in a consulting or floating capacity to help level-up skills. I remember we had a highly specialized frontend engineer at App-Folio who would nomad from one team to the next, and he would hold open-learning sessions to level-up others' frontend development skills.

Reteaming is a forcing function for learning. Encouraging people to be T-shaped is part of this discussion, and we can be deliberate about that. It is most likely the case that someone has deep knowledge of a particular area of expertise. That is the vertical part of the T. Next, they learn and expand their abilities to do even more in other areas, which is the horizontal part of the T. Changing teams encourages us to learn.

Collective code ownership versus strict code ownership

When the teams share ownership of the codebase, and any team is able to work on any part of the application, you have a lot more liquidity in the organizational design. When new work emerges as a priority in the organization, there are more teams that have the readiness to do that work. This gives incredible flexibility to the organization to respond to changing customer and market demands. At AppFolio, we were closer to the collective code ownership side of the spectrum from the start of the company. Throughout the years, pockets of specialization cropped up, and certain teams wound up "owning" certain areas of the code from a certain perspective. In particular, the teams that handled the processing of money come to mind—as new work came into that realm the teams that knew enough about it got the new work.

Sharing code across many teams does not come without its challenges. When you don't have explicit owners to sections of your code, you might feel like there is less accountability. In our revision-tracking systems we can see who the most frequent code contributors are. After about eight years into this type of scenario at AppFolio, we felt the need to introduce the concept of "code steward-ship." Some industrious engineers rallied people to claim stewardship, or oversight, over different areas of our codebase. These engineers developed guidelines for what it meant to be a steward. They did talks about it with the entire engineering group. They served as helpful resources of knowledge for anyone who wanted to extend different areas of the codebase. A lot of care was taken in this endeavor to be clear that the stewards were friendly guides and not domi-neers of their section of the codebase.

Age of the code

If we switch teams and now need to become familiar with a codebase that is quite old, and the people who wrote it are nowhere to be found, it will take some time to get up to speed and learn that environment. If you are instead switching to a team working on software created from scratch, without the need to connect to any existing code, it's a different situation. You don't need to spend that time as a "code archaeologist" trying to decipher how things work so that you can extend or transform it. When you are switching to a team that has legacy code, no matter how old it is, it will require taking some time to understand the code environ-ment that you will be changing or extending. Teams that practice Scrum and are refining their backlogs might come up with the adaptation that you do technical refinement of work before giving estimates. The emergence of this is a nod to the fact that there is indeed ramp-up time needed to extend your legacy code.

Test automation, or lack thereof

If the existing codebase has tests in place, we can get to know the codebase faster. We might also feel safer in making changes to it because we will get feedback on whether we have broken any tests when we commit changes.

Jon Walker, CTO of AppFolio, cites the presence of test-driven development as well as pair programming as factors positively influencing the ability to reteam at that company. He said:

> *Pair programming and test-driven development have really helped reteaming, in that you can bring someone new into the team. If you wanted to put in just one new person, they instantly have people that can bring them up to speed quickly through pair programming. It's a really quick way to do that. Test-driven development is also a great safety net where people can go in and change code in an area they don't understand. They've got a harness of tests. The test will fail if they've broken something. I think both those things have really helped. I think without those it would be a lot harder to reteam.[5]*

If you are a QA engineer used to working on a team that has a strong test-writing culture and you switch to one where that is nonexistent or lacking, then your workload will be impacted, and it will likely be more challenging.

How the team collaborates—soloing, pairing, mob programming

If your current team is soloing (coding alone as individuals), and you switch to a team that heavily pairs or practices mob programming, then depending on your viewpoint, it will be easier or harder for you to adjust. The same goes for a switch in the other direction: if you are on a team that heavily pairs or mob programs, and you switch to a soloing culture, it could be difficult. It could also be a relief, however, if you do not like pairing or mob programming.

If the people on the impacted teams pair or mob program, it is even easier to reteam or move people around those teams. There is less siloing of the work within the team, since two or more people understand the work. When someone

---

5 Jon Walker, in an interview with the author, February 2016.

leaves to go to a different team, there is still some domain knowledge that remains in the team. Jason Kerney, a full stack software engineer at Hunter Industries in California, talks about the group memory present on teams that mob program. When first getting into the practice of it, he would feel hesitant to take breaks, worrying that he would miss something in the mob programming session and would not be able to easily get back into it when returning from his break. To his surprise, after taking regular breaks, he learned that there is a group memory that enables the work to go on when people step away, and that it is entirely possible to reenter that work when coming back. He said, "It wasn't until about two months in that I realized that breaking away from it and coming back didn't actually cause me to lose context. The context was built from the communications that we'd been having all day."[6]

In addition, bringing aboard a new team member is less disruptive, especially if the coding language remains constant. When people reteam and need to learn a new programming language from scratch, it is a setback for the integration of the person into the team. Pairing and mob programming help to ease that transition and raise the confidence of the engineers. If the coding language is constant, but the domain area of the work is new or different, there is still a learning curve. Again, it can be eased with pairing or mob programming.

When teams mob program or pair program, the organizations are more resilient to team change, which is an inevitable thing. People will come and go from companies. If you want to build a sustainable company, practice pair and mob programming. Build it in from the start or adapt your way over to it, as described earlier in this chapter. Hire people into that setup or way of working, so they know what to expect. Learn from the stories in this book from Menlo Innovations and Hunter Industries. They pair and mob program, and are highly adaptive and resilient organizations.

Colocated teams versus distributed teams, or hybrids

When the team is dispersed, and people from each of the groups are sitting in separate places in the building or are distributed across different offices or time zones, it's a lot more challenging for the coordination of any coding effort. Reteaming will be more challenging unless you come up with some really good norms for relationship and team building. It can be done.

---

6 Jason Kerney, in an interview with the author, January 2017.

If you have the chance to start your organization from scratch like we did with AppFolio, you can make a concerted effort to have people not only colocated, but also coseated. It's a tremendous advantage to the company. Things can get done faster. People will socialize with their teams on a daily basis. People will socialize by the kitchen. Friendships will form. Reteaming will be easier.

If everyone's remote, you need to put in the effort to help the relationships build across the distance and rely on online communication to do so. Many of us had a crash course in this with COVID-19. It takes effort to foster the communication across distributed teams, but with some commitment it can happen. Video and asynchronous chat are the tools to rely on in order to create the spaces that make you feel like you are together in one place.

Hybrid situations where many team members are in one location with a couple of team members elsewhere can be particularly challenging. The people who are not located with the majority might feel excluded. Leveling the playing field by having everyone on individual video is recommended.

If you are going through a reteaming situation, and people for the first time are switching into a remote team or a hybrid team, there is a learning curve there for the new people. You need to reset on your team and communication norms.

If you are going through a reteaming, and the people are switching from one remote team to another, one hybrid team to another, or one colocated team to another—in essence, situations of parity—your reteaming will theoretically be easier.

Complexity of the domain

If your new team works on an area of the codebase with complex business logic and you do not know that in advance, it will take longer to get up to speed when you reteam. For instance, if you switch to a team that is responsible for accounting features and you do not know accounting, there is an inherent learning curve there. There was for us when we created the initial AppFolio Property Manager software. We brought in outside educators to teach us the ins and outs of accounting. We also had a standard set of books to read to level up our knowledge. It took time. People working on features other than accounting who would switch over to an accounting-focused team would have additional onboarding to get a decent mastery of the domain. This is a good learning challenge for those who seek it. I think managers who allocate people to different teams need to keep this in mind and build the learning into the reteaming plans.

Same or different manager?

When changing teams, will you keep the same manager or have a new manager? If changing teams means that you get away from a "bad" manager, it could be a net gain. If leaving an awesome manager with whom you are in sync and have great synergy and positivity, it could be a negative unless the benefits of the change outweigh the cost. When people are going through this, I usually coach them to see the situation as a learning opportunity. And it's not like they can never talk with their former manager ever again, especially if they are at the same company. Having an open mind and giving the new manager a chance can prove to be fruitful. In some companies there is less coupling between the team you are on and who your manager is. It might not matter what team you are on—you have the same manager regardless.

Familiarity with the people on the team already

If you want a flexible organization in which people can switch teams, it pays to encourage deliberate relationship building across teams. If you buy Tuckman's model for team development (which you might remember from "Larger-Scale Splits" on page 82)—forming, storming, norming, performing[7]—then conceivably some of that can already take place if you foster people knowing each other across teams. There could already be a sense of respect and trust present that enables the reteaming to be more successful. Conversely, if you know the people beyond the team and you don't like or have respect for them, the reteaming will be more challenging. I suggest that you prime people for future reteaming and build that into your culture, since it really is inevitable that your teams will change as your company exists through time. See the community-building tactics later in this chapter.

Choice in the matter versus being forced to change teams

As individuals, some of us want less change, and some of us are open to more of it. If we are on a team now that is jamming and we love the experience, we might not want to change teams. I don't see a problem with that. If the team is delivering value continuously, is building the right things for the customers, and is an engaging and enjoyable experience overall, then by all means keep the team together.

---

7 Tuckman, "Developmental Sequence," 66.

But sometimes we are forced to change teams when we don't want to. That makes the reteaming harder for us. When it's our own idea, it can be easier. If we volunteer to change, if it is our idea, and if we know what we are getting into, it will be easier because we are opting in. We have control and choice in the matter. Most likely we think it is a good idea and a positive thing. When companies decide on the change for the people without their input, it could go either way.

Managers can advocate for matching the people with mutual interests. Recently I was with some directors who wanted to start a new team to do some future-oriented research. Initially we tried to figure out who from our teams would be assigned to be part of this short-lived team. Instead, we wound up sending a chat message to all of our engineers describing the opportunity and inviting people who were interested in it to volunteer in. With that input, the managers then created the final team.

Mindset about growth and learning

In the Carol Dweck "mindset" sense, if we feel that we are people who have the ability to grow and change and learn on the job, versus having the fixed mindset of feeling that we do not have the ability or capacity to do that, then we will probably have an easier time reteaming.[8] If the people around us also share that outlook, then we will have a sense of parity on the team that can help the reteaming be more successful. Promoting an environment of learning and the idea that "we are never done learning" can help. Leaders can model the philosophy and speak about it. This can be part of the learning and development strategy at your company.

In this chapter, we first explored the ecocycle tool to get a shared mental model of our company's placement on it. This can help start discussions about whether the context is ripe for reteaming, like when we sense stagnation, and it can show us that we can shift out of it by catalyzing some reteaming in creative destruction.

Next we looked at a host of variables, which may or may not be present in our companies, that make it easier or more difficult to reteam, starting with a deep dive into collaboration dynamics, which I feel is one of the more critical areas to consider if reteaming and fluidity is your goal.

---

8 Dweck, *Mindset*.

There are some social hacks that you can employ to foster a readiness for dynamic reteaming in your company so that when you want to reteam later, the people are more prepared for it or even primed for it. This brings us to community building and role alignment.

Prime the People for Dynamic Reteaming

Foreshadowing is a technique that fiction authors use to give hints as to what may transpire in the future storyline. There are similar things that we can do at work to hint at future reteaming. We can incorporate these priming techniques into our hiring, our community building, and our role-alignment strategies. Let's dig in, starting with priming during hiring.

INCORPORATE DYNAMIC RETEAMING INTO YOUR HIRING

Earlier, in Chapter 5, I shared examples of how Menlo Innovations has prospective employees really experience their dynamic re-pairing, and how Hunter Industries has its prospective new hires experience mob programming. Both of these companies are priming their candidates and are giving them a glimpse into what working in their context is like. Then, if they get hired, there are no surprises. This provides awesome expectation setting, and it also helps to continue on their cultures of incredible collaboration.

In the same section, Damon Valenzona of AppFolio told us how he does that, simply by having a talk with the prospective new hire before they start at the company. It's nice to know what you're getting into when you join a company, and if you think about it, the employee experience really starts before our first day.

Nonetheless, there are other ways to prime people to expect that dynamic reteaming is the norm at your company. And, after people arrive and are integrated into the regular working rhythm, you can continuously prime for reteaming simply by deliberate community building, as we'll see in our next section.

CULTIVATE COMMUNITY

When you know and care about the people you work with, everything else is easier, including reteaming. In my experience, if you try to gel the wider community, then when people reteam later they are not strangers, so it helps. This section suggests some proactive ways to nurture and build relationships in your organization.

The common thread of all of these examples is that they give the people a shared social experience. The shared experience is like currency they can draw on later when working out complex team challenges like reteaming.

What about doing this within the immediate team? Some people might say that if the team is really solid, it will not be as accepting of newcomers. I tend to ignore that because I've found that it's important at the team, tribe, and higher levels to encourage knowing each other. So let's look at some approaches.

Design events to build relationships across the organization

I've whitewater rafted, camped on islands, and have even gone to Disneyland with teams. I remember going on the Tower of Terror ride with an assortment of team members and having the shared experience of screaming at the top of our lungs as the ride dropped us vertically—it is something I'll never forget, and neither will those teammates. Talk about an ice breaker. I was instantly connected to a site reliability engineer who was sitting next to me on that ride; I had met him that day for the first time. We would reminisce about this shared experience for years after. Taking epic trips together with your teams is something that you'll never forget, and it brings people together in a strong way. It is completely worth the investment. It's the secret sauce.

We had an annual tradition at AppFolio to have a tech retreat. It was a way to bond as a team, to have fun together, and get to know each other. We'd take these trips across our whole R&D organization. So you would get to know people across many teams, and then later when we changed teams for whatever reason, more people knew each other and had a shared experience, so things were easier. We would also deliberately invite our product team members to our engineering retreats. Keeping both teams together and healthy gives your company a strategic advantage. We closely collaborate across both groups in R&D, so why not spend the extra money and time to build and strengthen these relationships?

Once you get to a scale in your company where you can't easily take your entire R&D organization on a trip, you subdivide into smaller experiences, like encouraging tribes to bond in this way.

Give teams funding to create their own social events

At AppFolio, tribes would have money budgeted to use for celebrating key milestones. Each engineering director who was in charge of the tribe would have these funds ready to use to acknowledge successes. Teams would decide what they would want to do in the local area together. Some teams rode Segway scooters in Santa Barbara. Others went wine tasting. Others went to cooking school together. Some went to sporting events in Los Angeles. The key here was that the money went to celebrating a real work accomplishment, and the team chose how to spend it.

What if you can't get the funding? You can get creative. Teams can go for walks, hikes, have potlucks, or anything else in their local area that is free. I was with one team that chose to go to a local monarch butterfly preserve to observe some natural wonder, while also taking goofy photos of the team. The key here is taking the time to stop, choose an activity to do together, celebrate, and be with each other as a team. This builds camaraderie and shared experience.

And, empower the team to determine the social event. You can do it using the "1,2,4, all" pattern from Liberating Structures: Have each person think independently and write down some notes about what the team could do. Next, have them discuss their ideas in pairs and choose one idea to next discuss in groups of four. The groups of four can narrow down the ideas to one idea to serve up to the entire group. Then, each group shares out their top idea. Finally, the entire group can "dot vote" to determine the top idea. To dot vote, sum up the total number of items you're voting on, divide by three, and round up. That is the number of dots to use per person. Then, place the dots next to the items and see if you've come to an agreement.[9]

Many of us have teams that are distributed across different locations and time zones. It might require travel to have a shared social event. We got around this at AppFolio in the early days when the whole team was in Santa Barbara, and two engineers were in Portland. We would often fly the Portland people to our home office. But sometimes we would do a social event in Santa Barbara like a boat ride, and we would arrange for them to do a boat ride on the same day up in Portland. And we would make it a point to do bidirectional in-person visits with our distributed team members, as discussed next.

You can also set up virtual lunch gatherings by using videoconferencing software if it's not possible to get together in person.

Bring remote workers into the office and send team members to them

As companies grow, they might get spread out geographically. The people might not be colocated. This is really an obstacle for communication; however, it's a reality that many of us face in our companies. So how do we make the best of it?

---

9 Visit Liberating Structures (*http://www.liberatingstructures.com/*) for additional directions on the "1,2,4 all" pattern. Credit to Diana Larsen, who taught me the dot voting technique.

In the case of an organization that is largely colocated, but has a variety of remote workers, it helps to bring those remote workers into the context on a quarterly or more frequent basis. When you're remote and it seems like everyone else is not, it can feel pretty isolating. You just don't have the casual encounters with people in the kitchen or other common areas of your office. This is a threat to team gel.

I worked with some engineers at AppFolio who lived in Portland. Jim, a very senior engineer, would visit our Santa Barbara office on a regular cadence. And when he did, he would visit for a while and spend time with different teams at each visit, pair programming with different engineers not only to share his systemic knowledge of our codebase, but also to get to know people. Jim was our first engineer after our founders.

It also helps to go the other way and send key people out to work with remote workers in their context. We would regularly send people to Portland from Santa Barbara when I worked at AppFolio. It feels more inclusive to have "two-way visits" to connect the team members that are working in different locations. Early on at AppFolio, the tradition of eating chicken feet at a Chinese restaurant emerged out of sending people to visit these engineers in Portland. When team members would do that, photos would be shared with everyone, and the whole experience was memorable and fun. Traditions like this build a sense of *culture*.

Other things you can do is get all of your people to travel together to a different location in order to build the community in person, and then go back to your home countries, like in the next example.

Bring distributed employees together for a shared event

A global company that creates software to track PR campaigns and more had an annual retreat for its Agile coaches. I had the privilege of hosting a day-long coaching-skills workshop for this group. The coaches flew into Berlin from across more than four countries. Many of the people met for the first time, whereas others caught up with each other in person after a while. The three days they spent together focused on coaching strategy, skill building, and forming stronger relationships with each other. There was even a bowling event at a local establishment. Doing all of this gives you a greater sense of "teamness."

We can extend our community building outside of our department, to bring an even closer-knit feel to our companies, and here's how one company did just that.

Create opportunities for teams to get to know key leaders in different departments

Mark Kilby, Agile coach at a DevOps tooling company, told me how at his company, they started to have events called "coffee chats" with key leaders in different parts of their organization, such as "the chief marketing officer, VP of the product group, or key product owners." Having these types of events set up helps the teams build connections within the organization in order to strengthen it. In his words, "It also makes the reteaming a little bit easier. They know some of those senior people."[10] This almost primes the reteaming, in my opinion, because when you move to the different part of the organization, you've already started building the relationships needed to succeed.

At AppFolio, VP of Engineering Jerry Zheng created an event to encourage open Q&A between him and any team member. Every other Friday he hosted an informal meeting where anyone could come and bring any questions to the room. The meeting had a casual tone, as they had refreshments there, and the event had a "happy hour" vibe. Other department heads would come to this event over the years, providing opportunities for connection.

These are just some ways to build community across your teams. If people are comfortable with each other and have had a shared experience of some sort, then later when they reteam there is just one less obstacle. Besides deliberate community building like this, another way to set the stage for reteaming at your company is to develop greater role clarity across your teams.

ALIGN ON ROLES ACROSS YOUR TEAMS

If you are working in a cross-functional team, knowing what each role on the team will contribute can provide an anchor to help you cope with changes in team membership.[11]

Knowing role contributions can help when you have new people join your team and also when you switch to another team, assuming the role definitions are somewhat consistent. *The Scrum Guide* (*https://www.scrum.org/resources/scrum-guide*) by Ken Schwaber and Jeff Sutherland, for example, details roles used in the Scrum framework and is a decent guidepost to align on roles across

---

10 Mark Kilby, in an interview with the author, October 2016.

11 I did not make up this idea, I learned it from organizational development research cited in Valentine and Edmondson, "Team Scaffolds," and Wageman et al., "Changing Ecology of Teams," and have applied it in my work as a coach of software development teams.

teams that follow that framework. You don't need to be practicing Scrum, however, in order to align on roles.

No matter what you do, I think it is worth the effort to do a one-to-two-hour activity with the team to define and align on roles. In this context you can also strategize as a team on what you will do if you have incomplete role membership on the team, or if a person in a role is shared beyond your team—both situations put strain on teams unless the teams are comprised of people with entrepreneurial mindsets who can see beyond their roles to get the work done. You can start to make agreements as a team and plan for likely team-change scenarios. Here are some ideas that you can implement in your company to gain greater role clarity and alignment.

Get vertical alignment within the role hierarchy and among managers

If you are working in a cross-functional software development team that is beyond the startup phase, and there are multiple people in each role, they are probably reporting to someone who is experienced in that role. In other words, the software engineers usually report to software engineers, and the tech writers report to tech writers, and testers report to testers. As companies grow, hiring expands, and you could have sizable amounts of each role. Beyond startup, job descriptions emerge, as do career ladders that detail the progression from entry level in a role, to senior, to principal, and so on. So starting within the role hierarchy, there should be some alignment about the meaning and success criteria for the role. And, in the case when these departments of people are so large that you have a community of managers for each role, getting clarity and alignment on the meaning of each role with the managers is important, especially considering the pressures that managers will have to deal with regarding promotions and pay.

Get horizontal alignment at the tribe level

If you are working in an organization where you have clusters of teams grouped into a community akin to a tribe in the Spotify sense, or even in a product or platform area of work, you can get horizontal alignment across these communities.

For example, if you have a tribe with four cross-functional teams, you can do the Tribe Role Alignment activity.

Tribe Role Alignment Activity

If you are in the same physical location, bring each role together into different regions of the room. If you are virtual, put them in breakout rooms using your online meeting software. For example, product managers are in a group, user experience engineers are in a group, software engineers are in a group, and so on.

Next, within each group, have the people make posters or a presentation slide in a shared slide deck with these parts:

1. The outcomes of our role

2. What you might observe us doing in our role

3. How we offer to help other roles

4. What we need from other roles in order to succeed.

Next, have each role present their poster or slide to the other roles, who listen carefully. Instruct the people who are listening to write down ideas for how they can help the role that is presenting to succeed. In person you can do this on sticky notes. In a virtual meeting, tell the people to write their comments into the speaker notes section of the shared slide deck. After writing their ideas, they can read them off.

This type of activity fosters role empathy and gives people an opportunity to share publicly how they want to help each other. I find that this raises positivity, which can only help us when reteaming later.

If any conflicts come up when doing this activity, you can try to work them out on the spot, or follow up on them at the management level after the exercise. Then follow up with teams.

Tribes can have written agreements for how they want to operate as an organization.

In addition to role alignment at the tribe level, I encourage you to focus at the team level.

Get alignment at the team level

The activities described previously can also be done at the team level and can be very useful when a team is getting together to recalibrate how it works—especially in the case when a team might have split into halves or thirds from the grow-and-split pattern in Chapter 6. I've even simplified it in some cases where I facilitate a discussion in which people share only this: "I'm in X role, here's what I need from others." We then go role by role, and answer back how we can help the person in that role. Often in the team-level context one or more managers who are not active contributors to the team are present. I integrate them into this activity because it provides them the opportunity to state publicly how they want to help the team as the person in the manager role, and it gives the team the opportunity to request help from the managers in a public way.

Getting alignment on roles and what to expect as you switch teams is not that hard to do if you devote some time to exploring it. Each of these activities can take two hours or less, in my experience.

This chapter has covered a wide terrain in order to get your organization to analyze its context using the ecocycle tool and to analyze the constraints and enablers to reteaming, including a discussion of a myriad of variables that might come into play. We've also gone over how you might cultivate or prime your company for reteaming, before we finished with a discussion of role clarity.

As I have said throughout this book, sometimes dynamic reteaming is going to happen to you, and it can be unexpected. You are essentially forced to change if you want to remain at the company. Other times you take the effort and energy to catalyze your own reteaming and make it happen. What follows next is a discussion about deliberate dynamic reteaming, starting with some specific planning tools.

12

Plan Your Dynamic Reteaming Initiative

It's no small feat to plan a large-scale reteaming event that spans multiple teams. You might be changing the organizational structure and moving the people around within that new structure. Or, it could be that you are keeping the structure the same, but you're just moving around the people within it.

It could get even more complex. Maybe your company has acquired another company and you are blending together, as described in Chapter 8.

Or, maybe hierarchies are emerging in your context, and there are many shifts related to people management and structure. Peers might be promoted to manage their former peers, and the familiar, flat structure you knew before is now getting reshaped into a top-down triangle.

It could also be that your company priorities have changed, and because of that, some work must be paused or cancelled altogether, and the people need to be reassigned to different, higher-priority efforts elsewhere in the organization.

Whatever the case, doing larger reteamings takes careful planning and consideration for the people.

Even with the best intentions, we can be unskillful with this type of situation. Sometimes it feels like no matter what you try, someone is still upset and is feeling that things should have been done differently. This stuff isn't easy, and it often garners a lot of fear. People fear the loss of role, status, or their jobs—even when they are as safe as they can be. Change triggers fear.

So what can we do? I think we need to recognize that it's inevitable that you will restructure as your organization grows and evolves. It's very much worth the time investment to plan and anticipate scenarios that might come up in order to increase your chances of success, which is the purpose of this chapter.

Remember the ecocycle metaphor from Chapter 1, as shown in Figure 12-1?

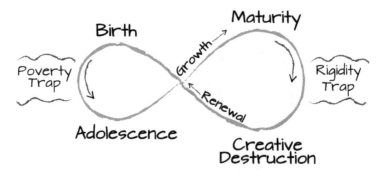

Figure 12-1. An ecocycle based on the adaptive cycle by Gunderson and Holling, Panarchy; *and Keith McCandless et al.,* Liberating Structures

When you catalyze a reteaming, you are really igniting creative destruction. Some people will be ready for it and might even crave it, while others would prefer to not go through that disruptive change and instead want things to stay the same.

In this section, I pose a variety of questions for you to consider when planning large-scale changes so that you can formulate your own plan, and bring in any outside help you may need in order to finalize and execute on your plan.[1]

There is no "one size fits all" reteaming. Reteaming is complex and shows up in the patterns described in this book. You can't just install dynamic reteaming into your organization. Frankly, it's quite nuanced and challenging. When you ignite reteaming deliberately, you need to prepare. So let's get started by analyzing what you're trying to do when embarking on a reteaming initiative. I suggest that you keep track of your approach by creating a Frequently Asked Questions (FAQ) document that explains your initiative. The rest of this chapter is built using that lens.

---

1 See chapter 10 in the "Guide to Managing Human Resources" (*https://hr.berkeley.edu/hr-network/central-guide-managing-hr/managing-hr/managing-successfully/reorganizations*) from the University of California, Berkeley, which digs even further into this subbject. There is also an interesting 2010 McKinsey report on reorgs titled, "Taking Organizational Redesigns from Plan to Practice: McKinsey Global Survey Results" (*http://www.mckinsey.com/business-functions/organization/ourinsights/taking-organizational-redesigns-from-plan-to-practice-mckinsey-global-surveyresults*). These materials, as well as years of experience, have definitely inspired my thoughts on planning larger reteamings.

Create Your Dynamic Reteaming FAQ

An FAQ document is a tool that helps you get really clear on what you're trying to accomplish with your reteaming initiative by anticipating the questions that might come up.

The act of creating this FAQ, which is comprised of questions and answers stored in a shared document, will bring alignment within your leadership group that is in charge of the reteaming, and it will bring some clarity about the plan to the people who are impacted.

Here are some question areas for you to explore and consider integrating into your own FAQ.

WHAT ARE THE PROBLEMS SOLVED BY THIS RETEAMING?

When your organization changes, the people want to know why. Is it due to growth? Are you preparing to go public? Are you trying to have a more scalable structure for the future? Or is it that you need to change your structure due to budget constraints? If you don't anchor to why, your reteaming initiative will not make sense, and it will appear as if you are doing it for the sake of doing it without any good reason. Articulate the *why* to show respect for the people in your organization who will be impacted by the reteaming.

HOW WILL PEOPLE GET ASSIGNED TO TEAMS?

As we saw in Chapter 3, there are different approaches to assigning people to teams. Determine how much inclusion in team assignment you are willing to give the people impacted by the reteaming. Are the managers going to determine the final structure and cascade the decision to the teams? Are the managers going to first seek input from the people and then determine the final team structures? Or is the organization wanting to embark on a more inclusive reteaming event, such as visualizing potential changes on whiteboards, or by having an open reteaming event? Align on this approach within your reteaming leadership team, and then articulate your plan in your FAQ. For step-by-step instructions on how to do a whiteboard reteaming, see Appendix A. To learn how to run a marketplace for team selection, see Appendix B.

HOW WILL PEOPLE FIND OUT WHETHER THEY HAVE A NEW TEAM ASSIGNMENT?

When you begin a reteaming initiative, you need to have clarity on what the impacts are to every person involved. In some cases, you need to consider questions like the following:

- Does anyone get a new title?
- Is anyone changing roles?
- Is anyone becoming a manager who wasn't one before?
- Is anyone getting a new manager?
- Is anyone now shared between teams who wasn't before?
- Is anyone getting a promotion and raise?
- Is there a need to hire new people into the company because of the changes?

You also need to be sure that you don't forget anyone in the change. It probably seems odd to read that, but I've seen it happen.

There are upsides and downsides for people during some reteaming events. Knowing and predicting how each person will be impacted is imperative so that you can talk with them about it and understand their needs. If people keep the same manager, it's generally less disruptive.

HOW ARE EXISTING TEAMS IMPACTED IN PARTICULAR?

Another dimension to consider is whether any existing teams are going to stay the same, or if they are going to change with your reteaming initiative. In particular, the following questions come to mind:

- Are any of the teams splitting or dissolving?
- Are any teams acquiring remote employees that they didn't have before?

If a team was colocated and now it has remote team members joining, there are collaboration obstacles that they will need to overcome. The day-to-day norms of the teams will change if their team membership changes extensively. They could use a *calibration session* if this occurs. See Chapter 13.

HOW IS EXISTING WORK IMPACTED?

More than once in my career I have seen work "paused," either temporarily or indefinitely. Even with the best of plans to come back to work later, that some-times never happens. It is extremely demotivating to have worked months, and sometimes years, on a product or service and then it's terminated. It's happened to me. It's happened to colleagues. If that is a repeated problem at your company, there are larger problems. Validating customer need is where I would look in order to stop the *pause work and reallocate the people* anti-pattern. On the other hand, drastic changes in work focus could be a pivot to save the company, like in the case of the Expertcity marketplace dissolution mentioned the preface. So at times it's completely necessary. Nonetheless, you need to address any work impacts within your FAQ.

WHAT IS THE COMPOSITION OF THE NEW TEAMS?

Sometimes new teams are seeded with one to two people while the company is hiring for the rest of the people. Know what you're getting into with this by rereading "Seeding Teams" on page 41, and, by all means, include the team members in the hiring of the rest of their team. Partially staffed teams can be a challenging situation that is stressful to people if they don't have all of the skills required to do the work of the team. I would avoid it if possible.

Also, avoid excessive sharing of people between teams. The more cross-team sharing of people, the more meeting overhead these people will have, as well as context switching. If you do have a lot of people shared between two teams, for instance, you might consider what it would be like if they were one big team instead. And if you do that, be mindful of facilitation during meetings—you will need it.

WHAT DOES THE ORGANIZATION LOOK LIKE BEFORE AND AFTER THE RETEAMING?

Create a before-and-after visual representation of your reteaming. Make a copy of your *before* picture. Denote any changes in another color so that they stand out. You can do this on whiteboards if the scope of change will fit. You can do it in an online document that you share. Figure 12-2 shows a very simplistic example of visualizing team changes.

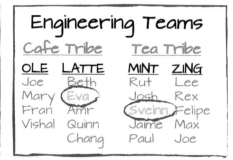

Figure 12-2. Example of visualizing the before and after

Even if you're not reteaming right now, having a visual of who is on what team can help people when they forget each others' names—which happens a lot when your company is growing fast.

WHAT TECHNOLOGY SYSTEMS OR OTHER EQUIPMENT NEEDS TO BE UPDATED OR ACQUIRED WITH THE RETEAMING INITIATIVE?

Once your teams change, you want them to be able to start working together immediately. With some advanced planning, you can make this go smoother. Getting any tooling ready in advance is what comes to mind. What do your teams rely on to get their work done? Think about the tools that your teams use, as well as any adjustments you will need to make to the tools to ensure the workflow gets off to a good start. For example, consider updating the tools your company might use for tracking management-to-direct-report relationships, for managing your code repository, for managing your work tickets or user stories, for managing documentation, and for managing online communication such as chat or email.

WHAT SEATING OR OFFICE CHANGES WILL TAKE PLACE ALONG WITH THE RETEAMING?

If you work in a physical office, there are likely IT and facilities implications of your reteaming, so plan for them in advance. It would be great if all of our work facilities were set up so that we could move our desks around whenever we want. For some that is not so easy because furniture is relatively fixed in place. Working with your IT and facilities departments in advance can help get any desk moves coordinated in step with your reteaming time line. If your entire team is remote, this whole situation is quite simplified, except for time-zone implications if people are located around the globe.

WHAT TRAINING OR EDUCATION IS NEEDED WITH THE RETEAMING?

Many times your newly formed or changed teams are a forcing function for learning. In particular, consider what new areas people need to grasp in order to be successful. For instance, do your engineers need to learn how to code in a different programming language? Is there a new domain area that they need to understand and master, like accounting? What is the age, quantity, and quality of any existing code that they will be working with in the new team? Have they seen anything like it before? Does it have tests? Taking these thoughts into consideration is kind to team members and attempts to acknowledge the reality that they need some ramp-up time in order to be fully productive.

WHAT IS THE COMMUNICATION PLAN FOR THE RETEAMING INITIATIVE?

Besides coming up with your new reteaming structure, you need to communicate really well about it. In particular, take into consideration questions like the following:

- Who needs to know what, and when?
- How will you inform the team members impacted by the changes?
- How will you inform the people who interact with those impacted?

Planning the communication is not to be taken lightly. Some organizations even have communication specialists who are skilled in crafting "the messaging."

Reteaming is change, and it can cause fear in your organization. In one reteaming I've been involved with, a team member heard about it and asked if there were going to be any layoffs. That was so incredibly far from the truth because our reteaming involved *hiring* more than 20 people. People make assumptions when they hear partial information, and fear kicks in. This is what you are trying to prevent, and frankly it's tricky.

In his book, *The Advantage*, Patrick Lencioni advises communicating about any key issue or change at least seven times. This can't be underemphasized.

Include in your FAQ the list of forums where people can find out more about the reteaming. Consider having daily standups about the reteaming offered in the same location and inclusive of any remote team members. You could also have a weekly all-hands meeting with your department to go over key information about the reteaming with an "ask me anything" component to it.

WHAT IS THE SCHEDULE FOR THE RETEAMING INITIATIVE?

Ideally you will have a lead for the reteaming initiative who will be the overall project manager for this change. That lead can create a time line with milestones and drive it so your reteaming moves along and does not stagnate. This lead can send regular updates on the status of the reteaming to the pertinent online channels. Here are some key milestones from a reteaming initiative I was part of, shown in Figure 12-3.

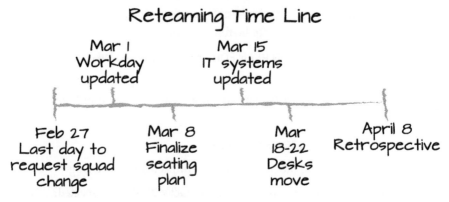

Figure 12-3. An example reteaming time line

Structure and communication about your reteaming initiative is important so you can try to decrease the uncertainty and confusion that will always be present.

WHAT IS THE FEEDBACK PLAN FOR THE RETEAMING INITIATIVE?

Plan a retrospective or survey that will be conducted when you declare the reteaming to be done. Ask: How did it go? What did you learn? The step that is sometimes forgotten is *closing the loop* and learning how we can do reteamings better next time in our organization. Taking the time to send a follow-up survey, or holding an in-person retrospective meeting after the fact is suggested. Refer to the survey template in Appendix C as a baseline to modify and send out in your organization.

Although this list of questions to consider for your reteaming is extensive, it's likely not exhaustive. You most likely have context-dependent requirements for organizational change like this. Take the time to think it through with your collaborators and communicate often.

If you haven't embarked on a larger-scale reteaming before, maybe this section has shed some light on the complexities of the endeavor. Invest the time to plan for a larger reteaming. You'll be glad you did. I always try to operate such that I can give it my all, with the goal that I will look back on the reteaming and feel proud of how it was planned and executed. Be kind to yourself and know that things will go wrong. This stuff is not easy to do.

Once you have reteamed, you might think your teams are ready to hit the ground running. While that may be true for some teams and individuals, it could be that, for others, there is still a great deal of transition happening. That, as well as how to deliberately start up your teams, is the subject of the next chapter.

13

After Dynamic Reteaming: Transitions and Team Calibrations

After you've reteamed, the work is not over. In fact, it could very well be that even though your teams have changed structurally, the people are still emotionally transitioning over to their new team realities. Don't forget that you're dealing with humans. You can't just snap them into place and expect them to adapt as quickly as you might want them to.

As with any organizational change, things take time. People need to get used to changes and settle in. This is not always easy. I've been reteamed without my input more than once, and sometimes it's really hard to shift into the new reality.

On the flip side, imagine if you included the people in the reteaming decision-making process—like through a whiteboard reteaming or marketplace reteaming described in the appendices to this book. They would most likely feel greater ownership of the change and, I'd argue, would be further along in their acceptance of this change. In that case, some of this preliminary processing of transition might not be needed. You can probably jump ahead to the tactics described in "Team Calibration Sessions" on page 198.

In this chapter, I will first share some personal stories of times when I've been reteamed unexpectedly and had to transition over and deal with it. I give advice for others who are going through this, and I hope that leaders will glean some empathy about what might happen in their teams when they engage in a top-down reteaming initiative.

Following that, I have some tips on how leaders in organizations can coach teams through dynamic reteaming, along with an exploration of the concept of transition. So let's explore some ways to cope when you get surprised by reteaming.

Coping with Unexpected Dynamic Reteaming

More than once, I've been reteamed out of teams or had changes inflicted on me. These were situations in which I really wasn't ready for a change; however, the changes happened, and I had to deal with them or move on. This can also be viewed as *surprising* creative destruction—a concept alluding to the back loop of the ecocycle that includes an unsettling, disruptive, or destructive phase, as described in Chapter 1. I have found that it can be quite common, especially in companies experiencing hypergrowth, to get disrupted unexpectedly unless you are higher up in the organizational chart and privy to the information.

When I was reteamed out, things felt bad—at least initially—and I didn't like what was going on. I felt like I had no control over the situation. As the years have passed, I've developed a bit of perspective, and I like to think that my coping abilities have advanced and that I've become more resilient; however, it's still hard for me when this happens, and it takes a bit of time to get over the hump of acceptance of the new reality. Here are some tactics that I have acquired along the way that have helped me deal with unexpected dynamic reteaming.

NOTICE THE TRIGGERING, THEN CHANNEL YOUR THOUGHTS

When I was at Expertcity, the first startup I joined, and our first product failed, we needed to kill it and pivot over to doing other things, as explained in the preface to this book. When this happened, I was so distraught. I was working as an interaction designer, and together with the engineers on my team, I had dreamed up other features and future directions for this product. All the hopes and dreams I had for it were taken away. I was so emotionally upset and tearful about this. Little did I know, I was about to be reteamed over to a new team, using the isolation pattern described in Chapter 7. That shift forced me into a new beginning, and I thrived in it (and so did the company), but at the time of the reteaming I didn't know it would play out like that. Here's what happened.

When this was going down, and I heard that our product was killed, I told a colleague that I thought I would "fight for the product." That I would "show some passion." So I wrote a long email to our leadership explaining why we shouldn't kill the product.

A day or so after I sent the message, I calmed down and didn't feel the rush of emotion like I had felt days before. And then I became uncomfortable. The situation kept me up at night. What were leaders going to think of me? Am I going to be perceived as dramatic or difficult? Did I just make a big mistake? Some might say that I probably felt psychologically safe to express my thoughts in this way, and that is a good thing. That could be, but days after, as I was reflecting on this situation, I felt like I did not want that behavior to become my "style," and I did not want to be known for behaving like that.

My takeaway is this: When you get upset about how things have changed, whether it's your team assignment or the work your team is doing, the adrenaline is most likely pumping strong through your body. Notice that energy within you. For me, it shows up as my heart pounding, and I get anxious to respond and feel like I will be incredibly articulate if I *do* respond in the heat of the moment. What I have learned from experience is that I am not super effective when my emotions are high and I feel triggered.

My advice to you is to first start with your own self-awareness. How are you feeling physically? Do you notice any tension? Notice your breathing and heartbeat. Are they different than when you are in a normal state? If so, give yourself some time to process what is going on. Literally, take a breather. Maybe a day off. If exercise is your thing, this is the time to lean into that.

If you feel compelled to respond publicly in the situation, you have the right to choose to do so. Your style might very well be different from mine. Maybe you will be more articulate than I can be.

But if you're not sure, instead try writing your thoughts in a safe space like a text document or on paper to get them out. Do it until you feel empty, like you have no more thoughts to express. Channel your ideas. Later, when you notice that you have calmed down physically, read what you wrote and determine what to do with it. You can always get a second opinion from someone you trust before sharing widely.

One-on-one discussions are another technique that I have found to be helpful when going through dynamic reteaming that I did not expect.

TALK ONE-ON-ONE WITH LEADERS ABOUT THE CHANGE

I was at a company on a team for a couple of years, and then I was reorged out of that team and onto another one. It hit me hard emotionally because I had been with that team for two years. Suddenly I was not in the biweekly standup, I was not in the Slack channels, and I was not in the tactical meetings. Whenever I'd look at my phone to see what was going on, the channels were gone on Slack. I really felt dismissed and left out.

I was reorged over to a group where I had an opportunity to have more responsibility, but I was personally hurt that I had been booted out of that original team. It kept me up at night. I thought it was the beginning of the end for me at that company. I was really distraught. It was the opposite feeling of belonging.

After a day or so, I chatted with the leader who had asked me to leave. She pointed out that the topics of discussion among her group did not pertain to my goals anymore, and that I was in a different part of the organization now. Both facts were true. She said that she thought I was probably wasting my time in her meetings, and that when she's in a meeting that doesn't help her to attain her goals, she excuses herself so that she can make the best use of her time.

And then she said this: "First figure out the impact you want to make at the company, and what outcomes you need to have happen in order to create that impact. Then, get the people together who will partner with you on the outcomes. That is a better use of your time." And she was right. She had just essentially unlocked some tools for me to become self-directed.

After about three days, and this leader's sage advice, I saw this whole situation differently. I saw that I had an opportunity, and that I could draw the lines of meetings differently than I had done before. My perspective on this situation had changed completely. What if this leader hadn't told me to leave? I would have wasted hours each week just due to habit. It probably would have dawned on me at some point to excuse myself. But I'm glad I didn't stagnate there. I'm glad I had moved through creative destruction (in Chapter 1 terms) and was starting my phase of renewal. You can, too—try the *What's Your Impact?* activity that follows.

Sometimes we have people we can reach out and talk to about changes that are happening around us, like I did in this case. The manager's role is to be there for us to try to help us succeed in our roles within our companies. That is the natural person to turn to when there is a lot of reteaming going on. I chose to talk with a key leader who was closer to the reteaming that I was experiencing.

You could also talk with a coach or a mentor. I suggest finding a coach that could work with you and help you make sense of your own professional growth. This coach does not have to work in your organization. There are a variety of coaches that work either over the telephone or the internet who can help you succeed if you make the investment into hiring them. Call a few and have a sample session with them. Then choose a coach who resonates with you.[1]

What's Your Impact? Activity

You've just been reteamed. Even if you're not thrilled about it, you choose to press forward. Here is one proactive path to consider:

1. What is the biggest impact that you can make going forward? Write down some ideas. Talk with colleagues, your manager, and other trusted advisors. Pick one idea that is meaningful and motivating to you. Write it on a sticky note. Put it on your monitor.

2. Make a list: What are three outcomes you need to create in order to make that impact?

3. Find partners. Talk with them about the impact and outcomes. Choose one outcome, and start working toward it.

Here's my example:

1. Impact: Software engineers work at a sustainable pace, and give more predictable forecasts of when their work will be done.

2. Outcomes:

   a. Engineering managers understand and are aware of how cycle-time stability connects to forecasting.

   b. Managers coach their teams to visualize their workflow and stabilize their cycle times.

   c. Teams leverage their stable cycle times for forecasting when work will be done.

3. Partners: To get this to happen, I form a coalition of people who think this is important in my company: an architect, a project manager, a QA engineer, and a key engineering manager.

---

1 To find a credentialed coach, check out the Find a Coach resources at the International Coaching Federation website (*https://coachfederation.org/find-a-coach*).

GET SOME DISTANCE—PHYSICALLY OR MENTALLY

When I was consulting, and the client was being taken over by a competitor, the full-time employees were told that we would know "what the changes were going to be" in engineering in two weeks, as I wrote about in Chapter 8. The management was essentially saying that you'd know whether you still have a job after two weeks because they did not have enough capacity to lay people off all at once.

As you might imagine, this was a tense and frightful time for many people. People assumed they were going to be laid off, even when their jobs were potentially "safe." My body felt physically bad in that environment due to all of this dysfunction. And I could imagine that others felt physically bad as well. People certainly vented about the situation when we had group lunches. Maybe that released some of the fear and tension that many of us were experiencing.

Looking back on this situation three years later, here is what I would advise to these colleagues now if I could turn back the clock. I would suggest that, if they can, they should try to get some physical distance away from the workplace. If you need to have your "butt in the seat" at work, this might not be possible.

If you must be there physically, however, maybe your mind can be elsewhere. Dive into learning something new. Read that book that you have wanted to read, the one that would help you attain mastery of your craft. You can apply that learning whether you stay or leave your company.

I think some people like to, and can, stay focused on the actual work. If that's you, go for it.

If none of those ideas resonate with you, maybe you can take some sick days. Over the years I've taken sick days when I have had emotional challenges. Sometimes being at home and lounging around is just what is needed.

People will respond in different ways when reteaming happens. It's important to recognize the human factor in all of this, which brings us to the next topic: empathy.

EMPATHY IS ESSENTIAL WHEN CATALYZING DYNAMIC RETEAMING

When reteaming happens to us and we are not ready for it, it can be extremely emotional, as I have shared here. I think leaders need to remember this. If leaders have the personal experiences of being reteamed without their input, maybe they will have greater empathy.

If people are included in the decision making around reteaming, it could be that the fear and discomfort is still there, but at least they can have a say in how it plays out. I think it reduces some risk. That's why I like the inclusive ideas of organizing reteaming with whiteboards and as a marketplace as described in Appendix A and Appendix B.

If you think about it, after you undergo a structural change of your teams, there is some follow-up movement of how the people actually acclimate to the changes. I've shared my personal stories in this chapter so far, and from that experience, and from 20 years of dynamic reteaming, I'll now share some perspective on how to coach people who are going through dynamic reteaming that they didn't necessarily sign up for.

Transitions—Coaching People Through Dynamic Reteaming

If we think about the ecocycle metaphor again, as shown in Figure 13-1, we can imagine that creative destruction is the place where dynamic reteaming happens. In this particular visual, you can see the bumpy line that I've inserted in that part of the diagram to represent the confusion, uncertainty, and in-between space that exists around the time of the actual changes. Maybe there are more bumps when we are caught off guard, or when we are having a hard time dealing with the change.

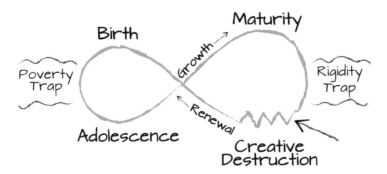

Figure 13-1. An ecocycle highlighting the bumpy path of creative destruction, where dynamic reteaming takes place

Many people would like to think that they can reteam a group of people, by applying the patterns in this book, for example, as a mechanical process, and then they can just get on with it and start over as a new team without some processing time. That is shortsighted, and is one of the reasons I wrote this book—so that we can get better at reteaming, and make the shift from managing as a mechanistic process to bringing more humanity into our reteaming instead.

It may be that the reteaming is unemotional for some people in teams. For others, I think it's important to recognize that the path to renewal and starting again as a new team might be far from smooth, especially if they didn't want the dynamic reteaming to happen. People could be experiencing great feelings of loss, as if experiencing a type of death. There could also be a lot of uncertainty and fear as they wonder what their new reality might be like. Thoughts of COVID-19 and its cascading, unknown effects come to mind.

Moreover, think about the case of getting fired, being laid off, or moving to a team that you didn't want to join. In that case, instant acceptance of the new situation is not likely. It takes time to get through and start renewal. You need to first pass through some transition.

Transitions are a concept discussed in depth by William Bridges in his seminal book on the topic. In particular, he talks about change as a concept that is abstracted into three general phases: the ending, the neutral zone, and the new beginning. However, he also points out that these aren't necessarily linear, and that you can get stuck in the neutral zone.

The neutral zone is the space between the ending and the new beginning, and it's often a strange time of "confusion and distress." Bridges credits this neutral zone concept back to the Dutch anthropologist Arnold van Gennep, who wrote about it in terms of "rites of passage."[2]

Teams are, at best, coached through dynamic reteaming by managers and team coaches. Investing the time into deliberate activities to help teams through change will help your dynamic reteaming initiative have a greater chance of success.

The following are the topics to focus on when coaching teams through change:

- Talk about the ending
- Mark the ending with a ritual
- Suggest what to bring forward
- Calibrate as a new team.

The rest of this chapter is devoted to sharing practical ideas on each of these topics, starting with having open discussions about the endings.

---

2 Bridges, *Transitions*, 141.

TALK ABOUT THE ENDING

The announcement of a reteaming may be cascaded to us from on high in the organization through an all-hands meeting, or in a meeting within our immediate department. We might hear about upcoming changes from our manager, or from a rumor started in our team area. When we hear about impending changes and take them in, our minds can wander into dark spaces, and we can make up scenarios that just aren't true, like in the story in Chapter 8 of the engineer who thought he was getting laid off but wasn't.

Talking as a team about the reteaming changes that are forthcoming is what I recommend. I was in a leadership team once, and some of our peers got promoted, and we started reporting to them. These changes had happened gradually over a couple of months, but we hadn't talked about the situation all together as a group. It was almost like a silent reteaming, managed outside of our public team space via one-on-one discussions. Once we had a collective discussion about what happened, during an offsite meeting with a consultant, I was able to start the process of getting over the change and moving on. A couple of my colleagues who were in a similar position expressed the same sentiment.

Sometimes you just need to *name it* together in order to process it and get over it. We needed to accept that things weren't going to change back to the way they used to be. We needed to adapt and move on into our new hierarchical structure, and we all didn't foresee or want things to evolve in that way, but they did. Talking about it helps, although I will admit that, for me, the act of doing so was incredibly painful in my chest for two days, as I apparently took the change very hard. After that time, however, I felt better and was really able to move on. Hiring a consultant to help teams adapt to new reporting changes or dramatic reteams is highly recommended. I suppose we could have processed this change individually with our managers or coaches; however, there was something important about discussing the changes with our preliminary team system. Hearing from other team members about the changes was revealing for me, and helped me to feel closure to that chapter.

Being able to shift over to new reporting structures, and other organizational changes like reteaming, is a skill for your organization to develop. One senior engineering VP once mentioned to our leadership team that we need to get better at our "time to adapt" metric—that is, our ability to shift forward into the changes that must take place to get our company to the next level. It's not that we were collecting a metric about this per se, it was just the idea that we needed to deal with change in an expedient fashion. Doing that can indeed be a strategic advantage.

Alas, it's not always that easy, since we are dealing with sentient creatures. We do the best that we can. Taking the time to acknowledge the ending of how things used to be is kind to the humans, and it helps us shift forward. Another thing you can do along those lines is to mark endings with rituals.

MARK THE ENDING WITH A RITUAL

A ritual is a thing that you do to mark a transition or a passage in time. One ritual that we are probably all familiar with is the birthday party. Throughout our lives, when we have a birthday, we might also have a party to commemorate and mark the occasion. In western culture, symbols like the birthday cake and the ritual of blowing out candles are a part of that tradition as well. Funerals and memorials mark the ending of people's lives in a public recognition of the end.

You can incorporate the idea of ritual into the endings you experience at your company, like Rachel Davies told us about, as you might recall from Chapter 6. She told the story of her first team at Unruly Software. The team split in half, and one of the members decided to mark the occasion and bring in a cake inspired by *The Lord of the Rings* as a symbol of the splitting of the fellowship, or in their case, their company's first team. They were marking the ending with the ritual of a party, with the symbol of a cake.

Another way to mark an ending is to have a retrospective where you celebrate the accomplishments of your team as it is dissolving. You might consider doing the activity called *The Story of Our Team*, described in "Team Calibration Sessions" on page 198. In this activity, you make a shared time line as a team, either in person, or online via a shared document or whiteboard. You list the key milestones and accomplishments you shared as a team. As such, it's a great exercise to look back, appreciate what you did together, speak about it out loud to really acknowledge it, and then get ready to move on. A less formal activity would be to have a happy hour or a team dinner to mark the ending of your team. If you do that, have a toast where people share their thoughts on what they are proud of from being on the team.

Marking the ending with a ritual helps you and your team remember that although things are done, there are likely some things that you want to "take with you" to your new team, which is discussed in the following section.

SUGGEST WHAT TO BRING FORWARD

As we saw in Chapter 5, when someone leaves your team, the remaining members might take the time to make a list of the things the team member did that were outside their job description, and that the team wants to continue doing and carry forward. Maybe Joe used to bring the donuts to the team meeting on Fridays. That was not in his job description, but it became a part of the team culture. Having the discussion of what to carry forward and continue doing as a team is the idea.

You can also do a deliberate team transition activity, if you just went through a large and disruptive dynamic reteaming, like a reorg that created brand-new teams out of people from other teams. This exercise, inspired by William Bridges, is designed to give each person time to think about some key questions individually, and then have pair discussions to process the situation. Sharing beyond the pair is completely optional. Here's how I like to do it.

Team Transition Activity

First answer the questions individually, then discuss in pairs. Then invite, but don't force, sharing with all. See what you can uncover together. You can also go through questions like these during a one-on-one coaching session with a team member who has switched over to a new team:

- What do you need to let go of from your past team as you transition over to our new team?
- What are you happy to leave behind?
- What will you miss?
- What is important from your past team experience to import into your new team?

Invite someone on the team to make a list of the actions to take in your new team going forward. Have you uncovered any team agreements? Get a consensus and move forward as a team in your new beginning.

At the end of this activity, consider asking each person to write down how they will "be there" for their new team going forward. Ask people to finish this statement: "Going forward, you can count on me to..." Then ask people to share, one by one, what they wrote.

The team transition activity can be used as a segue into more team calibration exercises. You've likely already acknowledged your ending with a team, and have talked about what you want to bring forward. Now you are ready to design your new team deliberately. Let's move on to how to run team calibrations.

Team Calibration Sessions

When teams come together for the first time, or when their composition changes so much that it really feels like a *new* team, there are things you can do to deliberately help the teams understand the history of the change they've been through as well as understand each other better as people. You can also help them to align on their roles, to understand their new areas of work, and to gain clarity on their workflow for collaboration.

Sure, you could leave all of these things to chance, or you could help reduce your risk and encourage the team gel and scaffolding proactively by investing in team calibration sessions. These are facilitated sessions that focus on how to work effectively as a team.

There isn't a one-size-fits-all set of activities for a team calibration. Each team is different and has different needs and personalities. What I do in my day-to-day work is talk with a couple of team members beforehand, get an idea of what the team is like, learn how much time they want to invest in a calibration session, and then propose a set of activities to see if it resonates with the team. I encourage the product manager and engineering lead to get a sneak peek at the calibration plans to foster alignment before meeting with the entire team. Once the plan comes together, either I facilitate the activities for the team, or I train an interested team member or two who are motivated to run the activities themselves.

Having calibration sessions is a time investment. You can bundle team calibration activities together into a half-day or day-long offsite meeting, or you can gradually do the activities over a week or so in two-hour chunks. It's up to your team.

So let's dig into four calibration areas: history, people and roles, work, and workflow. That schema serves as the organization of the rest of this chapter.

CALIBRATE ON HISTORY

Teams that merge together, like we read about in Chapter 8, can benefit from telling their new collective team about their roots. What are people proud of from their previous teams? What are they excited to share about their past with their new team entity?

In addition, if you are in a context that has doubled in size, like you will read about in "After Your Team Doubles in Size" on page 211, it's a good idea to "connect together" the team members who have been there for a long time, even years, to the people who might have just joined the team in the last couple of months. You do this with a facilitated activity that I call *The Story of Our Team*. It is inspired by an activity called *The Epic Tale*, which is credited to Grace Flannery, Leigh Marz, and Judith MacBrine.[3] It's also related to the concept of "myth change" in the Organization and Relationship Systems Coaching (ORSC) tradition.[4]

Keep in mind that when teams merge together, and when people join a new team, there is a period of transition. I think this particular activity helps people get closure on the past, as it were, just by visualizing and vocalizing the past. That's an important step toward integrating into a new team situation.

Outcomes you get from doing this activity are an acknowledgment and celebration of milestones and accomplishments from the past, respect for teammates, inclusion of new team members into the existing storyline, and an overall greater sense of being "one team."

The Story of Our Team Activity

Create a time line that tells the history of your team. Use it for team cohesion and as a team artifact for future new hires. This activity can be done in person or virtually. If you are in person, the best place to do this activity is in a room with ample space on the walls or windows. It

---

3 A write-up of this activity can be found online. (*http://www.orscglobal.com/.ee82b1a*) To learn more about these three collaborators, visit their web sites: Leading Spirit, (*http://leadingspirit.com*) MarzConsulting, (*http://leighmarz.com*) and The Mirror Group (*http://themirrorgroup.com*).

4 In Organization and Relationship Systems Coaching (ORSC™), your team's original myth is the founding story of your team. It's why and how you came together. *Myth change* relates to changes to your team entity. In this case, it's helpful to anchor back to your origin story in order to process changes and to raise positivity in the new team situation.

also works in a long hallway. If doing this virtually, you can use a shared drawing or whiteboard, along with individual video, and a breakout room feature so that you can put people into small groups. It works like this:

1. Tell the team that together they will be creating a shared history of their team by creating a time line and then making a low-fi video of them telling the story of their team.

2. If in the physical world, as the participants are entering the space, ask them to help you put flip-chart paper on the wall— each page side by side. Then, using a bold marker, draw a horizontal line across the middle of the conjoined papers. On the far right of the line, write *today*. If you are doing this online, just do the same thing in a document or whiteboard, like Miro or Mural. You can also use a Google drawing or even a shared Google slide deck to do this. See what you have available, and test out the technology beforehand. If you are doing this with teams or companies that have merged together, start by drawing one line, and then later encourage the people to draw branches connecting to the main line, which represent the groups that have merged in.

3. Ask participants to physically stand, walk to the time line, and line up along the time line corresponding to when they joined the team. This is an activity that is bursting with dialogue as people talk to each other to figure out when each person started at the company. There's typically a lot of excitement as people "find each other." Next, tell them to write their names and start dates on a sticky note, and place it on the time line. If doing this virtually, have each person individually type their names and start dates on the virtual time line. Your time line is coming alive!

4. Next, group the people based on their start dates. Depending on the size of the team, groups of three to four work best. Tell them to have a conversation, and to write down significant events and milestones on sticky notes to place on the time line that tell *the story of our team*. Have them also list team members who joined and left along the way, and any happenings from the company or world as a whole that had significance to them. We do this with sticky notes because people like to move things around during

this activity, and to pile up duplications. If you are virtual, you can place people who started on the team at about the same time into breakout rooms to do this task.

5. Once the time line seems relatively filled out (it only takes about 8–10 minutes), tell them that you will next record them telling the *story of their team*.

6. Invite one of the participants to be the camera person, and have them record on their phone with airplane mode on so their video does not get interrupted. Instruct them to walk the time line, and record the people telling the story, along the time line, one by one. I do not force everyone to talk; instead, I just see what happens. If you are virtual, share your screen and click *record* in the remote meeting tool that you are using.

7. When they are finished telling the story of their team, take the time to debrief. I ask questions like: What was surprising about this activity? What did you learn that you really want to celebrate? Why is the work of this team important?

8. Then I typically get the team into dreaming about and vocalizing what they want the future of their team to be like by asking something like: What are your dreams for the future of this team? What do you want it to be like? If you are doing this in person, have people write down ideas individually, and then share. If online, have people type their ideas into the chat tool of your online meeting platform. This mixes up the modalities so it's not all speaking out loud. Then, debrief that.

9. To close, have the team stand in a circle. Ask each person to complete this phrase: "Going forward, you can count on me to..." Then instruct them to toss a ball or soft object to the next person to do the same, and so on. If doing this online, have people type their thoughts in the regular chat tool that people use for their team. Then have them read off what they wrote, one by one.

Doing this activity really helps to set the context for the changes that have happened in your team or across multiple teams or groups. It's a kind of team glue and positivity raiser.

Once you have created this shared history for the collective team, you can dig into accelerating the relationships on the team, which is the next section.

CALIBRATE ON PEOPLE AND ROLES

Sharing information about ourselves at work can help accelerate the gel of our teams. Sharing across multiple teams can be even more powerful as a tactic because it's easier to reteam later when people aren't complete strangers, as we discussed in Chapter 11.

Each team that comes together is comprised of unique personalities. Celebrate that and appreciate the differences. The go-to activities I rely on to accelerate getting to know each other are *Market of Skills* and *Peak Experiences*.

Market of Skills is an activity that takes under two hours, depending how many people are on your team. I was introduced to a variation of this activity by Lyssa Adkins, who cites Bent Myllerup as the originator in her book *Coaching Agile Teams*.[5]

I've modified and adapted this activity for years. I've used it with teams of 12 people or fewer as a centralized activity, and I've also modified and scaled it to use with 30–50 people. You could even go beyond that. And, you can do it in person or online. I often extend this activity to help teams get greater role clarity, as you will see.

The outcomes you get when doing this activity include common ground, a celebration of our differences, increased respect from learning what others can do that you can't do, visibility of learning goals, offers to help each other, positivity, role clarity, and closer relationships as a team. The following describes how I do it.

Market of Skills Activity

Have each person write down the following about themselves, either in a shared online slide deck—one slide per person—or on a poster if in the physical world (7 minutes):

- Name

- Role on the team

- Skills I bring to the team

---

5 Adkins, *Coaching Agile Teams*, 153–154.

- Hobbies and special interests
- What I want to learn in the next three months
- What I offer to teach you
- What I need from others to succeed in my role

When finished, have each person present. (2 minutes)

After each person presents, have everyone else take a minute to respond to what they said by sharing the following information:

- The other skills and talents that you know they posses, but did not mention
- Kudos, appreciations, and "bingos" for when you share their interests
- Book recommendations and resources you think they might like
- Specific ways that you want to help them to succeed in their role

If you are doing this online, people can type their reactions into the speaker notes portion of the slide deck, or if in person, people can write on sticky notes to affix to posters. Give the group one minute to create these reactions after each poster is presented.

If you have 10 or more people for this activity, have people first create their virtual or physical posters, have them share what they wrote in pairs, and then switch pairs three times. Then have people write their reactions to what they heard. Recently, when doing this activity with 65 people in a large workshop room, I played music while people walked from poster to poster to write their reactions. It really feels like a lively marketplace.

To conclude this activity, debrief as an entire group. You can ask questions like, What surprised you? What did you notice that we have in common? What are you learning about our team? Based on what you learned from your teammates, what do you want to do now?

I find that some teams like to have a team outing based on their interests, or start book clubs, or decide to have lunch-and-learn sessions to teach each other what they know. The information discussed in this activity could also feed into individual development plans or collective team development plans.

A third activity that I love to do with teams goes a little bit deeper than the others. It is the sharing of peak experiences.

Getting beyond the "surface" when you first reteam with someone can sometimes be challenging. In the Peak Experience activity, each person shares an influential and memorable story from their past and explains how it impacted their life.

After sharing our peak experience with our partners, our partners summarize our peak experiences with the whole team. After each person presents their partner's story like this, we then write down the values that are present in the stories told. Then we have a discussion and talk about the frequency of our collective team values.

I've done this activity with teams in conference rooms and online using breakout rooms, but I love it more when I do it with teams outside: going for a walk or a hike in nature, pausing at the peak or midpoint to share our partner's stories, and then walking back with free and open conversation to where we started.

Peak Experiences Activity

Have each person find a partner, ideally someone they don't know very well. Tell people that as they start their walk, they will tell their partner about a peak experience in their life—it could be a very significant event that transpired, a key learning or realization that they had, or even a challenge that they overcame. Tell the person who is listening to pay attention because they will summarize their partner's peak experience later in the activity. If you are virtual, you can place the pairs in breakout rooms for this discussion.

After the first person finishes telling their peak experience, their partner shares their own. If you are out walking, allow 15 minutes for each person to tell their story. If you are inside, allow 10 minutes for each person. Next, reconvene as the team. If you are outside, stand in a circle, or sit, and have each person tell the gist of their partner's peak experiences. If you are inside, just have the group together at a table, or online together. After the recounting of each experience, ask the group what "values" they think are present in the story they just heard. Write the values on a shared list. Examples of values might include things like trust, honesty, courage, leadership, and bravery.

After you hear the recounting of each peak experience, review the complete list of values together. These are the values that are present on this team. Put them in order of frequency. This list of team values can be pinned to the team's chat channel, or written down and put up on the wall if the team has a physical space. Ask the team members if they want to adopt this as their team values.

So far in this chapter I have shared four team activities that anyone can facilitate to help teams gel faster and become more comfortable with each other. I would most likely do only two of these activities with a team that is getting started. And I don't inflict these activities on a team. If a team has no interest in doing activities like these, we don't do them. The general rule is to invite and not force things on people.

Resources

The following are a couple more resources to help with team gel:

- Personal Maps (*https://management30.com/practice/personal-maps*), by Jurgen Apello, are a visual way to introduce yourself to others. You can create your own mind map with yourself in the center and branch out with family, friends, and hobbies, or you can get with a partner, tell them about yourself, and they can draw the mind map.

- *Constellation* is an interactive activity that I learned from Co-Active Training Institute (CTI) and Lyssa Adkins. You can do it in the following way: Ask the team to stand in a circle, then place an object in the center. Say a statement like, "I am a morning person." If that is true for you, walk toward the center. If it's not, walk away from the center. Then look around the room and debrief. Continue with other statements to help the team get to know each other and then ask people to write down their own statement, and then constellate like this. You can do this online by using a shared drawing document or whiteboard. Just draw an object to represent the center of your constellation, and have each team orient an avatar or virtual sticky note close or far away from the center of the constellation.

Who we are as people and what our preferences are is one vital component of a team calibration, but why does our team even exist in the first place? The next part of a team calibration session is getting clear about what the team is paid to do.

CALIBRATE ON WORK

It's always a good idea to get really clear on why your team exists, and why your company is paying you to do the work of your team. When we're motivated about the work we get to do, and our company really needs that work, it's really the sweet spot of professional life.

Here are the basics that I like to cover about "the work" during a team calibration. It starts with digging into several questions in what I call the *Work Alignment* activity.

I've worked with these questions for years, usually partnering with engineering managers and product managers who often like to create and present slide decks to answer some of the questions in advance, and then get with the teams to figure out the rest. Many times for this activity I'm behind the scenes, coaching the product and engineering managers to cover this material with their teams.

Work Alignment Activity

As a team, work through the answers to these questions and document your answers in your shared online space. Or, if you are in a colocated space, create a board or wall that showcases this information.

- What is the mission of our team? What are the outcomes that we are expected to produce to attain our mission? Who are the people and their roles on our team? For many teams, this information is a given and might connect to objectives and key results (OKRs) or higher-level company goals. However, I've worked with other teams who own particular software tools in their organization, and who really need to come together and drive their identity and impact. I coach these teams to experiment and learn rapidly via customer interaction.

- What are the current "big rocks" or epics the team is working on, and what are the top three priorities in that work? This information is typically driven by a product manager and engineering lead, in my experience. It's important to encourage engineers during these discussions to always illuminate the work that is "under the hood" that needs to be prioritized, like an equal citizen to feature work. This could be, for example, larger-scale refactorings that really need to be done, that are discovered while doing other work.

- What existing code and tools does our team own and maintain? How will we balance maintenance and identification of engineering-driven work that must be prioritized along with our product-driven work? We create new things, and we maintain things that were there before us. It's important to acknowledge that we can't just add new things without care and feeding of the code that is already there. Moreover, we need to discuss how we will handle tickets to fix issues that get reported to us from our customer service friends. Managing that relationship for our team can be deliberate, and I've seen teams do it in different ways—in some cases it's handled by quality assurance, and in other cases it's funneled to the product manager.

- How does our work get prioritized, and who owns that decision making? In frameworks like Scrum, there is a product owner role that officially owns the work priority. In practice, I've seen this play out in the best case when that product manager works with the engineers on the team and encourages healthy discussions about priority. It may be that changing the order of the product manager's priority list makes the most sense from an engineering perspective. Having open conversations together as one team and fostering a shared understanding of the best way to approach work is the key here.

- How will we as a team communicate the status of our work to others outside of the team? We don't exist as islands with no communication with the outside world. Each team needs to keep the rest of the teams and leadership informed of the progress of its work. Mature companies have this built into their structures. In many evolving companies I've been a part of, the teams take the ownership to radiate out their accomplishments, deliveries, and future road maps. It's a good team discussion to have if your organization does not have this built in. Own your communication plan.

- How will we know if we've built the right thing for our customers? How will we "close the loop" on the success or failure of what we delivered? Things aren't considered *done* in my mind once you've shipped them. You need to figure out how you are going to close the loop and not just move on to the next thing. What are you learning about the features and value that you deliver? Are you building the right thing? How will you know? In the best case, you have an idea of what success looks like at the beginning of development, and then you collect data after you deploy to find out how it went.

Resources

In addition to focusing on the topics that I have previously suggested, there are other resources that you might consider reviewing to dig deeper into work management. They are as follows:

- For digging into the purpose of your work together if it is not predefined, consider doing the *Purpose to Practice* activity from Liberating Structures (*http://www.liberatingstructures.com*).
- For making your big rock initiatives clear within your team and beyond, consider creating an opportunity canvas for each of them. See Jeff Patton, *User Story Mapping: Discover the Whole Story, Build the Right Product* (*http://http://shop.oreilly.com/product/0636920033851.do*) (O'Reilly, 2014).
- For getting "the work" kicked off and chartered, see Diana Larsen and Ainsley Nies, *Liftoff: Start and Sustain Successful Agile Teams*, 2nd ed (Pragmatic Bookshelf, 2016).

We've gone over some activities to get to know each other as people, and we have also covered how to dig into the work of the team. The final area that I suggest you consider for team calibration sessions is about your workflow.

CALIBRATE ON WORKFLOW

Once we are clear on the work of our team in general, we can discuss how we want to manage our work as it flows through our team system, assuming that our work is shared. Depending on our contexts, this could be as simple as a visual Kanban board on the wall, or online using a variety of tools.

Either way, our work most likely goes through phases. Each phase has an entry and exit point. Defining how you will handle work that enters your flow, and what it means to be "done" at the exit of each phase is imperative.

I figure this out with teams by doing an activity that I call *Own Your Workflow*. The outcome of doing this activity is to get alignment on the agreements you have as a team in terms of collaboration. You also get alignment on the function of different meetings, as well as what it means for work to be considered "ready" and "done" along the way.

Own Your Workflow Activity

Allow two to three hours for this activity. You can do it online using a shared slide deck, whiteboard, or drawing document. If in the physical world, you can do this by drawing on a whiteboard and then taking a picture of the whiteboard as documentation.

- First, ask people to write down on their own a list of how work enters your team system. Talk about it with the group, and come up with one shared list. Sometimes your work comes from product, other times from customer success, and other times from sales. Maybe you even get work directly from your customers. It can come from engineers on your team or in other parts of the organization. The point here is discovery of all the various ways things get into your team system. Should you embark on every piece of work that comes to your team? No. The point of this exercise is to have the discussions about how you will handle the entry points of work areas into your team system, and who will decide the work that carries forward into your flow, or not.

- Next, as a group, write down in your shared document or whiteboard the phases that each type of work passes through in order to be considered finished or delivered to customers. Phases might include things like discovery, grooming, in progress, ready for code review, in code review, ready for testing, in testing, merged, and so on. It could be that in your workplace you have a standard set of phases across all of your boards. That's OK. Write down the phases. The main idea here is to get alignment on how the phases work. When I do this virtually with teams, we use a shared slide deck and list out one phase per slide. Next, dig into each phase, and talk about what it means for work to enter that phase, as follows:

— "For something to be <in progress>, what needs to be true?" or "For something to be <ready for testing>, what needs to be true?"

- Answer this question for each of the phases and write down the answers in your shared slide deck. In doing this step, you will essentially gain alignment and come to some agreements on how your team will collaborate. This is the heart of this activity. Many teams have unspoken agreements about the passage of work, and this activity brings things to light and enables later change.

Through this activity, teams come to agreement on how they want to function as a team, especially across the different roles on the team. It's another way to bring role clarity to the team, in the context of the work that we will do together. Along the way, on each slide, when it becomes clear to me that the team has a proposal for how that workflow phase should function, I teach them how to "poll for agreement" on what they wrote, using the fist of five technique I described in Chapter 8. Using your hand, if you show five fingers it means "I wildly support this idea," four means "I support this idea," three means "I don't feel strongly about this—I'll defer to the team," two means "I have the following clarifications needed before I can support this," and one means "I don't support this." Teaching teams this consensus tool enables them to use it later throughout their team life span.

After articulating the workflow and what it means for work to pass from one phase to another, in subsequent team coaching sessions, I start coaching teams on how to remove delays in their workflows, stabilize their cycle times, lower their work in progress (WIP) limits, and ultimately lower their cycle times. In other words, I teach them how to manage their flow by using Kanban techniques, which is what this approach really is.

Resources

The practices that I have introduced here on flow management are really only a brief pointer to the vast world of managing work that flows through team systems, and it was not my intention to write a thorough Kanban book inside this dynamic reteaming book. Instead, I point you to the following resources for further study:

- For techniques you can use to manage the flow of work through your system and even forecast when work will be done, see: Daniel S. Vacanti, *Actionable Agile Metrics for Predictability: An Introduction* (Daniel S. Vacanti, Inc., 2015), and *When Will It Be Done? Lean-Agile Forecasting To Answer Your Customers' Most Important Question* (Daniel S. Vacanti, Inc., 2020).

- For basics on Kanban and how it relates to Scrum, download "The Kanban Guide for Scrum Teams" (*https://www.scrum.org/resources/kanban-guide-scrum-teams*) by Daniel Vacanti and Yuval Yeret. It's a nice companion to *The Scrum Guide* (*https://www.scrum.org/resources/scrum-guide*).

This section contained the main activities that I draw from when I run a team calibration session. It is quite rare that I do all activities with a team. Sometimes, I do only one of the activities with them, and advise on the other material. Each team system is unique and has different coaching needs. We invite people to do activities like these; we do not force them onto people.

Thus far in this chapter, we have gone over what to do as teams transition into their new team systems, and what to do after they've joined their new team. Taking a step out in our vantage point, let's dig into some techniques to use when your team had doubled or maybe even tripled in size.

After Your Team Doubles in Size

When your organization doubles in size it can sometimes feel surprising, like it has snuck up on you—especially if the growth had followed the one-by-one pattern and was predominantly gradual. One day people notice that there are all of these "new people" around. To the new joiners, they are in a sea of mostly unknown people and are hoping to fit in and be recognized. They see the current state of the company as how it normally is, whereas the people who've been there for a while feel like the company is different from how it's been.

If you are colocated you can see these new people in person, walking around the building. It becomes awkward when you don't remember most people's names. If you are distributed, maybe you notice different names popping up in certain channels in your chat tool. Things become more formalized around you as the organization deploys systems to manage all of the people.[6]

I think a lot of the time people just let the feelings about doubling drift by and don't acknowledge them or do anything to name them or process them. But that's not the way it has to be. I think talking about this team change is healthy and proactive.

In fact, I think you can face this doubling head on and get better at bridging the past and present communities of people together. You can try to unify perspectives on the context. Here are some ideas I have gained from experiencing this personally at three companies.

HELP PEOPLE "SEE" THE ORGANIZATIONAL GROWTH AND KNOW EACH OTHERS' NAMES

We went through some heavy growth phases at AppFolio in product development. I remember when Paul Tevis and I were the two internal coaches resident at the company. One day, as we were discussing our teams, we decided to make a huge visual board so that we could better grasp all the people that were there with us at the company already, and those who were about to join. I think there were nearly 10 teams of roughly 7 people around then. These teams were organized into tribes.

We knew there was a spreadsheet somewhere that managers were using to keep track of this information, but it was not found easily. So we found a whiteboard and pens, and across the top row wrote the team names. In columns under the team names we wrote the names of the people who were on each team. People walked by and commented on the board. They erased names and moved them over to better reflect who was actually on which team since the teams had changed. We did the research to find out who was joining our organization and then displayed the names of the new people next to the teams they were about to join, or we put them in a section that was labeled "coming soon." Later, we would even announce special cross-team events on this board. The board helped people make sense of the changes in the context, and looked similar to the visual shown in Figure 13-2.

---

6 Examples of systems: Workday, to keep track of reporting structures; Okta, to manage the entitlement of software; intranets containing official company information from your People department; and tools to manage performance reviews. And more.

Figure 13-2. An example of visualizing teams on a whiteboard

Later on in our growth at AppFolio, we created an engineering life and culture specialist role who took over the visual board. The written names became low-fi printed and laminated photos of team members. This board essentially converted into a tool for existing people and new people to use to learn each others' names and roles, or *re-learn* this information if it had been forgotten since we had such a fast hiring spurt.

This doesn't really work in the same way, however, if you have a lot more teams. It's not scalable. At another company where we had 50 teams distributed between multiple office locations in the same and different cities, we relied on a centralized spreadsheet to keep track of who was on which team, and it was part of an administrative assistant's job to keep it up to date. After a while, managers were required to update Workday, which is the software this company used to be the single source of truth regarding employee information. From this tool, we could generate a squad list containing the names of the team members across the organization. You'd essentially run a report to see the teams. This depended on the managers updating Workday. Regardless, this artifact was pinned to our main channels in our organizational chat tool. It's what we had. I like the solution Pivotal Software had, as described by Evan Willey in Chapter 9, as a preferred solution to this organizational "seeing." As you might recall, in Pivotal's solution you can see who is on which team, and for how long.

For most of us in larger organizations, we usually find out who is on which team in the moment by asking a point person for the team that we are curious about, or asking the manager of the team. We can search for people in our online chat tool and then inquire if we need further information.

In addition to helping the organization make sense visually and understand who is on each team, I have found it quite useful to stimulate cross-team guilds to launch organizational initiatives as a way to weave the organization together. This can be done as an event to kick-start these connections, as described next.

HELP PEOPLE FIND SHARED CAUSES AND FORM GUILDS

Another tactic for sensemaking and community building when your team doubles in size is helping the people form connections across the organization based on shared interests and action. This can start out as basic as creating "channels" in an organization-wide chat tool and hoping that different interest groups catch on. That is indeed one way that people connect inside organizations on shared ideas, and it's not to be overlooked. People can develop a shared understanding, get answers to questions, share what they are working on, and meet each other this way organically. Announcing the groups that emerge through an organizational announcement can help to draw membership into the channels.

If you want to catalyze a shift in your organization, almost like deliberate creative destruction described in Chapter 1, you might consider having an event to stimulate and kick off some 90-day guilds and initiatives by finding the people who are passionate about them.

At Procore Technologies we held an Operational Excellence event where we hosted an open space conference for 350 people, in conjunction with Dan Mezick, who is a consultant and leader in the open Agile movement.[7]

In our open space conference, we tapped into the intelligence of the people to determine the discussion topics for the day. In structuring that, we posed a challenge similar to this one: "How can we collaborate better going forward across our tribes and squads?"

After opening the event and posing that challenge, participants came up with a variety of 50-minute sessions that they held themselves throughout the day, in an attempt to solve that problem.

We held the event in a large warehouse on our campus, which we divided into sections with numbers. The discussions throughout the day were held across this warehouse—each discussion took place in one of the numbered-off

---

7 See the Procore blog (*https://engineering.procore.com/operational-excellence-one-way-optimism-is-constructed-at-procore*) for a writeup of this event. For information on open space, check out *Open Space Technology: A User's Guide* by Harrison Owen. To read about Dan Mezick, see the Open Leadership Network (*https://openleadershipnetwork.com*).

sections. During each session someone took notes, which were compiled into a book of proceedings that was discussed the following morning.

After that, I facilitated an activity called *25/10 crowdsourcing* from Liberating Structures. I asked all 350 people to write down on an index card the one most important idea from the day before that should be put into action.

We played music. I asked everyone to walk around the space and exchange index cards with each other continuously. Five times throughout that card exchange, I told people to stop, look at the card they had, and on the back of it give it a vote from one to five, with 5 being the highest score. After they did this five times, I asked them to add up the numbers on the back of their cards. The highest possible number to get on a card was a 25.

Accordingly, I called people forth with the highest rated cards. "Who has a 25?" I did this 10 times. And then we had the top 10 ideas that were voted on in the room. Some of the ideas included addressing technical debt, involving QA earlier in the dev process, and cross-squad pollination, to name a few. These essentially became guilds in our context for 90 days (and some of them lived on for at least a year later).

This is not a perfect voting mechanism, but it is a lively way to crowdsource, and it seemed to work well for our purposes that day.

Once we had the top 10 ideas, we took a break, went over the ideas with our leaders for alignment, and then came back as a group and asked people in the crowd who would like to lead a guild on each of the topics. We gave some parameters around what this meant. And then people ran over to the posters for the guilds that they wanted to lead. If there was more than one person who wanted to lead, we asked them to work it out because we wanted one point person for each initiative.

Next, we invited the rest of the people who were interested to join the guilds, and people went over to the physical locations for each guild. We did not require that anyone join. People did what they wanted and that was fine for us, and people could participate in more than one guild.

The newly formed guilds spent the rest of the day strategizing on what they could achieve in the next 90 days, and they created a one-page plan by the end of the day that was compiled into another book at the end of the event for later follow-up.

For the 90 days following, we had a Kanban board with the guilds across the top in columns, and also *to-do, in progress,* and *done* within 3 swim lanes of 30, 60, and 90. We had weekly standups by this board, and we had leadership presence at the standups to unblock the guilds and to provide attention and support for what they were trying to achieve.

After the 90 days, some of the guilds lived on, and some of them faded. We did not have a formal follow-up for them anymore.

Overall, what this event did for our community building was to enable people to find shared causes that they believed in and that they felt passionate about working on together. Without this event, the people probably would not have gotten into action together nor would they have formed the guilds.

Besides helping connect people to shared interests and problems to solve, you can also do an activity for them to get a sense of shared history.

HELP PEOPLE GET A SENSE OF SHARED HISTORY

When your organization doubles in size, there is an even greater need to connect people to a sense of history. The Story of Our Team activity, which I described in "Team Calibration Sessions" on page 198, is a fantastic activity to use not only at the team level, but also at the organizational level. I've used it with different office locations for Procore Technologies, for example. I once visited our London office and worked with a sales team. Their office had doubled in size, and during a lunch-and-learn slot as a visiting colleague, I ran this activity with them.

I've also used it with around 65 people in our user experience group, which had an offsite meeting. Their team had also doubled in size, and this activity was a perfect way to bridge the gap of the past and the present. It is really cool to see the camaraderie that emerges when people organize themselves according to when they joined the company. They have shared experiences together.

Connecting to *why* we joined the company in the first place—in other words, connecting to our origin stories—raises positivity and is also a binding agent for organizations. This concept, also called *original myth* and related to the concept of *myth change* by CRR Global, Inc. (*http://crrglobal.com*), is another handy concept to draw on to bring people together after their teams have doubled in size.

Along with discussing the *why* of joining the company, it simply helps for the processing of such organizational change to face the topic head on, by talking about it.

TALKING ABOUT CULTURE CHANGE DIRECTLY

Remember when we discussed how at a certain point in your company's growth, especially with doubling, that people will ask the inevitable question, "How do we maintain our culture?" We addressed this back in "What It Means When You're Asked, "How Do We Maintain Our Culture?"" on page 87. When you feel like this type of thing is brewing in your company, it's a good time to proactively make sure that the people who were at your company early on have a bit of extra attention.

I was part of two "first teams" at two startups. For many of us who some might consider "the old guard," this job is most likely not "just a job." We have helped to birth the company. Seeing it mature and change can be difficult to comprehend, especially if it's the first company that we've been a part of in our professional careers.

I like to have extra one-on-ones and to reinforce with people the notion that organizations grow and evolve. How lucky we are that our company is successful and growing. Jon Walker, CTO and cofounder of AppFolio, would always say, "Everything's easier when you're at a successful company." And there's a lot of truth to that. We have a lot to celebrate when our company has doubled or tripled in size. That in itself is very challenging, however, so we need to understand what's going on and get everybody moving in the same direction, aligned as one team. And those who are not energized by being at the company because it has become so large either self-select out and leave or, at times, might be asked to leave if they are becoming disruptive. It's how I've seen things play out for 20 years. For more on this, reread "Larger-Scale Splits" on page 82.

In this chapter we learned ways to bridge the gap between past and present teams when your company has doubled in size. We can tap into techniques to visualize our team change, and talk about it deliberately. In this way, we have looked back in order to make sense of our present state, so that it's easier for us to go forward together.

In a similar vein, one of the best ways to get better at dynamic reteaming, no matter what the pattern is, is to do just that: take time to reflect on what has transpired in your team or organization, in order to better tackle the future. Accordingly, the next chapter digs into the important concept of retrospectives and other feedback loops.

14

Reflect and Determine How to Shift

Reflecting on how things have gone in the past to derive the ways we want to change going forward is at the heart of being a learning organization. This can happen at multiple levels: across many teams, within teams, and through one-on-one sessions. When we encourage the people in our organization to own their own growth and development through experimentation and learning, they are on the road to becoming empowered.

The following are stories about and techniques for team retrospectives, multiteam retrospectives, initiative retrospectives, and one-on-ones, followed by a discussion of survey tools and metrics to apply as feedback loops.

So let's get started, with a discussion of retrospectives at the team level.

Team Retrospectives

We can learn, grow, and change as people, teams, and organizations. One way we do this is by having regular retrospectives with our teams. These can be facilitated by coaches or anyone who wants to *hold the space* for teams to reflect on what has happened in their teams in the past in order to make decisions about how they should be different in the future. Teams themselves can be empowered to derive the experiments they want to try out in order to change.

Reteamings can be experiments that fall out of retrospectives, which might lower the fear of trying out team changes, especially if the team compositions have been the same for a while. As one of my interviewees, Mark Kilby, put it, "If it doesn't work out, no problem—we'll go back. So far this hasn't happened. But we try to couch things in terms of experiments so that nobody feels like they failed."[1] Keeping the experiments *informal* is also important. According to Mark: "We try not to have too much formality around it. We've talked about having more tracking than we do now. But we have found that when we started turning the knob up there is reluctance to experiment." I fully agree with the strategy of experimentation, as Mark suggests. It helps to reassure people that we are a learning organization, and that we might not have all the answers. We can experiment and learn together.

At another company, I worked with a team that grew quite large to include about 15 people. The people reflected on their size and looked the work that they had on their backlog. They determined that the best thing for them to try was a concept they called *strike teams*. In their case, they re-formed into three short-lived teams to complete their work, and then they re-formed back into one larger team. After further reflection, this team also experimented by splitting in half and then rotating the two iOS developers back and forth between the resulting two teams. This way, these developers could pair with each other and work on the highest-priority items across the two teams. Later, this team wound up morphing again into two separate teams, splitting the iOS developers. The key part of all of this team-driven transformation is that the team was in charge of its destiny. It was on the quest for higher performance and fulfillment based on experimenting and really owning the team structure.

Along the same lines, Hunter Industries has a very strong retrospective-based culture that has illuminated different reteaming options to try over the years. This is a very people-centered approach to organizational development and change.

Chris Lucian, director of engineering, told me about how they work. Across the department as a whole, they have a retrospective monthly. Within project teams, they reflect weekly. These are projects that involve more than one mob working together to achieve a shared goal. Topics like reteaming across mobs might come up, and within individual mobs they are continually reflecting and tuning the way they work. As Chris described, "Individual mobs kind of naturally end up starting to have their own retrospectives impromptu, just because you're all working together on the same thing and it's just right in your face."[2]

---

1 Mark Kilby, in an interview with the author, October 2016.

2 Chris Lucian, in an interview with the author, August 2016.

So what are the topics in these retrospectives? In Chris's words, "We reflect on anything that we're currently working on and we come up with an action item about what to change and we do this regularly. [...] Since we started hiring a lot of people [...] we put in mandatory retrospectives [...] because people need to know that they can call out something and change it."

He went on to describe a common technique they call the *happy, sad* retrospective, which is done at the team level: "It's just things that are going well and things that are going poorly, and then we affinity group the items [...] then we dot vote them. If something gets a whole lot of votes, we talk about it and then we try and come up with an action item around it. That action item becomes a change to our process."

On the department level, they have done these in different ways. People might be encouraged to find someone that they don't normally work with and then go do a retrospective with them. In this way, they mix up all of the mobs to reflect on topics together, and then those groups will bring the results back, and the department will "dot vote" the results as the target for the wider, departmental discussion. The topics that come up in the departmental retrospectives are things that impact all the mobs as a whole. It could be anything from "the placement of a vending machine, to some technical distraction that's coming from Windows updates, or something along those lines," according to Chris.

I really like the way that they retrospect at multiple levels at Hunter. Reflecting across teams and coming up with shared policies is a great way to spread decision making about process to the people who are doing the work.

Multiteam Retrospectives

When you have multiple teams that work in the same area of code, or that typically have a lot of dependencies between them, it's a good idea to have regular retrospectives to reflect on how things are going. You can then make and update team agreements for use with the set of teams. The teams might decide that it's better for them to join some of the teams together. They may decide that some regular switching between teams would help them attain their goals. The question, "How might we adjust our team composition in order to achieve our goals?" is one you can consider asking. When the leader poses this question, it gives the people the permission to organize or reorganize to best attain their goals.

At one company I worked with, the teams engaged in a lot of dual-squad development. Platform components were being developed in one team, and were then being implemented in a feature set that was developed by a different team.

Working out the logistics of this development is important. You can kick it off by doing a joint-team calibration as described in "Team Calibration Sessions" on page 198. Then, after you start working together you can meet at regular touch points to monitor the team health of the situation, followed by a retrospective at the end of the initiative.

Multiteam retrospectives can get quite large. Once your retrospective becomes 10 or more people, you need a scalable facilitation strategy so you don't have two people talking, with 20 people listening. To meet this challenge—trust me, as I've facilitated hundreds of people at once—become a student of Liberating Structures. These are open sourced techniques that scale. They are my go-to facilitation strategy for 10 or more people, whether in person or virtual.[3]

It doesn't have to be a cross-functional team, or a group of them for that matter, that engages in retrospectives. They can also take place among other groups of people.

Initiative Retrospectives

Getting other groups of people together who are working on joint efforts is a way to drive continuous improvement in other areas of your work. Maybe these people are working on a program together, like onboarding new summer interns. Or perhaps they put on an event together and want to reflect on how it went so that it's easier to deploy the next time. Beyond that, maybe this group of people was in charge of a large-scale reteaming effort that reorganized hundreds of people. No matter the initiative, it pays to take the time and talk about how it went. The following example shares some perspective on this.

At AppFolio, we started an incredible *double-loop* retrospective so that we could continuously improve our onboarding of new people in engineering and product development. We would have regular retrospectives with new hires beginning 6 months after they started (the first loop), and then again after 12 months (the second loop). This was managed via a calendar invite so that we would not forget to do it. Two Agile coaches pair-facilitated a feedback session on what it was like to come up to speed as an engineering team member at the company. From that feedback we would derive initiatives for our Engineering Academy guild. Then, when getting that same group or class of new hires together after 12 months, we could share with them how the changes and feedback they

---

3 Visit the website (*http://www.liberatingstructures.com*) and join the Slack channel to start experimenting and learning.

had suggested were put into action for future new hires. It was an awesome experience to show people the impact they had made on an organizational program. This is one example of how to tactically build a generative learning organization.

You will also learn how to get better at the large reteaming initiatives that you plan, like those discussed in Chapter 12, if you schedule a facilitated retrospective on them. One way you can do this is to get the planning team together for two hours. You can use a frame for the generation of ideas to discuss. One frame is to write on a whiteboard, either in person or online, the following words in four quadrants: *Like, Learned, Lacked, Longed For.*[4] I have used this for years with teams as a way to look back and structure thoughts. Each person generates ideas for each section. Then, you can cluster the similar ideas together, and as a group go over each section. In doing so, action items will come up that you can note for future reteamings.

You could also do a version of the sailboat retrospective. Draw a sailboat with an anchor going into the water, and some visible rocks showing under the water, on a shared in-person or online whiteboard. Near the anchor, write, "What held us back or slowed us down?" Near the sails, write, "What was the wind that carried our initiative forward?" Near the underwater rocks, write, "What were the obstacles and surprises that we encountered?" Then you will gather ideas from people, kind of like in the previous activity, and have a discussion, writing down your takeaways.

A third way you can run an initiative retrospective is my favorite way—by creating a shared time line of what happened. You can do this with just the planning group, or better yet, with members from the wider community that experienced the reteaming. Using a shared online or in-person whiteboard, draw a horizontal line. On the rightmost side, write *today*. Then, talk with a partner about what happened and, using physical or online sticky notes, write down the milestones and events that transpired over the course of your initiative on the whiteboard. Then take a look at the filled-out time line together as a team. Using red, yellow, and green dots (just draw dots with colored markers or online markers), indicate how you felt at different parts of the time line. You will see patterns emerge when things went poorly (red), when things went *meh* or just OK (yellow), or when things went well (green). Have a discussion and then bridge into a conversation about what the key takeaways are for future initiatives like this. Ask

---

4 See "The 4 L's: A Retrospective Technique." (*https://www.ebgconsulting.com/blog/the-4ls-a-retrospective-technique*).

people to pair up and have a discussion about takeaways, and then have them share with the wider group.

RESOURCES FOR RUNNING RETROSPECTIVES

These are just a few ways that you can run retrospectives. And there are many other ways, as detailed in a quick Google search. Here are some favorite resources that I use when I design retrospectives.

- The classic reference for running retrospectives in the Agile space is the book *Agile Retrospectives: Making Good Teams Great,* by Esther Derby and Diana Larsen (Pragmatic Bookshelf, 2013).

- Retromat (*https://retromat.org/en*) is a website that details a wide variety of activities that you can use to reflect with and beyond teams. There is also a print version.

- Liberating Structures (*http://www.liberatingstructures.com*) are scalable facilitation patterns that you can use to fully include people in discussions. If you need to facilitate a retrospective with hundreds of people or fewer, you can use these patterns to include everyone.

Besides reflecting on reteaming initiatives, and other event-based initiatives and happenings in your company, you can also connect with people individually as an additional feedback loop.

One-on-Ones

On a different level, staying in touch with how the people in your company are feeling as individuals is a great feedback loop to have in addition to the team- or organization-level retrospective loops described already. It's critical to know how people are doing in your company. Are they excited to come to work each day? Do they feel fulfilled with their current work assignments? Do they need a change?

In some places, managers serve the role of "temperature taker" and meet regularly with their direct reports in this capacity. That's fine; however, there is a power dynamic at play. I find that having a team member other than the manager tap into the sentiments of people is a valuable thing to do. This person can be a member of a dev enablement team. They can be a coach. The key is that it is an empathetic person who does not have direct influence over the person's salary or review. Trust needs to be built in these one-on-ones.

There can be a trap with one-on-ones. If managers use one-on-ones as their only communication with team members, then the communication can be obscured and under too much invisible control. For example, I once worked with a manager who, at the quarter's end, assigned work for the quarter by meeting with his team members one-on-one. Since the team did not have healthy practices of meeting together as a team, the people complained that they had no idea what their other team members were working on. This can shut our opportunities for collaboration. It's better for teams to come together and choose their work foci as a coherent group. One-on-ones are not a replacement for open team communication.

Further, one-on-ones are also not the channel for the exclusive communication of organizational changes. When something potentially disturbing to the team and organization is about to be announced, or when a topic is sensitive to people (like the departure of a team member), I've seen managers first meet with people one-on-one and then make public proclamations of these changes. This is a risk reduction technique to not surprise people in a more public forum. Again, the private one-on-one forum is not a replacement for other communication channels. Instead, it is a companion or addition to them.

Technology deployed to help us manage our organizations has advanced, and we now have access to tools to help us get better at understanding how people feel. Tools like these are important to consider when you are a larger organization.

Survey Tools

When you are working at a larger scale—and here my experience is with about 50 teams—you can use commercial tools to attempt to gather the sentiment of individuals across multiple teams. Gathering this information can inform your reteaming needs, and it can also provide feedback on how reteamings went. Two examples that I'm familiar with are Culture Amp (*https://www.cultureamp.com*) and Peakon (*https://peakon.com*). One company I worked with deployed surveys quarterly, managed by the HR department, to keep a pulse on the reporting structures and people's overall engagement. When getting the results from these quarterly surveys, each department would respond to the feedback to their groups with prioritized action items. These surveys were given anonymously. At a later point, this company deployed weekly five-question pulse surveys so that managers could get even more frequent feedback from their employees that they could respond to individually.

If you start surveying people on a regular basis but do not acknowledge or take any action on the feedback, then your usage of these survey tools will fail because no one will take them seriously. My advice is to figure out how you will process the results from any survey tool before you deploy any surveys. If you do not do this, you will likely regret it. I've witnessed survey fatigue in my career, and it can become a type of "organizational health theater" that can do more harm than good.

Moreover, be sure you do not *over survey* people. That's another dark pattern of surveying for sentiment. If people get too many surveys, they will likely just delete them or not respond, which defeats the purpose of having surveys in the first place.

In addition to using surveys as a window into how people are feeling, you can also take the metrics route as a feedback mechanism.

Metrics

At every company I've been at, we always get to the point where we want to try to track the *health* of our organization using metrics to help guide our attention and decision making.

There is a wide range of metrics that you can track, and it really depends on what you want to look at and who is going to use the metrics for analysis. For our purposes here, I want to draw your attention to some research-backed, industry standards on software delivery performance, as well as some lean techniques for looking at workflows.

First are four key metrics of software delivery and operational performance, by the Accelerate team, as articulated by Forsgren, Smith, Humble, and Frazelle, in the Accelerate State of DevOps 2019 report.[5] These four metrics focus on the system level and include the following:

- Lead time for changes (from code committed to running in production)

- Deployment frequency (how often you deploy to production or release to customers)

- Change failure rate (what percentage of your changes result in degraded service and need remediation)

---

5 This is a downloadable report (*https://services.google.com/fh/files/misc/state-of-devops-2019.pdf*). You can also read the book *Accelerate*, written by Forsgren, Humble, and Kim. I like to get the reports each year to read the latest findings of this research team.

- Time to restore service (how long it takes to restore service from incidents or key defects)

The 2019 report defines elite, high, medium, and low performers according to their research.[6] For example, elite performers have lead times of less than one day, deploy on-demand multiple times per day, have a change failure rate of 0–15%, and can restore service in less than one hour. How does your organization compare to that?

In my view, no organization is perfect, but we need to have vision and strive to be the best we can be. The first steps are to define what excellence means to your organization, get set up to see metrics that connect to your definition of excellence, and then strive to pursue excellence by experimenting and seeing how your metrics get impacted.

So, if these metrics resonate with you, get a team together and fund it to study this report, read *Accelerate*, and build in the capacity to analyze these metrics for your environment. Don't have this as a side project—fund it deliberately. Being able to see your system performance is a window to guide your improvement efforts and your deliberate reteaming.

As your company evolves and changes through dynamic reteaming, you can see how your software delivery and operational performance is impacted by looking at these metrics.

Besides these metrics from *Accelerate*, for coaching team effectiveness, I recommend coaching teams to pay attention to cycle time and cycle-time stability of work items like stories. Many of us track our work in ticketing systems, which we can augment with other tooling to enable the analysis of lean metrics like cycle time.

In teams I work with, we define *cycle time* as the time it takes from when you start a ticket to when you deliver the ticket. Teams need to see their cycle time in order to understand it, stabilize it, and lower it. Using tools like Actionableagile.com with Jira, teams can view reports to visualize their cycle-time stability. Once the team stabilizes its cycle time, it can leverage it for forecasting using Monte Carlo and other techniques. These practices give the team a better strategy for answering the question, "When will it be done?" than other techniques such as estimation and velocity tracking. These are metrics for the team to use to pur-

---

6 Forsgren et al., *Accelerate State of DevOps 2019 Report*, 18.

sue improvement. They enable data-driven retrospectives that the team can strive to impact, by better workflow management.

You need to set up a system to view your cycle time. Once you do, you will see most often that when you reteam, your cycle time will probably increase in the short term because, if it's a one-by-one reteaming, you are training a new hire to get up to speed or you just lost a team member, so work has slowed.

In the case of growth, once your squad is calibrated and off and running, you might see cycle time decrease, especially if you talk about aging tickets in your standup meetings and then take action to move things along. I don't emphasize lowering cycle time right away in the teams I coach; I emphasize visualizing your cycle time and trying to stabilize it. I do this because I want to encourage working at a sustainable pace, and I want to encourage squads to own their cycle-time stability by reflecting on it in their retrospectives. If they are aware of it, then they can come up with experiments to try in order to stabilize it and then later lower it.

If you have just reteamed into a brand-new team, the advice that experts in this area like Daniel Vacanti suggest is that you can start leveraging cycle-time metrics with as few as 12 to 14 data points. So you set up your ability to see your cycle time, work a bit to collect the data points, and then start looking at cycle-time stability.

You can dig into this topic, and more, by studying the work of Daniel Vacanti in his books *Actionable Agile Metrics* and *When Will It Be Done?*

In this chapter we've talked about retrospectives, survey techniques, and metrics as essential feedback loops that can help you see the health of your development organization, guide your reteaming, and help you get better at it.

We've covered a lot of ground in this book. *Dynamic Reteaming* is the lens I've developed that articulates my view of software development. Just like our teams, this book has evolved and changed over the five years of its being, and it now will come to an end.

PART IV

Conclusion

Companies, teams, and people evolve and change. Sometimes changes just happen and we need to adapt to them or leave. Other times we catalyze the change with the hope that we are going to have a better outcome in our workplace.

In this book I have gone over what dynamic reteaming is, why it happens, and how it shows up as regular patterns: one by one, grow and split, isolation, merging, and switching. I've also gone over anti-patterns and have shared some rather sad, and what I think are upsetting, stories about reteaming.

I've shared several tactics from the trenches that you can employ before and after dynamic reteaming to help you become more successful with it, such as planning your reteaming initiatives, transitioning over to your new teams, calibrating the new teams, and having retrospectives to propel your learning around this concept.

What really amplifies reteaming and makes it feel more dynamic is when it happens on multiple levels, simultaneously. We might be part of a growing startup that is doubling or tripling in size. Changes in that situation happen at all levels of panarchy: the individual level, the team level, the tribe level, the company level—and even at the global level. The more it happens on the different levels, the more dynamic it might feel. As humans, sometimes we might feel excited and motivated by all of this change. Other times, change feels like a punch in the gut, and it takes time and empathy from our leaders and teammates to pull through.

One day we might realize that our company has doubled in size, and we may feel the need to come together to gel as one company again, or we might feel like things have changed so much that it's time for us to leave. And at other times we have no choice but to adapt to the changes in order to survive. I hope this book has given you ideas so that you don't just survive dynamic reteaming but thrive in it.

On the flip side, we might be in an organization that moves as slow as a glacier, and then the work to be done is trying to catalyze change to bring renewal to our stagnating situation. We desire, more than anything else, to get some creative destruction, a.k.a. dynamic reteaming, in order to bring some life back into our company. It can be done.

These two extreme examples typify dynamic reteaming. Sometimes the reteaming is dynamic and multilevel, and other times we try our darndest to "reteam the dynamic" or shift the dynamic to get out of our organizational funk. Doing either involves humans, and can get messy. People want different things, and our uniqueness is a blessing, but also makes reteaming hard to do and quite complex.

The fact is, some of us prefer more change and stimulation, and some of us prefer less. Maybe that's why we join different types of organizations—some of us want the crazy speed of high change, and others prefer a more serene setting with less change. It's not that one setting is better than another; it's more about choice and preference, if we have that luxury. If we are lucky, we will join a company that has great parity in its hiring, with the actual experience working at the company. That way, we'll have an idea of what we're getting into.

Human emotion can shine brightly through reteaming. It can feel primal. And, sometimes reteaming feels like it rips our hearts out. Our friends get laid off, we might get fired, or the company hires a leader that we do not prefer for whatever reason. Other times reteaming feels like it relieves pressure, or that it liberates us from undesirable situations like the diffusing of a ticking time bomb, or the firing of a colleague that we abhorred.

Results may vary. Some of our reteamings are going to go well, and some of them are going to fail. This stuff is hard. And the more people we try to deliberately reteam, the trickier it might be. Other times, even what seems like a manageable reteaming might not work out. But many times it does. The key is to learn your way forward together, and build the capacity of becoming an adaptive organization. Be brave.

And that's the key—reflection and learning. Invest the time to plan out your deliberate reteamings. Include the people in the decision making and have respect. Consider your individual contributors as partners in your efforts to improve your workplace. Because that's what we're trying to do with reteaming—have a better, more effective working life.

Use the power of the retrospective to talk about how things went with your reteaming. Share what you are learning with your colleagues. Don't just move on and pass over the process of learning, even if you feel that you are too busy to stop and care. Schedule the time on the calendar to process what happened, and carry the learning forward.

It's my hope that this book has helped you to see the software industry a bit differently. The quest for team stability is unrealistic and not helpful in companies where change is more the norm than ever. It's my hope that you will go forth, reflect on your own team compositions, and catalyze the changes that you and your teammates believe will help you get to a better place. Take charge of your teams. If you don't, someone else will. Because, whether you like it or not, "Team change is inevitable. You might as well get good at it."

Whiteboards to Enable Open Dynamic Reteaming

I was involved in a reteaming event that impacted around 80 people. We were in the final stage of shifting a mobile-only tribe into three separate infrastructure tribes. We had a lot of discussions in our engineering and product directors forum about how to go about this large structural change and what we wanted it to look like. We had the realization that we weren't as open as we could be about this large-scale change, and we wanted to change that. So, we chose to visualize that baseline structure on a set of whiteboards, as I had learned from Kristian Lindwall.

Visualizing the changes on the whiteboards helped us bring a greater sense of inclusion in this reteaming with all of the other people in our organization.

The following is a general guideline for how to go about visualizing reteaming changes with whiteboards, and using them as a tool in your reteaming.

Supplies and Artifacts Needed

- Whiteboards: one or more to visually represent all of your current and planned teams (we used three horizontal whiteboards on wheels in the physical space), as shown in Figure A-1. You could also do this with an online whiteboarding tool, like Miro or Mural.

- Information for the whiteboards: team names, team missions, list of people currently on each team, understanding of how many "open slots" you have for hiring (if applicable).

Figure A-1 contains an example format that you could use to illustrate the concept for one tribe. The squares above the team names represent sticky notes with the missions of the team written on them.

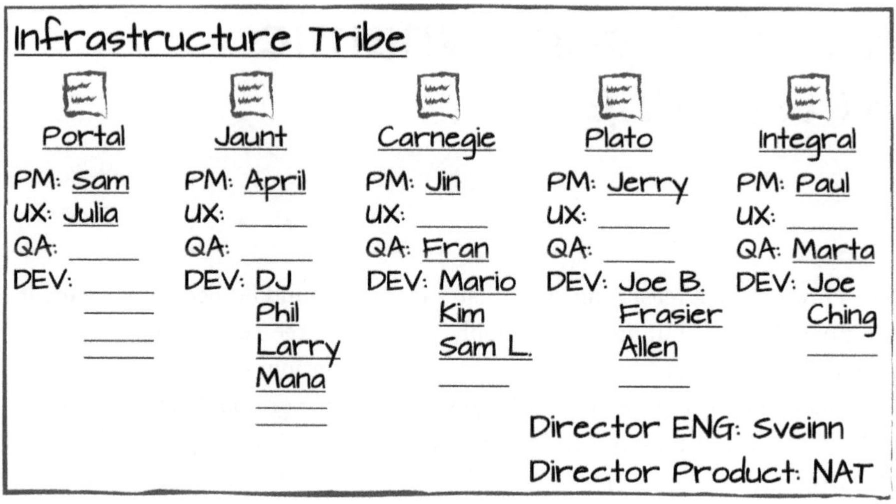

Figure A-1. Example of a reteaming whiteboard for one tribe

How to Do It

- Prepare whiteboards containing the names of all of your teams, the current team members, and lines representing the "open slots" for new hires, or for people who want to switch to those teams.

- Prepare mission statements for each of the teams and put them up on the whiteboards.

- If your teams are grouped into larger units (like tribes) include the tribe name and tribe mission on the whiteboards.

- Include another whiteboard that contains instructions on how to interact with the boards. Information on this whiteboard should be sufficient to "stand alone" to give anyone who walks up to the board background information about the reteaming. The reason for this is that you're not going to be by the whiteboards all the time ready to field questions about them.

- Create a baseline FAQ with questions and answers that you think might come up, and put this on your instructional whiteboard. Be prepared to iterate on this FAQ as more questions get illuminated. See Chapter 12 for ideas on what to include in your FAQ.

- Have a time line of activities and make it known to the people. They need to know how long the boards will be up. Include dates for when the team change decisions will be finalized, and when the new teams will go into effect.

- Have an all-hands meeting with your organization about what you are doing. Have a live Q&A about your reteaming activity.

- Send an email and chat message about what you are doing. Point people to your FAQ.

- If you are in the same physical location, you can sit by the whiteboards and work whenever you have free time. Any of the team members who are "running" the reteaming should discuss and determine how to "staff" the area for Q&A. You can also do this online by having office hours with the purpose of discussing your visual. Just schedule an open virtual meeting and have the whiteboard shared using screen sharing.

- Take down the whiteboards.

- After the fact, collect feedback from participants on how this event and overall reteaming went. It could be a retrospective or a survey, for example.

An even more open way to enable people to select their own teams is to get more synchronous and have an event. The marketplace concept is an idea like this—each prospective team has a booth staffed by the seeds of these teams, which are most likely the product manager and lead engineer. See Appendix B for more on this concept.

Team Choice Marketplace

A team choice marketplace (also called a self-selection event) is a lively event where people go from booth to booth to "shop around" for the team they want to join. They indicate three preferences—first, second, and third—for which teams they want to join. After the marketplace is over, some time is allocated to work out the final teams with the managers. Once the teams are set, they can start their calibration sessions according to recommendations in "Team Calibration Sessions" on page 198.

This approach is inspired by Sandy Mamoli and David Mole's book, *Creating Great Teams*, and is also influenced by the team self-selection approach used with a 75-person team at Redgate Software in Cambridge, England, as recounted by Chris Smith, head of product delivery.

In a blog post (*https://medium.com/ingeniouslysimple/how-redgate-ran-its-first-team-self-selectionprocess-4bfac721ae2*), Chris details their event, which included follow-up one-on-one meetings with each team member to help finalize their team assignments.[1]

The entire process took place over 20 working days, and a lot of care was taken to help reduce the people's worry and fear about changing teams. Only 33% of his employees elected to actually change teams. And that's fine. The goal is not to change everyone around for the sake of changing, but rather to provide opportunities to change.

---

1 Smith, "How Redgate Ran Its First Team Self-Selection Process."

In my view, the spirit of self-selected reteaming events is to help people pursue the learning goals that they feel will motivate them, while still meeting the needs of the company.

The following are some basic steps for how to run a team choice marketplace.

Supplies and Artifacts

- Flipchart posters: one for each team
- Sticky notes: one pad for each person
- Black pens: one for each person
- Slide deck for the event
- If doing this online, prepare a shared slide deck, open to editing by participants. You can also do this activity with a shared whiteboard like Miro or Mural. See what online tools you have access to at your company, and try them out beforehand to see what might work best.

Location

- Choose a location such as a large offsite ballroom or event space where all of the people who are choosing teams can mill around and look at posters on the walls.
- After the marketplace, you will hang the marketplace posters in a location near your work area where people can visit them and have discussions about the team membership for a week or two via one-on-ones with managers and other team members.
- If doing this online, join from anywhere.

How to Do It

- Identify who the product manager and key technical representative are for each of the teams.
- Ask each of the product managers and tech lead pairs to work together and prepare an elevator pitch for their team at the event, using a visual aid like a poster.

- Create a slide deck with high-level instructions to kick off the marketplace. This is really only a few slides:
  — A title slide
  — A slide that states the goal of the marketplace
  — A slide that tells the participants to write their name on three sticky notes to indicate their first, second, and third team choices
  — A slide to show the next steps after the marketplace—how you are going to come together after the marketplace event in order to finalize who is on each team.
  — If you are doing the whole event virtually, also include one slide for each team that you are putting together, using one of the formats suggested next.
- In terms of format, to make the pitches easier, have the leads create one poster for their team, which will be put on the wall at the event. Or if doing this virtually, contribute this information to a shared slide deck, one slide as the "poster" for the team.
- The format of the posters is up to you. At the minimum, they can write the name of the team, the product manager's name, the tech lead's name, and the high-level product and technical challenges or points of interest. The posters can also include the roles they are seeking for the team, such as four software engineers, one QA, one UX, etc.
- There are other options for poster format. For instance, your posters could have draft "opportunity canvases" filled out, describing the goals of the work focuses. In his book *User Story Mapping*, Jeff Patton includes a baseline opportunity canvas with the following sections: "1) Problems or Solutions 2) Users and Customers 3) Solutions Today 4) User Value 5) User Metrics 6) Adoption Strategy 7) Business Problem 8) Business Metrics 9) Budget."[2] This is worth checking out.
- Another format to consider is one from Redgate, as shared by Chris Smith, head of product delivery. The company has devised the template shown in Figure B-1.

---

2 Patton, *User Story Mapping*, 170–172.

[Team Name] Team Charter – [Date]

redgate

Why does the team exist?	**What will life be like in this team?**	**You'll be a great fit for this team if...**
What's our purpose?	*What will the team need to succeed?*	*What are the attributes that'll make you really enjoy working with this team?*
What impact will this have for [company name]?	*How will they work?*	
	What practices & principles will they apply?	
What does the team own?	*What are the biggest challenges this team will face? How will they tackle them?*	
What's the scope of the work?		**What are the constraints around team membership?**
What does the team cover?		*What skills, roles and experience do we need in the team?*
What's ruled in/out?		*What skills, roles and experience would be a bonus?*
What's our strategy?	**What help do we need?**	
What outcome will the team aim for in the next 3 to 6 months?	*What does this team need from other teams and people around the division/[company name]?*	
Longer-term, what are the team trying to achieve?	*What external dependencies are there?*	

Figure B-1. Team charter template from Redgate

- And here's an example of what a Redgate team created, based on the template, shown in Figure B-2. Notice the personality that shines through with this team, not only with the naming of the team after a Harry Potter concept, but also with the illustrations incorporated into the team's poster.

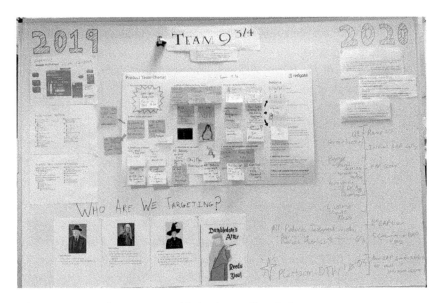

Figure B-2. Example team poster with the charter, from Redgate

- You could also consider including the life cycle phase of the work of the team. For example, Redgate sometimes uses the following life cycle phases to classify their team opportunities:
  - — Explore: ideas searching for a market fit
  - — Exploit: products and solutions looking to widen their serviceable addressable market
  - — Sustain: successful products that have reached maturity and now need to maximize return on investment

I like the idea of using these categories because they hint at the type of work to expect on the team. There is undoubtedly more discovery work and ambiguity in focus when working in a team in the Explore phase. In the Exploit phase, we already have a clear direction and track record—we need to exploit it. There might be more re-factoring when in the Sustain phase. Team members can better identify what might appeal to their interests with illuminating these phases:

- If some of the teams existed before this reteaming, you might think to yourself, "Well, I'll just include the names of the existing team members on the posters." But it could be that those team members feel like they are stagnating and that they need a change. Depending on your context, the people might hesitate to bring that up. You might consider taking all of the names off of the paper and enabling people to place themselves onto the teams as they see fit. They can then put themselves back on their current teams or on a new team. The decision to take all the names off or keep them on existing teams takes thought and consideration. Discuss with your planning team. If you want to encourage more team change, then take the names off of the posters. If you want to encourage less change, then leave the names on the posters.

- After the event, you might consider putting all of the posters from the event up on the walls near your team areas and allowing some time for people to have one-on-one discussions and work out with the management what the final teams will be. If you are doing this virtually, share the slide deck again and have one-on-ones scheduled. You can also have open Q&A sessions for either the physical or virtual running of this.

- After the fact, collect feedback from the participants on how this event and overall reteaming went. It could be a retrospective or a survey. Redgate puts up whiteboards where people could leave their feedback on sticky notes.

Variations

I've run these events multiple times during 24-hour hack days that we would have at AppFolio. The difference there is that the topic of the teams is entirely made up by the participants, and anyone can do anything that they want. The stakes are lower because it's a one-day event, so there are fewer constraints. Testing out a marketplace during an event like a hack day is recommended. It helps people understand the concept, and it lowers the fear that might be present with doing this event.

As is mentioned throughout this appendix, you can also do this marketplace online. If you do that, besides providing the slide deck, you can also connect using an online meeting tool that has screen sharing. Each product manager and tech lead can present their slide about the team they are building. People have an opportunity to put their names down on the slides indicating their preferences. They can put their names in the speaker notes section of the slide representing the team they want to join.

Resources

- Jeff Patton, *User Story Mapping: Discover the Whole Story, Build the Right Product* (O'Reilly, 2014)
- Chris Smith, "How Redgate Ran Its First Team Self-Selection Process" (*https://medium.com/ingeniouslysimple/how-redgate-ran-its-first-team-self-selection-process-4bfac721ae2*)
- Sandy Mamoli and David Mole, *Creating Great Teams: How Self-Selection Lets People Excel* (Pragmatic Bookshelf, 2015)
- Dana Pylayeva, "Let's Run and Experiment! Self-selection at HBC Digital" (*https://tech.hbc.com/2017-05-31-self-selection-hbc.html*)

  This is a case study of a self-selection event at HBC Digital. An interesting component they've added is called *team ingredients*, where when making their team selections, participants indicate their skill level and interests in learning eleven proficiencies identified as pertinent to the teams.

Survey Template

After your reteaming initiative, I recommend that you collect feedback on how it went. So often I see companies reteam and then they just "move on," and don't learn from what happened. I think it is critical to collect feedback in order to iterate and learn. You can do this via a survey, and you can also do it by having an open retrospective, as discussed in Chapter 14.

Here is a short example survey for you to build on and customize for your context.

Reteaming Survey

Please take a minute to fill out this survey so that we can improve our reteaming initiatives in the future. If you have any questions or would like to discuss in person in more detail, please reach out to <insert name here>.

- Please rate your level of satisfaction with our communication about the reteaming.

  Very dissatisfied 1 | 2 | 3 | 4 | 5 Very satisfied

- Please rate your level of satisfaction with our use of whiteboards as a tool during this reteaming.

  Very dissatisfied 1 | 2 | 3 | 4 | 5 Very satisfied

- Please rate your level of satisfaction with our new organizational structure.

  Very dissatisfied 1 | 2 | 3 | 4 | 5 Very satisfied

- Did you take the opportunity to change squads? Why or why not?

  <text box>

- We will continue to grow the company in the coming year. What advice do you have about how we conduct future reteaming initiatives?

  <text box>

- General feedback and comments:

  <text box>

After you circulate this survey and remind people to actually fill it out, report back to your organization on the results so you can learn to be more effective with all of this going forward. Don't forget this crucial step of sharing your survey results. Otherwise people won't care to take your surveys in the future.

Bibliography

Adkins, Lyssa. *Coaching Agile Teams: A Companion for ScrumMasters, Agile Coaches, and Project Managers in Transition.* Boston: Addison-Wesley, 2014.

Anderson, N. and H.D.C. Thomas. "Work Group Socialization." In *Handbook of Work Group Psychology*, edited by M.A. West, 423–450. Chichester: John Wiley & Sons, 1996.

Beck, Kent. *Extreme Programming Explained: Embrace Change.* Boston: Addison-Wesley Professional, 1999.

Bridges, William. *Transitions: Making Sense of Life's Changes.* Cambridge: Da Capo Press, 2004.

Brooks, Frederick P. *The Mythical Man Month: Essays on Software Engineering.* Anniversary Edition. Boston: Addison-Wesley Professional, 1995.

Brown, Brené. *Dare to Lead: Brave Work, Tough Conversations, Whole Hearts.* New York: Random House, 2018.

Brown, Brené. *Daring Greatly: How the Courage to be Vulnerable Transforms the Way We Live, Love, Parent and Lead.* New York: Avery, 2015.

Cable, Daniel M., Francesca Gino, and Bradley R. Staats. "Breaking Them In or Eliciting their Best? Reframing Socialization Around Newcomers' Authentic Self-expression." *Administrative Science Quarterly* 58, no. 1 (2013): 1–36.

Carmeli, Abraham, Daphna Brueller, and Jan E. Dutton. "Learning Behaviors in the Workplace: The Role of High-Quality Interpersonal Relationships and Psychological Safety." *Systems Research and Behavioral Science* 26 (2009): 81–98.

Conway, Melvin. "How Do Committees Invent?" In *Datamation magazine*, April 1968. Retrieved May 20, 2020 from *http://melconway.com/Home/Committees_Paper.html*.

Coyle, Daniel. *The Culture Code.* New York: Bantam Books, 2018.

Deming, W. Edwards. *Out of the Crisis.* Cambridge: MIT Press, 2000.

Derby, Esther and Diana Larsen. *Agile Retrospectives: Making Good Teams Great.* Raleigh: Pragmatic Bookshelf, 2013.

Dunbar, R. "Coevolution of neocortical size, group size and language in humans." *Behavioral and Brain Sciences* 16, no. 4 (1993): 681-694. *https://doi.org/10.1017/S0140525X00032325.*

Dweck, Carol. *Mindset: The New Psychology of Success.* New York: Ballantine, 2007.

Edmondson, A. C. "Psychological Safety and Learning Behavior in Work Teams." *Administrative Science Quarterly* 44 (1999): 350–383.

Edmondson, Amy C. *Teaming: How Organizations Learn, Innovate and Compete in the Knowledge Economy.* San Francisco: Jossey-Bass Pfeiffer, 2014.

Fitzpatrick, Brian W. and Ben Collins-Sussman. *Team Geek: A Software Developer's Guide to Working Well with Others.* Sebastopol: O'Reilly Media, 2012.

Flannery, Grace, Leigh Marz, and Judith MacBrine. "The Epic Tale: Weaving the Story of Multiple Employee *Generations* Together." (*http://www.orscglobal.com/.ee82b1a*) Accessed June 3, 2020.

Forsgren, Nicole, Jez Humble, and Gene Kim. *Accelerate: The Science of Lean Software and DevOps: Building and Scaling High Performing Technology Organizations.* Portland: IT Revolution Press, 2018.

Forsgren, Nicole, Dustin Smith, Jez Humble, and Jessie Frazelle. *Accelerate: State of DevOps 2019.* (*https://services.google.com/fh/files/misc/state-of-devops-2019.pdf*) Accessed May 20, 2020.

Freire, Paolo. *Pedagogy of the Oppressed.* 30th Anniversary Edition. London: Continuum, 2000.

Gorman, Mary and Ellen Gottesdiener. "The 4 L's: A Retrospective Technique." (*https://www.ebgconsulting.com/blog/the-4ls-a-retrospective-technique*) June 24, 2010.

Gunderson, Lance H. and C.S. Holling. *Panarchy: Understanding Transformations in Human and Natural Systems.* Washington DC: Island Press, 2001.

Hackman, J. Richard. "The Design of Work Teams." In *Handbook of Organizational Behavior,* edited by J. Lorsch. Englewood Cliffs, NJ: Prentice Hall, 1987.

Hackman, J. Richard. *Leading Teams: Setting the Stage for Great Performances* Boston: Harvard Business Review Press, 2002.

Heidari-Robinson, Stephen and Suzanne Heywood. "Assessment: How Successful Was Your Company's Reorg?" *Harvard Business Review* (February 2017).

Izosimov, Alexander V. "Managing Hypergrowth." (*https://hbr.org/2008/04/managing-hypergrowth*) *Harvard Business Review* (April 2008).

Kaner, Sam. *Facilitator's Guide to Participatory Decision-Making*. San Francisco: Jossey-Bass, 2014.

Kozlowski, Steve W.J., Stanly M. Gully, Patrick P. McHugh, Eduardo Salas, and Janis A. Cannon-Bowers. "A Dynamic Theory of Leadership and Team Effectiveness: Developmental and Task Contingent Leader Roles." In *Research in Personnel and Human Resources Management*. Vol. 14, edited by Gerald R. Ferris. Institute of Labor and Industrial Relations. University of Illinois at Urbana-Champaign, 1996.

Kozlowski, S.W.J. and B.S. Bell. "Work Groups and Teams in Organizations." In *Handbook of Psychology (Vol. 12): Industrial and Organizational Psychology*, edited by W. C. Borman, D. R. Ilgen, and R. J. Klimoski. (2003): 333–375. Retrieved May 7, 2020, from Cornell University, ILR School site. (*http://digitalcommons.ilr.cornell.edu/articles/389*)

Larman, Craig and Bas Vodde. *Large-Scale Scrum: More with LeSS*. Addison-Wesley Signature Series, edited by Mike Cohn. Boston: Addison-Wesley, 2016.

Larsen, Diana and Ainsley Nies. *Liftoff: Start and Sustain Successful Agile Teams*. 2nd ed. Raleigh: Pragmatic Bookshelf, 2016.

Lencioni, Patrick. *The Advantage: Why Organizational Health Trumps Everything Else in Business*. San Francisco: Jossey-Bass, 2012.

Mamoli, Sandy and David Mole. *Creating Great Teams: How Self-Selection Lets People Excel*. Raleigh: Pragmatic Bookshelf, 2015.

McCandless, Keith, Henri Lipmanowicz, and Fisher Qua. "Ecocycle Planning." Liberating Structures. (*http://www.liberatingstructures.com/31-ecocycle-planning*) Accessed May 20, 2020.

McCord, Patty. *Powerful: Building a Culture of Freedom and Responsibility*. Jackson, TN: Silicon Guild, 2018.

Organization and Relationship Systems Coaching (ORSC™) from the Center for Right Relationship.

Owen, Harrison. *Open Space Technology: A User's Guide*. 3rd ed. Oakland: Berrett-Koehler, 2008.

Patterson, Kerry, Joseph Grenny, Ron McMillan, and Al Switzler. *Crucial Conversations: Tools for Talking When Stakes Are High.* 2nd ed. New York: McGraw-Hill Education, 2011.

Patton, Jeff. *User Story Mapping: Discover the Whole Story, Build the Right Product.* Sebastopol: O'Reilly Media, 2014.

Pentland, Alex "Sandy." "The New Science of Building Great Teams." *Harvard Business Review* (April 2012).

Pink, Daniel H. *Drive: The Surprising Truth About What Motivates Us.* New York: Riverhead Books, 2011.

Ries, Eric. *The Lean Startup: How Today's Entrepreneurs Use Continuous Innovation to Create Radically Successful Businesses.* New York: Viking, 2011.

Rød, Anne and Marita Fridjhon. *Creating Intelligent Teams: Leading with Relationship Systems Intelligence.* Bryanston, JHB South Africa: KR Publishing, 2016.

Scott, Kim. *Radical Candor: Be a Kick-Ass Boss without Losing Your Humanity.* New York: St. Martin's Press, 2019.

Schwaber, Ken and Jeff Sutherland. *The Scrum Guide: The Definitive Guide to Scrum.* (*https://www.scrum.org/resources/scrum-guide*) November 2017.

Scrum PLoP. "Stable Teams." (*https://sites.google.com/a/scrumplop.org/published-patterns/product-organization-pattern-language/development-team/stable-teams*) Accessed May 20, 2020.

Sheridan, Richard. *Joy, Inc. How We Built a Workplace People Love.* New York: Portfolio, 2015.

Sinek, Simon. *Leaders Eat Last: Why Some Teams Pull Together and Others Don't.* New York: Portfolio, 2017.

Smith, Chris. "How Redgate Ran Its First Team Self-Selection Process." (*https://medium.com/ingeniouslysimple/how-redgate-ran-its-first-team-self-selectionprocess-4bfac721ae2*) *Medium.* September 22, 2019.

Spotify Training and Development. "Spotify Engineering Culture (Part 1)." (*https://labs.spotify.com/2014/03/27/spotify-engineering-culture-part-1*) March 27, 2014.

Tabaka, Jean. *Collaboration Explained.* Boston: Addison-Wesley Professional, 2006.

Tuckman, B. W. "Developmental Sequence in Small Groups." *Psychological Bulletin* 63, no. 6 (1965): 384–399.

Turner, C. "Catalyst SYNC Features Klaus Schauser and Jim Semick: Market Validation." *(https://www.noozhawk.com/noozhawk/print/111811_cata lyst_sync_klaus_schauser_jim_semick) Noozhawk.* Updated November 18, 2011.

Vacanti, Daniel S. *Actionable Agile Metrics for Predictability: An Introduction.* Ft. Lauderdale: Daniel S. Vacanti, Inc., 2015.

Vacanti, Daniel S. *When Will It Be Done? Lean-Agile Forecasting To Answer Your Customers' Most Important Question.* Ft. Lauderdale: Daniel S. Vacanti, Inc., 2020.

Valentine, Melissa A. and Amy C. Edmondson. "Team Scaffolds: How Meso-Level Structures Support Role-based Coordination in Temporary Groups." Working Paper 12-062, Harvard Business School, Boston, MA, 2014.

Wageman, Ruth, Heidi Gardner, and Mark Mortensen. "The Changing Ecology of Teams: New Directions for Teams Research." *Journal of Organizational Behavior* 33 (2012): 301–315.

Wikipedia. "Bus Factor." *(https://en.wikipedia.org/wiki/Bus_factor#cite_note-3)* Accessed May 20, 2020.

Whitmore, Sir John. *Coaching for Performance: GROWing Human Potential and Purpose: The Principles and Practice of Coaching and Leadership.* London: Nicholas Brealey, 2009.

Index

About the Author

Heidi Helfand coaches and influences fast-growing companies using practical, people-focused techniques. Her approach is based on experience at highly successful startups. The first was Expertcity, Inc. (acquired by Citrix Online) where she was on the development teams that invented GoToMyPC, GoToMeeting, and GoToWebinar. Heidi helped the company scale from 15 employees to 800. Then she was Principal Agile Coach at AppFolio, Inc., makers of workflow software for property management and law verticals. There, she built a coaching group that supported dynamic, cross-functional teams as the company scaled from 10 people to 650. She is currently at Procore Technologies—a leading provider of cloud-based applications for construction. At Procore, Heidi is Director of R&D Excellence, coaching and consulting on software development and reteaming best practices as this company scales globally.

Find out more about Heidi:

> Website: *https://www.heidihelfand.com*
> Email: *heidi@heidihelfand.com*
> Twitter: *@heidihelfand*
> LinkedIn: *https://www.linkedin.com/in/heidihelfand*

Colophon

The cover illustration is by Randy Comer. The cover fonts are Gilroy Semibold and Bebas Neue Pro. The text fonts are Adobe Myriad Pro, Adobe Minion Pro, and Scala Pro, and the heading font is Benton Sans.